Gonneville of the Cuirassiers

AYMAR OLIVER LE HARIVEL DE GONNEVILLE

Gonneville of the Cuirassiers

The Personal Recollections of a French Cavalryman
of the First Empire

TWO VOLUMES IN ONE SPECIAL
ILLUSTRATED EDITION

Countess De Mirabeau

LEONAUR

Gonneville of the Cuirassiers
The Personal Recollections of a French Cavalryman of the First Empire
by Countess De Mirabeau

TWO VOLUMES IN ONE SPECIAL
ILLUSTRATED EDITION

FIRST EDITION

Leonaur is an imprint of Oakpast Ltd

Copyright in this form © 2017 Oakpast Ltd

ISBN: 978-1-78282-692-7 (hardcover)
ISBN: 978-1-78282-693-4 (softcover)

http://www.leonaur.com

Contents

CHAPTER 1

Entrance into the Service, 1804

I am going to collect in their order, as well as I can, the remembrances of a long military career spent at a memorable time. This last fact alone can give interest to what is to come; and if I allow myself to add a few words on my personal impressions, they may be set down either to that slight satisfaction that is very commonly felt in speaking of oneself, or to the desire of being of use to those who, when I am gone, may find something to learn from these remembrances. I am now seventy years old, and must recall things which happened when I was twenty. It is not very easy, and no doubt there will be numerous omissions in my stories: but I am quite certain that they will be true and never exaggerated in their truth.

I believe my taste for soldiering arose from the reading of the *Jerusalem Delivered*, and thus dates from my childhood; for this book, which I have read twenty times, and hope to read again, was in my hands before I had reached my twelfth year. It made so deep and definite an impression on me, as to withdraw me, as it were, for a time from actual life.

I made myself one with the heroes whose prowess it relates, and my enthusiasm was most excited by Tancred and the old Raymond Count of Toulouse. I was so overcome while reading the passage where he replies to the challenge of Argantes, when all the knights around Godfrey were silent, that I burst into tears, and would gladly have given my life to have found myself also in the presence of Argantes. From this it is easy to fancy that everything relating to the art of war found favour with me; but I groaned for a long time over the invention of powder, and regretted the shield and the lance.

At last I entered the service in 1804, I was nearly twenty-one and was of the class that the law of conscription called upon in that year.

I anticipated the summons, and entered as a private in the 20th regiment of Mounted Chasseurs, (20th Chasseurs à Cheval), where two of my friends, Vaumel de Livet and Le Termelier, had preceded me, and were already sergeants. I had obtained my parents' consent—but a consent so mingled with evidence of regret, and of fear of what I might become, that to prevent my resolution from wavering I required the support of all that could revive my ideas of glory, and also of the disgust that arose in me at the idle, useless life I was leading with the youth of Caen, a fairly brilliant youth at that time, but restless, quarrelsome, and dreaded by families for fifty leagues around.

There was another feeling that I had to struggle with. My father and all my uncles, both on father's and mother's side, had emigrated and lost a greater or smaller portion of their property, as well as all their expectations, so the idea of seeing me in the service of the Republic and wearing the tricoloured cockade, was painful to them, especially to my uncles, in whom old-fashioned notions had struck much deeper root than in my father, who was infinitely superior to them altogether, and who, though full of the deepest devotion to the house of Bourbon, could not, at this time of the dawning of the Empire, see, like his brothers, any indication of a speedy and certain restoration in the most unfavourable conditions of political affairs.

So, I left Caen at the end of September, 1804, to join the 20th Chasseurs, whose headquarters were at Saint Brieuc. I was furnished with a letter of introduction from our prefect of Calvados, M. Caffarelli, to his brother the Bishop of Saint Brieuc, and another letter from M. de Montcanisy, a former lieutenant-colonel of the Queen's Dragoons, to a major of the 20th Chasseurs, called Rosières, Lastly our cousin, Le Clerc d'Osmonville, had written to Colonel Coutard commanding a regiment of infantry, also having its headquarters at Saint Brieuc, to beg him to give me a recommendation to his comrade M. de Marigny, colonel of the 20th Chasseurs.

This M. de Marigny came from Dauphiné; he was rather over thirty years old, of handsome person, had not a penny of private fortune, and spent a thousand a year; so, his poor regiment was his farm, and he squeezed it in every possible way, without any regard for justice. Afterwards an inquiry took place, orders were given for his arrest and trial, but he made his escape, and no news was ever heard of him till the very day of the Battle of Jena, when he rejoined his regiment with a perfectly regular order to resume the command. A few minutes afterwards a shot carried off his head.

When I arrived at Saint Brieuc not one of my expected protectors was there. All the regimental staff was gone to Paris as a deputation to be present at the coronation, and the regiment was dispersed over the country from Lannion to Saint Malo, under the command of Major Castex, and he was at Rennes with the depot. Nothing but the *compagnie d'élite*, commanded by Captain Fleury, was at Saint Brieuc; the lieutenant's name was Capitan, and one of the sub-lieutenants, Marigny, was the colonel's brother.

The first person I met was the chief sergeant, Guilmin; I gave him my marching order, and he took me to a somewhat poor-looking inn, where he presented me to Captain Fleury, who was there with other officers. The captain spoke to me in a haughty and ironical manner, and gave orders that I should be provisionally entered on the register of the *compagnie d'élite*. I was taken to the quarters in an old Capuchin convent, and placed under the hands of Corporal Henneson, a sort of Hercules, nearly six feet high, whose bed I was to share.

The same day I was so fortunate as to meet Galbois, *aide-de-camp* of General Vaufreland, who had been commander of the department of Calvados, and was now of the Côtes du Nord. I knew the general, and had been intimate with Galbois. Both of them greeted me in a very friendly manner, and this gave me a little importance in the eyes of my chiefs. I also remember with gratitude that when I was on duty as the general's orderly, Madame de Vaufreland sent me an armchair and some books.

I should like to observe here how much the position of any persons who are in authority over us is enhanced in our imagination by this very dependence. Before I became a soldier, a captain seemed to me to be but a very ordinary sort of gentleman, and as; soon as I joined the regiment he appeared to me perched on a pinnacle that I never could reach, there were so many steps between.

I was the last of a troop of a hundred-and-twenty men, most of whom had seen active service; many of them had weapons presented for good service. There was one named Robin, who had a silver-mounted carbine with a fantastic inscription, declaring that he, single handed, had rescued four hundred prisoners, escorted by two hundred Austrians. This Robin was a regular brigand, and looked like one; he had committed pillage, rape, murder, and this to the knowledge of the whole regiment. The rest of the company was pretty well supplied with men of this stamp, and the horrible stories they told of an evening in the rooms, made one's hair stand on end.

But among all these were also to be found admirable instances of their bravery, which they boasted of much less than of their misdeeds. I had become their comrade, even their inferior, as I had never seen fire; and when I found myself with them on my first evening in a great room, formerly a corridor of the convent, with thirty beds in a row, half of one of which was mine, with a solitary candle stuck in a potato by way of candlestick, shedding only a melancholy light—my family, my father's house, the care and sweet remembrance of my youth rose up to make a cruel contrast with the surroundings that must encircle me daily for an unlimited period. I managed to conquer this attack of discouragement and disgust, as well as similar failings roused by other matters.

Henneson, my bed-fellow, was an excellent man, very well-mannered for a peasant. I lost sight of him for twenty-four years, and found him at Verdun a retired captain; I was then lieutenant-colonel of the 12th Regiment of Chasseurs, and was really glad to see him again. He was married and had resumed his agricultural life, living in the country a few leagues from Verdun.

As soon as I joined my regiment, I threw myself ardently into all the exercises required to place me on a level with my comrades. I studied the theory as well, and as I could already ride pretty well I was soon able to take my place in the ranks.

We were then in training for a descent on England. In order to make provision in case of any emergency, artillery instructors had been sent to us, and once a week we had gun and mortar drill. At the end of six months I was made a corporal, without having to leave the *compagnie d'élite*. This was a great favour; for the interests of discipline usually require that a man when invested with this rank—so little above the soldier—should not be left among the persons who were his equals the day before. I saw the wisdom of this rule as soon as I assumed my new duties, but I was not wanting in a somewhat serious matter that then arose, and as there was no fixed order of promotion at that time, I was appointed sergeant a month later, and still in the same troop.

Just as I was given this step, one of my relations, M. d'Avenay, Colonel of the 6th Regiment of Cuirassiers, knowing that I was already a sub-officer, made a direct request to the Emperor Napoleon, at a review held in Italy, at Monteschiare, that I should be made a sub-lieutenant. An instance that destiny often hangs on a trifle, for if my appointment to the rank of sergeant had taken place a fortnight later the opportunity would have been lost, and heaven knows what would have become of me.

A few months afterwards, I received my commission, with an order to join the 6th Cuirassiers, quartered at Lodi. I received it at my father's house, where I happened to be, as I was one of a detachment of the 20th Chasseurs that had been sent to Caen for a remount. I started for Italy at the end of August, 1805, and soon reached Lodi.

War with Austria was imminent, the armies faced each other; those of Italy fronted on the banks of the Adige. We held Verona, and the Austrians Veronette. The bridges between them had been cut, and the passage was commanded by batteries and loopholed houses on both sides.

On arriving at Lodi, I only found the depot of my regiment, under the orders of a captain, as the major was away on some mission or other. Being a relative of the colonel, and probably by his recommendation, I was excellently received by the officers of the depot, who were most of them too old or infirm for active service. I was soon fitted out, and received orders to join the squadrons on active service. I left Lodi, for the first time in my life in command of a detachment. It was composed of thirty *cuirassiers* and some sub-officers, who had been left at the depot for various reasons, and were now to join their squadrons. I was very new to my duties, but very desirous to be equal to them, and much interested in my journey. I passed Pizzighetone, Cremona, Mantua, and joined the service squadrons at Isola della Scala, a town four leagues below Verona, in the midst of rice grounds, and therefore very unhealthy.

Colonel d'Avenay received me in a way that showed he had pleasure in seeing me, and on my side, I felt a great deal at finding myself with him, though we had never been very intimate, as he was fifteen years older than myself. But I had often seen him in Normandy; he came to visit my father at Caen, and also in the country where we were neighbours. He was the eldest son of M. Rioult de Villaunay, and his name of d'Avenay came from a property on which his father lived, and that was meant to be his. He had one sister, Madame de Magneville, and one brother, Adrian de Villaunay; we were related through their mother, who was my father's great aunt.

The family had a considerable amount of property that had increased day by day by the economies of its head, in excess of any ordinary moderation. Colonel d'Avenay was a splendid man in every sense of the word; his features were perfectly regular, and had a martial and

JUNIOR OFFICER OF CUIRASSIERS

imposing expression. In society he was not considered clever, because he often made far-fetched jokes, that sometimes were very heavy. His education had been so neglected that he knew neither French nor spelling, but his speech was ready and clear. He was possessed of an unwearied activity, which could not be daunted by any obstacle, and a determination that caused him to be ready for any responsibility; he inspired unlimited confidence in all those who served under his orders, and was extremely far-seeing in everything. His men worshipped him. Had he lived, he would certainly have become a marshal of France; for in addition to the qualities I have mentioned, he had the art of putting anything he did in high relief, and he was always inspired by a spirit of justice and quiet courage.

Our division was composed of the 4th, 6th, 7th, and 8th Cuirassiers; it was commanded by General de Pully, an officer of very ordinary ability, and a more than equivocal reputation on the score of morality. He was a regular old gossip in the ordinary ways of life, and used to make speeches to the soldiers, while they laughed at him.

We and the 4th Cuirassiers made up the first brigade, and as there was no General of Brigade, Colonel d'Avenay commanded it as senior officer. This seniority arose from his rank of Colonel of the Royal Normans in former times, which he had lost at the period when the nobles were excluded from the army by a decree. When he again reached the same rank, the eleven years that he had spent in retirement were reckoned as half-pay time.

The 6th Cuirassiers had been on the point of being disbanded and distributed among other regiments, on account of the evil influence diffused through every branch of its service by Colonel Cacotte, the predecessor of Colonel d'Avenay.

Before the formation of the twelve regiments of *cuirassiers* which, with two of *carabineers* then composed the heavy cavalry, there had been twenty-four regiments called heavy cavalry. The consequence was that two of these regiments had been united for the formation of each regiment of *cuirassiers*, and that only eighteen months before. Now Colonel Cacotte, a blundering and partial man, had permitted such an ill-feeling to get a hold in his regiment, that the officers of the old King's Regiment and the old 23rd Cavalry which composed it, lived in enmity, and were always fighting; the sub-officers and soldiers did the same, and in consequence there was no discipline, no drill, no smartness.

As soon as Colonel d'Avenay arrived, he changed all this with a wave of his wand; he called the officers together and spoke firmly to them, while giving them his promise to have their interest at heart when they deserved it. He caused the retirement of some poor old creatures, procured a promise that vacancies should be filled up from the corps, an extraordinary subsidy for putting clothing, accoutrements, and saddlery in proper condition, and for several horses to be cast and replaced. All this time drill went on energetically.

The old soldiers, who formed the majority, soon recovered themselves, and at the end of four months, at a grand review of the whole army, held by the Emperor in the plain of Monteschiare, the regiment showed off to such excellent effect that its chief got anything he asked for, and the result to me was the favour of being appointed a sub-lieutenant, an especial favour to one so lately made a sub-officer, and who ought not to have been promoted before others who had claims for promotion from serving in several campaigns.

When I joined the 6th Cuirassiers, the body of sub-officers was much superior to that of officers. The latter, although very brave men, were without education, and had not the least idea of manners or conventionalities. With the exception of La Nougarède, De Tilly, and myself, all the officers were no longer young men.

My life at Isola-della-Scala became entirely military, and I set myself to learn all the duties of my position that I did not know. The list was a long one, for the 20th Chasseurs had been dispersed over the country in Brittany, and never drilled together; and as long as I was with them my instruction had been confined to a very superficial knowledge of the soldiers' duty, and the services that the sub-officers have to perform in garrison. So, I set to work to study the theory and the duties of troops on campaigning service, and I soon found myself a match for my comrades on these points.

The army under the command of Marshal Masséna was waiting, before crossing the Adige, for information from the great army operating in Germany. The plan of the marshal was to force the passage at Verona, to march on Caldiero, a well-known position two leagues from Verona, on the road to Vicenza, which it seemed certain that the Austrians would hold, as they had always done in the preceding wars; this time they had improved the natural means of defence, by numerous field-works armed with a large force of artillery. During the struggle that would take place in the open country, the infantry division, Verdier, ten thousand men strong, was to pass the Adige three leagues below Verona, and so to turn the left flank of the Austrians and

CUIRASSIERS 1805

come on their rear. Our division was to follow this movement, but for that purpose we ought to have had a bridge prepared to carry us over at the appointed place, but General Verdier could not establish it.

The attack on the bridge of Verona took place on the 28th of October, 1805, and was successful. While on this topic, I ought to mention a specimen of the daring of our light infantry. The bridges of Verona are of ancient construction, and very highly arched, and, in consequence, the Austrian batteries had full command of the highest part, where the bridge was cut about six feet in width, but a few paces lower down on our side was exposed only to the fire of the loop-holed houses. Attempts had been made at night to place planks on the breach, but this work could not be done without noise, and then the guns, which were laid for night as well as for day, fired grape, and killed and wounded great numbers.

The *voltigeurs* in a body earnestly begged to be allowed to carry the position in their own fashion, and at the turn of the day the enemy might see our *voltigeurs* following another with extraordinary speed on to the side of the bridge he was holding; they ran at full speed, jumped the breach, and with the same rush carried the guns and seized the houses. This bridge is some thirty feet above the river, which is very deep, and runs like a millstream; two men only failed in the leap, and fell into the gulf. A few minutes after this exploit, the planks were fixed, and the *voltigeurs* properly supported.

On the evening of that day I had been sent by General de Pully to General Verdier for information as to what progress had been made in the construction of the bridge. There was a good deal of firing from both banks, but without any great injury being done to either side, for the combatants were covered by the embankments, and they are very high at that spot.

The Battle of Caldiero took place on the 30th, and was most sanguinary; the whole day was consumed in taking and retaking the various positions of chief importance. The Austrian Army was commanded by the Archduke Charles, having with him the Archdukes Louis, John, and Maximilian. The princes went wherever their presence could encourage the defence, and charged on foot, at the head of the battalions, to the recapture of elevated positions.

We beheld this battle like a play from the best seats. The left bank of the Adige at Verona is a buttress of the Alps; it rises rapidly like an amphitheatre, with successive ledges perpendicular to the river, coming quite down to the marshes that fringe it. Caldiero is situated on the last of these ledges towards Vicenza, and to reach it the natural and artificial defences with which the country bristled had to be carried. As we had missed the part intended for us, from the impossibility of establishing a bridge to carry us over, we remained on the right bank, following all the events of this action with the naked eye. It was very murderous, and lasted the whole day.

Some of the positions were carried, but the strongest, of which Caldiero formed the centre, remained in the hands of the Austrians, and we had on that day a loss of six thousand men killed and wounded. Marshal Masséna has been accused of having given battle on this occasion entirely for the sake of his private interest; he had just received information of the success of the grand army, the capitulation of Ulm, and the army of Italy had not yet done anything.

The sight of the battle, the sound of the guns and musketry fire, excited and impressed me very much. I had already heard the whistle of balls when I was sent to General Verdier, but without running much risk, and I suffered much all day at the passive duty to which we found ourselves condemned, so different from what I felt myself called by inclination to fulfil. My fancy created pictures; I exaggerated the intoxicating delight of success, which nothing in my imagination could obscure. Then I never conceived that devotion and heroism could pass unobserved; in my eyes all the chiefs were impartial men, always anxious to reward good actions duly. I could not understand envy among comrades, and I burnt to distinguish myself, with the belief that I should find sympathy everywhere.

On the evening after the battle, we passed the Adige above the line occupied by our troops, and we established our bivouac behind it, on the left of the road to Vicenza. All night we were on the alert, and the patrols continually exchanged shots. The next morning was occupied in feeling the enemy. We advanced a little, and I found myself for the first time on a field of battle. It was literally covered with the dead; which in spite of the shrinking of our horses, they were obliged to tread under foot.

We halted every moment, and in a hollow road where we stopped, besides the corpses beneath my horse's feet there were others on the hedges on each side, so close to me that I could have touched them. They were perfectly naked, and their hideous wounds visible; those at the bottom of the road had been mutilated and crushed by the wheels of the artillery. Their hair generally stood on end, and their faces were dreadful. I confess that this sight very much cooled my martial ardour,

Cuirassiers engaging with Austrian Cavalry

and my hair made some small imitation of that above-mentioned. I thought of my father, my mother, my brother, all so dear to me, whom I had left in Normandy, and sorrowfully considered that perhaps in a few hours I, too, should be dead, naked, and crushed by the artillery, and this was entirely beside the notions I had given myself of the honours paid to the brave who had fallen on the field of battle.

During the day the enemy gave up the rest of the positions he had retained, and commenced a full retreat. This confirmed the reports about Marshal Massena. This retreat was, indeed, the natural consequence of the march of the grand army upon Vienna, and the blood shed at Caldiero had been entirely and wholly wasted. The enemy's army was thirty thousand men stronger than ours, and conducted its retreat in capital order and without any notable loss. Northern Italy is an everlasting defile for an army, cleft by rivers, and near them alone is there any space for deployment. Thus, in the Venetian territory, from the Adige to Isonzo, the fields of battle are between Caldiero and Vicenza, on the banks of the Brenta, of the Piave, of the Tagliamento, and in the plains of Udine, in the midst of which is Campo Formio.

We followed the Austrians in their retreat, which they conducted deliberately, stopping at the passages of rivers long enough to allow their artillery and baggage to pass. The rivers had no bridges, for they inundate a considerable amount of country during the melting of the snows. We crossed the Brenta by a ford, and the Piave by a bridge of boats. These two passages were hardly disputed, and we made no figure in them; but that of the Tagliamento gave rise to a tolerably serious affair when all the cavalry was placed in line; there was a smart cannonade, and we were manoeuvring near enough to the enemy to give us hopes that we were at last coming to blows. I was ashamed of the sensations that I had experienced at the sight of the field of battle of Caldiero, and feeling the need of restoring my position in my own eyes, I prayed for an opportunity with all my heart.

I was on the main guard the night before the day of Tagliamento. During the march that we made to reach the spot, I was on the rear-guard of my regiment, and as it was cold we were wrapped in our cloaks. When we reached the Tagliamento, I saw the 4th and 6th Cuirassiers forming line of battle at the gallop and drawing swords. I conformed to this movement; but what was my consternation when, desiring to make my detachment draw swords, I found I had not got my own.

While trotting during the night, the upper clasp had given way, the sword had turned over and fallen from the scabbard, giving no notice of the misfortune, which seemed so dreadful to me, that I remember the feeling I experienced as if it had taken place yesterday. Happily, I saw our surgeon-major, who had no need for his sword; I hastened to him, and begged it of him in a way to make him feel that he could not refuse. Thus, I found myself armed again; but the incident served to make me take especial care of everything relating to the arms and equipment of a cavalry officer on service, and I may say that from that time forward I never experienced any misadventure of the kind again.

The Tagliamento, when at the fullest, is at least a league in width, but now it was only a plain of pebbles and sand cleft by two or three streams of water, the deepest not reaching to a foot and a-half. We made our bivouac in its bed under a dreadful wind, which enveloped us in whirlwinds of sand; we had nothing either for ourselves or for our horses, and it was a trying night. Next morning, I was detached with twenty-five men to search for oats and maize.

I went back, inclining to the right, and getting as far as I could away from the direction of our advance; I was successful, and in the evening rejoined our quarters in another place, on the other side of the Tagliamento, near Cadraïpa. I was well-received, for I brought ample provision. This was the first mission entrusted to me, and I was satisfied at having performed it well.

The main body of the Austrian Army retired by Carniola, and only a small portion of it by Carinthia. We followed the latter after having stayed some weeks near Cividad and Palma Nova, and then returned to Campo Formio, where we remained a fortnight, then mounting the gorge of the Tagliamento, passing Ponteba, Willach on the Drave, and Clagenfurth, and taking the road to Hungary, in order to rejoin the portion of our army that had taken the route by Carniola.

During our stay at Campo Formio the Prince de Rohan issued from the Tyrol, by the valley of the Drave, with an Austrian corps of ten or twelve thousand men. A sufficient number of troops to make head against him were thrown back, and among them our division, but still without finding any means of coming to action. Rohan's corps was too much isolated, besides being demoralised by the information received from Germany, and the retreat of Prince Charles. It was entirely defeated, and the Prince de Rohan seriously wounded and made prisoner.

During our march in Carinthia we advanced to the frontier of Hungary, and just as we were going to cross it we received orders to

Eugène de Beauharnais

return into Italy; the treaty of Presburg had just been signed.

So, we retraced our steps, the Alps had to be crossed in all the severity of Winter, and our passage took place without accident, though the snow was much drifted. The plains of Italy bear an aspect far from smiling at this time of year; they are so much soaked by the rains that as far as Treviso the roads are like rivers of mud. We met nine thousand Hungarian grenadiers, who composed the garrison of Venice. It was in the middle of a narrow road, where to make room for us they were obliged to march in open ranks at each side; our horses covered them with mud, our men laughed at it, and the Hungarians were doubly humiliated, and abused them.

At Fontana Freda, the last stage before reaching Trevisa, I discovered the body of a man recently interred in a little wood of willows connected with the inn where I was lodged; and when I examined the master of the inn about it, he seemed so dismayed at my discovery, that I immediately thought he had committed or permitted the crime. I told the colonel, we went together to the *podesta*, and next day at Treviso to a competent authority; we heard there that for some time the track of several travellers had been lost at Fontana Freda and that they had never been heard of again, and orders were given to apprehend the innkeeper; but as we went away the next day I never could hear any more of the matter.

We went into garrison at Vicenza, and whilst there the Viceroy of Italy, Eugène de Beauharnais married the Princess of Bavaria and brought her into his vice-royalty. Vicenza was the first Italian city where he stopped; I had been sent two leagues forward to meet him with twenty-five *cuirassiers* as an escort, and I was astonished at the beauty of his wife. Vicenza desired to distinguish itself; there was a ball, concerts, &c. The young and brilliant couple seemed pleased; everything at this time seemed to presage a happy fortune to them, but the sequel of their history is well-known.

We remained three or four months at Vicenza, and then went to join our depot at Lodi. I had a severe cold during the ten or twelve days' march we had to make, and suffered acutely from the first spring heat, which is very oppressive in this part of Italy. At last we arrived, and I had the delight, if the expression may be allowed me, of finding at Lodi a horse I had bought in Normandy before my departure, which had been brought me by a detachment of dragoons who had come from getting remounts at Caen. The horse had borne the journey perfectly well, and was in very good condition; he had been selected by M. de Montcanisy, who passed for a very good judge of horses.

Besides the horse's material qualities, he was my countryman, and persons who have not left their country cannot understand what value anything that comes from the native land acquires in the eyes of those who are expatriated. At that time distances seemed much greater on account of the time that was occupied in traversing them, and when measuring in my mind the space between Normandy and Italy it seemed almost impassable; my feverishness increased the dejection I experienced at such a separation, and I felt the approach of home sickness. I rebelled against my weakness; used every means to combat it, and my horse I must confess was a great assistance to me. He had been bought at the fair of Guibray, and I had travelled on him from Falaise to Maizet; he had been stroked and petted by my father, my mother and brother; he became my friend. I cared for him affectionately, and took especial pains with teaching him. My orderly was a *cuirassier* named Jouette, a man of forty years of age, who had passed through several campaigns, and was famous for the way he looked after horses, for he was passionately fond of them.

Jouette was a living instance of a particular type and deserves to have his portrait drawn, besides I only pay a proper tribute of gratitude in making mention of him. He was the nephew of a major who had left the regiment two years before, and he had always refused the promotion he deserved for his excellent conduct. Brave, gentle, of an honesty equal to any trial, his respect for his superiors was a kind of worship; he might be said to be an ideal soldier. He had a house and a small property in the Aube bringing in twenty-four pounds a year, and left the whole enjoyment of it in the hands of his sister, the widow of a man who had dissipated her property. He lived upon nothing but his pay, and put by anything I gave him.

If an officer of the regiment of any rank at all had appeared on parade with his arms and saddlery smarter than mine, or his horse better groomed, Jouette would have been inconsolable; but he never exposed himself to this vexation, and I was literally compelled, before going on parade, to submit to his inspection. He was accustomed every day to write down all he did, and anything that he noticed; he wrote it on loose sheets that he kept in the folds of his forage-cap, and in diaries which he shut up in his portmanteau, and gave in charge to some friend at the depot when he went campaigning.

We received horses and recruits from France; I was constantly employed in their instruction, and that finished my own. At the end of a few months we received orders to go into garrison at Piacenza, when the course of training was actively continued. War with Prussia became imminent and soon broke out.

CHAPTER 2

March on Prussia, 1806

In the month of November, 1806, the four regiments of *cuirassiers*, composing our division, received orders to march on Berlin without delay. Of course, the Battle of Jena and several actions had preceded the occupation of this capital by our troops. We had to march with speed, and we were only allowed three halts for a considerable distance. We went through the Tyrol, this being the third time I crossed the Alps in the course of one year, and each time I had gone by a different route. I saw Trent, Botzen, and Inspruck with the appearance of which I was greatly struck.

The town is commanded at a very short distance on the Italian side by very lofty mountains, over whose heights we had been marching all the morning in a thick fog that was nothing but cloud. When we left these elevated regions, we issued all at once out of this thick vapour, and saw Inspruck at our feet, but at an immeasurable depth, and the plain was lighted by a brilliant sun, yet a few minutes before we had been unable to perceive the least ray from it; on the north-east we could follow the course of the Inn winding through the mountains, for Inspruck is commanded by the Alps on all sides. We had the same day left the springs of the Eisach, an affluent of the Adige and come upon the Inn an affluent of the Danube. Possibly it is childish in me, but I have never passed Nature's tracings of grand lines of demarcation without peculiar emotion.

From Inspruck our march lay on Augsburg and Nuremberg, after passing the Danube at Donawerth; then on Bayreuth, Gera, Leipsig, Wittemberg, Potsdam, and at length we reached Berlin. General Clarck was commanding in the city, and it was perfectly quiet.

Our division occupied the barracks of the guard and the body-guard, and we spent a week there to recover ourselves a little, for we had considerable need after marching so long without a halt, and the more that after Inspruck we had a continuance of rainy weather, and had to pass by roads that were dreadfully broken up and inundated plains; among them there were some near Augsburg more than a league in length, that we passed at night; I never understood how it was we were not all stuck there.

We left Berlin about the middle of January, 1807, to join the army already beyond the Vistula; we passed the Oder at Custrin, and marched on Posen and Thorn. There are often remarkable contrasts in military life; after we left Berlin I had always been very miserably quartered, usually upon Jews or peasants, and for the very good reason that I was only a sub-lieutenant, and the four regiments of our division travelled together; the day before we reached Thorn I was summoned on duty to the headquarters of the regiment, and I found Colonel d'Avenay installed in a fine house occupied by seven or eight ladies, almost all young, and two of them remarkably pretty; they were elegant, and spoke French as well as we did; they received us most delightfully.

In the house among all these women there was one old man more than sixty years of age, for able-bodied men were engaged in raising soldiers and drilling them to come and join us afterwards. They asked me to remain, and I was only too glad to accept; they provided a very good dinner served in French style; in the evening they gave us some music, and the time passed so pleasantly that we did not go to bed till midnight, though much tired with a long day's march. We had a thick bed of very fresh straw to lie on spread in a gallery leading to the saloon. This is always the case in best furnished houses of Poland; no one has a bed who does not bring it with him.

We departed before our fair hostesses were awake, and we reached Thorn at night, for at this time of year and in this latitude, it begins at half-past three. We passed the Vistula on a hastily constructed bridge, the legs of the trestles were whole pine trees, and so the bridge was much elevated above the surface of the river, and loaded with enormous masses of ice that struck against the trestles, and caused a vibration of the bridge that was not reassuring, especially as it was enhanced by the irregular steps of the horses covering it from one bank to the other; besides this bridge was only twelve feet wide, and had no parapet.

However, the four regiments that came from Thorn crossed it safely on their way to cantonments in various directions, and we had three leagues more to go to reach our quarters, a village entirely stripped, we were two squadrons then under the orders of Commandant Chalus, a poor officer, and very pretentious.

Next day, the 3rd of February, I was in orders to go to get oats in five villages, named in the order where I had to go; my instructions were to despatch any vehicles that I could manage to get loaded from each village to that which we occupied, under the escort of two or three men. It followed from this that I had no military precaution to take, and that we were in perfect safety, for at the last village I had to search there would not be more than three or four men left me, as the others were to go away in proportion to our discoveries of oats. Besides, when we crossed at Thorn, we had been told that the line of our advanced posts was eleven leagues to the front, and no measures for protection had been taken the night before on our arrival at our cantonment.

My detachment consisted of twenty-three men, of whom two were sergeants and two corporals; having to return by nightfall I did not take my *cuirass*, and we set out in a cold of some eighteen or twenty degrees, but beautiful weather, while snow had continued to fall the whole time after our departure from Berlin. They found me a guide, and we made our way across a great plain covered with snow a foot thick, and quite untrodden.

As we left our village I saw at about two leagues distance a small town; that my guide told me was Culmsee, showing that the lake of that name was in the neighbourhood. I thought the town was occupied by our forces, I was separated from it by obstacles of the country that would have prevented my reconnoitring it, if I had ever thought of doing so; when we came opposite to it, half a league off, my guide showed me at a similar distance, in front on the right, a small house surrounded by a group of buildings, of fairly good appearance, and gave me the name of the first village I was to have dealings with.

We were separated from it by a valley and in the bottom, was a short canal connecting two lakes, and we made our way to a stone bridge thrown over this canal. Before we reached it, after having descended a steep bank, we came out on a road that evidently led from the village we were approaching to the little town of Culmsee. On the other side of the bridge was an escarpment like that we had come down, and at its top the nearest houses of the village could be seen; the road was bounded by enclosures four feet high, formed as is usual in that country, of two lines of horizontal planks firmly attached to stakes fixed in the ground. The house stood on the right of this road, and had a court before it which I entered, and drew up my detachment in it; this brought out a couple of men of rather distinguished appearance on the doorstep, and five or six women to the windows.

I dismounted and explained my mission, begging that in consideration of the shortness of the day they would make haste to load three vehicles with oats, saying that I would give a receipt for them; I asked besides for some bread and beer for my men. All was settled without dispute, and I was even very politely invited to breakfast. The horses were tied to a paling in front of the house, the *cuirassiers* went into the laundry to warm themselves, and a large fire was made there. I had been five minutes in the saloon when the master of the house told me that two hours before my arrival, he had already had a visit from a detachment of cavalry that came from Culmsee to inquire if there were French in the neighbourhood—this detachment was composed of Prussian dragoons.

The neighbourhood of the enemy required precautions that I had not taken, and that according to the tenor of my instructions I was not required to take. I went out that moment, called my men, ordered them to mount, and proceeded to reconnoitre the approaches of the village, and to place vedettes, when all at once a *cuirassier* rushed out of a building opposite to the entrance of the court-yard, crying out, "Here they are!"

The enemy came by the side that was masked by this building, and in the first place I had to find out what force I had to meet. This question was soon settled; the sergeant I had sent to the front was received by several carabine shots, and he returned to me at full gallop. Meanwhile I had come out of the court, with a view of forming to the left of the village at the junction of the two roads where they made a kind of open square; but taking a few steps in that direction, the ground that was covered by the barn was thrown open and my unpleasant situation revealed to me.

The enemy was coming by the road from Culmsee, and his advanced guard, composed of about thirty Black Hussars (Hussars of Eben), had passed the bridge, and were coming up towards me at a gallop, having already some men opposite the farm outside the palings, the very ones who had fired upon my quartermaster. Behind them, marching by fours, and occupying the whole breadth of the road, came a squadron of dragoons. I perceived all this from the height where I was, and saw I had to meet a considerable force; but I must say, for it is true, that I felt neither an impulse of fear nor a moment's hesitation. The idea of escaping by the opposite side, which was perfectly open, never occurred to me; besides I could not very well think of it for I should not have known what direction to follow in an unknown country without made roads, and with a hundred and fifty horsemen on my track. There was nothing else to do but to force a passage through the midst of them, push them back beyond the fork of the road they had passed, despatch one or two of the best mounted men to our cantonments to give the alarm, and with the rest do the best I could in the almost desperate position in which I found myself.

If I could have gained the road leading to the bridge it is probable that the pursuit would not have been long, for the Prussians would not have cared to approach too near to our cantonments. But an officer, followed by two dragoons, was already in advance in the road by the side of the houses of the village, and this officer came in front of the hussars, and made signs with his hand that he wished to treat. I had not a moment to lose, for the space widened at the opening of the road the enemy's column were coming up, and it was evident that if they reached that spot before I did, I should be surrounded, and lose all chance of safety. I said a word to my *cuirassiers*, made them draw swords, and charged at once. One thing came into my mind at this very serious moment, we had our cloaks, and from a distance they had taken us for dragoons because of our helmets; for the enemy's cavalry coming from Culmsee, where they had spent the night, had watched our progress ever since we entered the plain.

So, we had been counted before the attack! Now some weeks since a division of dragoons, the Division Milhaud, had had two or three unfortunate affairs that had discredited this body in the eyes of the enemy, and gave them a confident expectation that they would any way have an easy victory. But in drawing swords, my men threw back the right side of the cloak over the shoulder, discovering their cuirasses, and cuirassiers had a colossal reputation. So, I observed a very distinct movement of hesitation in the head of the column; some hussars moved to the rear, and this put their troop in disorder, besides they were coming up without keeping their ranks.

The two dragoons, with the officer whom I have mentioned before, fired at me and missed me; I wounded one of them and passed on. We came to the hussars and literally passed over them. I do not think that four of them were left on their horses, they were so overthrown by us and by each other. We met the head of the dragoons

CUIRASSIERS IN SPAIN BY DENIS DIGHTON

just as they were entering on the bridge. They were so closely compacted together as naturally to form an obstacle which it was difficult
to pass considering the depth of the column, and they found themselves stopped by us, while we having no resource but to regain the
road, made a desperate resistance. During this struggle the hussars had
passed to the other side of the palings that bounded the road and had
fired on us across the palings.

I could not possibly look round, but on hearing the shots and the
shouts that accompanied them, I easily imagined what was passing
behind me. Indeed, I should probably have received the honour of the
first of these shots had I not been engaged upon the bridge, and if they
had not been in danger of hitting the dragoons by firing obliquely
upon me. In order to get out of this position, it was absolutely necessary to mix ourselves up with the dragoons. I pressed my horse as
much as I could without cruelty, he penetrated into their ranks, and
for one moment I saw the senior sergeant by me, but we two were
alone, and he soon fell.

Probably Providence had its share in the business, as far as concerned myself, for while I was still in the midst of the turmoil striking and guarding more with the hilt than the blade, I did not receive
a single scratch. I took advantage of a weak spot on my right to get
out, and turning my horse sharply to the right, forced the escarpment
commanding the road we had come by, an attempt I should not have
made under any other circumstances. This escarpment was nearly vertical, and at least fifteen feet high; but the snow that covered it was
hard enough to give a foothold to my roughshod horse.

By good luck, at the moment I made the movement to the right
I have spoken of, an old sergeant who had thrown himself forward to
bar my passage, let his horse be caught in flank by mine, was thrown
down and formed an obstacle that gave me time enough to prevent
my horse being hamstrung when he made his first effort to climb the
escarpment. But at this moment a pistol-shot struck me on the right
side, the ball pierced my belt of two thicknesses of buff leather and
penetrated into the flesh to the depth of its own diameter, without
causing me more pain than a smart fillip. I felt I was hit and that was
all.

After two or three violent efforts, during which I was very near
falling back into the road, my horse reached the top of the escarpment, and I set off at the top of his speed, finding myself on the plain,
in the direction of our cantonments. I had cast a glance backwards on

the scene I was leaving, and had seen nothing but the remains of my poor detachment; the defeat was complete.

The first moment I was not followed, as no one attempted the climb that I had accomplished; but it was not long before I heard the gallop of several horses coming my way, and saw I was desperately pursued by an officer who was gaining ground on me, and by seven or eight dragoons. I had not much chance of escaping from them, and I made that discouraging reflection while all the time on the watch and digging in my spurs. Then an accident came to my assistance. There was ice upon some portions of the ground we passed over, I had already seen it when I perceived the officer's horse fall, and hoped he would rise without his master, but unhappily they got up together; the advantage I had gained during their short mishap was rapidly diminishing, and I heard them calling to me, in very good French, to surrender.

I was still some paces in front of my pursuers, when my horse fell in his turn. I had my leg caught under him, but did not let him go, and he managed to rise to his feet without my being separated from him. His croup was still on the ground when the officer, coming up with me, made a blow at my face with his sword, exclaiming, "Surrender then!" I should really have had nothing better to do, but the sword cut had been warded off, and as he had made me angry I hastily returned some blows, notwithstanding my disadvantageous position, and without in the least thinking of what must inevitably ensue.

The dragoons who were behind soon came up, and I then despairingly pronounced the solemn words, "I surrender." Those who have never found themselves in the position of saying this word, can never conceive the dreadful sinking of heart that it causes. It binds us to observe uncertain and perilous conditions, puts us at the mercy of unknown enemies, possibly abounding in insults and ill-treatment; it often breaks a career, and causes the loss of fair years in a sad captivity; lastly, it causes the deprivation of all intercourse with country and family, and presages long and painful anxieties on account of the sufferer. These reflections and many others quickly crowded upon my mind.

The dragoons who came up to us would certainly have killed me had not some of them been carried on beyond by the impetus of their horses, and if the officer and the old sergeant, whom I had overthrown with his horse, had not thrown themselves across to cover me with their bodies, and parry the blows which were not spared me in the first moments, some of which I also kept off as well as I could with the remains of my sword, which was broken a foot from the hilt. At last the tempest was stilled, and I handed the remains of my sword to the officer, when he gave some orders that I did not understand.

A dragoon took the reins of my horse, two others followed me, and we set off at a gallop in the direction of Culmsee, We met several dragoons who came at me in succession with raised swords and threatening words, and every time this caused a conversation or dispute between them and my three conductors. I remember that, as we neared Culmsee, I felt a moment of false shame at the notion of the sorry spectacle I should make on entering into this town; then a still more bitter feeling arose together with it, I was going for ever to lose my poor horse who had behaved so well, but had become the victor's prize.

On entering Culmsee I was speedily reassured as to the reception I should meet, the town is Polish, and the faces of all the inhabitants expressed interest and anxiety for me. I was conducted to the burgomaster's house, situated in the open square, and taken into a room on the ground-floor. Then my conductors took my cloak and my watch, and searched me to find my purse. I had none, for I had taken only one Frederick with me, and that was small enough to escape their observation in the place where it was put.

In half-an-hour I saw the whole troop I had met come into the square. They dismounted, and the room in which I was became filled with soldiers, who looked curiously but not impertinently at me. However, one came who wanted to take my epaulets, and this occasioned some struggle among them, for there were some opposed to it. I do not know what might have been the result of this contest, had not another interruption come to my aid; a dragoon of large stature, with his left side bared so as to display a large wound in his arm near the shoulder, came quickly up to me, and seizing the man who wished to take away my epaulets with his only serviceable hand, pushed him to the door with such ease that I must think that a well-established reputation for strength prevented any idea of resistance.

After this exploit he came to me, and made me and his comrades understand that I was the person who had wounded him, and this gave him a right to be my protector. He had a very nice face and I was sorry that I had wounded him.

It was he who had fired the first carabine shot at me, he was one of the men with the officer that advanced, probably to induce us to surrender without resistance. He showed me his wound with a smile, to mark that he bore no malice for it, as I had already understood from the nature of his intervention.

A few minutes after this incident the officer to whom I had given up my sword came in; he held a bloody handkerchief upon his left cheek, and carried my cloak in his other hand; he gave it to me, saying, in a proud tone, "We do not rob our prisoners, not *we.*" This *we* was an insult, a gratuitous insult, and in bad taste; moreover, it was a bit of cowardice considering my position. Blood mounted to my face, and I replied as I felt, but soon remembered that an hour before this same man had prevented my being put to death. So, we remained some seconds looking at each other; then he held out his hand to me with a cordial and frank air that removed the vexation he had caused me by his untoward *we*, which he subsequently explained to me.

I pressed the hand he extended to me and asked him about his wound; I learnt he had received it from me, for in the heat of action I had not been aware of it; he asked after my wounds, and seemed pleased to hear I had only one. Then he showed me that my cloak had seven bullet holes in it. Thanks to the cloak, the persons who shot at me had not aimed at the spot really occupied by my body. I heard that twenty of my men were taken, all more or less seriously wounded, and one of my sergeants so dangerously that they had been unable to think of bringing him in; he had been left in the village where the action took place. A corporal and two *cuirassiers* had escaped over the frozen lake on our right, and so must have reached our cantonments and given the alarm.

A surgeon had been sent for, but before he came there was a great commotion in the square; they mounted their horses, and made me mount mine, after having required my parole that I would make no attempt to escape, and we left Culmsee, followed by a dozen sledges carrying our wounded, and by our horses led by the hand. We reached two woods at a short distance, and marched fast for two or three hours; then we halted at a village with a good house near it, and the officers went there and took me with them. We were received by the master and mistress of the house, whom I recognised as Poles from their cool politeness to my introducers and cordiality to myself. They spoke French without any accent.

Whilst on the road from Culmsee to this house, I had time to become a little acquainted with my conquerors. Their leader, who had come forward to parley with us, was the Baron von Werther; the officer who had been the principal cause of my capture was the Count von Moltke; besides, there was a Baron Trenck, great nephew of the famous baron of that name, a young brother-in-law of Baron von Werther, and another, all belonging to the dragoon regiment of Haors.

The detachment of hussars was commanded by an officer who was not a gentleman, and whom the others treated with distant coolness, though he had very refined manners. His arm had been pierced by a ball, an accident certainly owing to the clumsiness of one of his own hussars, for my *cuirassiers* had no cartridges, and so could not use their pistols. He took no more notice of this wound than if he had not received it, and the other officers made no more of it than he did. As for me, I was the object of the most anxious attention; I was questioned on my country and family; the resistance I had made was magnified; in a word, all kinds of consolation were sought for me.

M. de Moltke wished to see my wound; he took me in a room adjoining the saloon, and I undressed. It was not a dangerous wound, as I knew by the small amount of pain it caused me. The ball had penetrated into the flesh to the right of the kidneys, the wound had bled but little, but it caused a swelling as large as an egg. On pressing this the ball could be seen. M. de Moltke removed it from me very cleverly and put a plug of linen in its place; when the operation was finished, he went out and I remained alone.

I had hardly resumed my clothes when a door opened opposite to that by which I had entered. The mistress of the house hastened towards me with such a business-like air that I perceived she came to propose to me some means of escape. At the same moment the Baron von Werther entered by the other door, and the poor lady's disappointment was so evident that the baron said to her in French, probably that I might understand, "I am afraid, madam, I am in your way." She retired without speaking, but casting on the baron a look that was anything but tender.

I was fetched to dinner, which I very much needed, not having eaten since the night before. I was assured that my poor *cuirassiers*, whom I thought of very much, should be carefully attended to. At table, notwithstanding my resistance, I was helped first, and the best selected for me. Then I asked to see my men, and Count Moltke led me into a large room, where they were all gathered round a good fire. They met me with so many exhibitions of affection, and showed so much pleasure at seeing me again, that I felt in a kind of way consoled: and I was also proud that a foreign officer should see what a French officer was to his soldiers. I made inquiries as to their wounds, but we were going to start again, and I had no time to examine them. One man alone was unwounded, some had suffered very severely; the only sergeant left me had his head cleft with a sword cut, a gash on his left hand, and his right arm twice thrust through with the point of a sword. The attitude of all these men displayed resolution and resignation.

We resumed our march, night fell, and we were in the depths of the wood. The sledges went heavily, for the snow was thick and unbroken, and our progress was slow through the thick darkness pervading the pine forest. I was again riding my own horse, with the sorrowful thought that we should soon be parted. The boughs were weighed down with snow and struck me in the face; it was horribly cold, and I was assailed by most sorrowful thoughts all through this night march. I had before me the prospect of a lengthened captivity, possibly in Siberia, for many prisoners were sent there, and with the help of fatigue my imagination exhibited pictures to me that were still more doleful than the sufficiently unpleasant reality.

Shortly before day we reached a dirty little town, and for some reason or other they would not tell me the name of it. I lodged with the officers in a house of mean appearance, and perceived that we were clear out of the reach of any pursuit, from a certain air of security that appeared upon their faces, instead of the anxiety and pre-occupation that I had observed the evening before, and which was shown during the night by halts and expeditions of sub-officers sent to listen, and come and report.

The town where we were must have been occupied by Prussian troops, for I saw two dragoon officers wearing a uniform different from that of the regiment of Haors. I began to suffer from my wound, and also from the leg that the horse had fallen upon; however, the day passed without its being impossible to bear it; the surgeon of the place had been fetched, and what a surgeon! He came with a great pot of grease, with which he rubbed the wound and the parts near it, as well as my leg and thigh, and his air of capability and importance made me anxious as to how he might treat other wounds more severe than mine.

In the evening straw was brought into the room where we had passed the day; mattresses were put on the straw, and we all lay down there except Baron von Werther, who, as commanding officer, had a separate room. Baron von Werther might be about forty years old; he had been lately married, and talked a great deal about his wife and his affection for her. The Count von Moltke was thirty-two, of handsome and distinguished appearance; he was tall and well made, but entirely bald.

My pain and my thoughts were overcome by fatigue; I slept soundly till day, and then I had great trouble in getting on my legs. My whole body was swelled, and the smallest movement painful. In the morning the officers went out on duty, except the Count von Moltke, and he wrote a long report on the occurrences of the day before yesterday, asking me to give him the correct spelling of my name and surname. I was questioned as to the strength of the division my regiment belonged to, but not pressed, on my formal refusal to say anything about it.

Then I was informed that I was to go with the rest of the prisoners under the escort of a detachment of hussars, and I felt a kind of sorrow at parting with the officers who had treated me so well; I thanked them for myself and for my men, whom they had not allowed to want for anything. I was to be carried along in a sledge carefully prepared and provided with blankets. Five other sledges were prepared for my men in the proportion of one to four men; they were well furnished with fresh straw, and as the cuirassiers had kept their cloaks, they must have been pretty well protected from cold.

The sergeant, whose wounds I have mentioned, was named Le Duc, and was son of the court coachbuilder under Louis XVI. He had received some education, was at most twenty years old, had a pretty beardless face, and in woman's clothes might have passed for a girl. His history, together with the courage he had shown in the action, had excited the interest of the Prussian officers, and I had arranged that he should be entered on the list as a *cadet*, a rank unknown in France; but in Prussia it removed him from the rank of sub-officer, without any further responsibility for him or for me, than the repayment of the difference of pay, on exchange or delivery, and no claim was ever made for it. I also requested that Le Duc should be placed in my sledge.

At the time of our departure all the Prussian soldiers assembled in the square; many of them had their arms in slings and heads bandaged. I came out at the same time as my *cuirassiers* were brought out to be put into the sledges awaiting them in the square. Only two of them could walk without assistance; I myself was supported by M. de Moltke and another officer, and though my mental and bodily sufferings were great, the sight I saw for the moment removed all my feelings. The Prussian sub-officers and soldiers paid the greatest attention to my wounded, brought them brandy, pressed their hands, and, in a word, when they saw them go away, seemed as if they were parting from old friends. As for me, I was overwhelmed with courtesies, and two of them even came and kissed my hand. I also parted from the officers very amicably, though with less demonstration.

We went under the escort of fifteen hussars commanded by a sergeant, who spoke French as well as we did. These hussars were of the regiment of Eben, and also bore the name of Hussars of Death, because their uniform was black, ornamented with white braid, and on their shakos and sabretaches were death's heads with cross bones. Their faces were not comforting, and we were at their mercy as to their behaviour to us, for I knew that much persuasion had been used towards them not to illtreat us. We had travelled the whole day, and night had fallen for two or three hours when we stopped in a village before a very large building; it was the mansion of the place.

I made my entrance into it, carried by the hussars and preceded by several women bearing lights and crying out "*Alas!*" Le Duc could walk, but I found it quite impossible to take a single step. At this first halt the anxiety excited by the appearance of the hussars was completely dissipated. They took the greatest of precautions to avoid hurting me; they walked quietly, questioning me by look, and showing attention, with a delicacy I could not have supposed them capable of. They laid me down in a large and very tidy room, while instant preparations were made for warming it, and a little table was set out close to me with a white tablecloth and places for two.

Half an hour later we had a dinner that would satisfy anyone at the best of times. Poor Le Duc could not use his arms, and he never recovered the power of the left, but two hussars stayed by us and vied with each other in waiting on us. While we dined, the one bed in the room was made up; I pointed to Le Duc to signify that I wished them to make up another for him, and they brought it immediately. There was one great difficulty, and that was getting our clothes off. At our first halt the sleeves of Le Duc's coat had been cut in order to dress his wounds, and he could get it off with a little assistance; but my clothes were uninjured except for the shot holes, and anything done to interfere with their condition would have caused me immense inconvenience, not to say pain.

So, I intended to get myself carried to bed with all my clothes on, though my swelled limbs had much need to be eased from the pressure. Especially my right leg gave me much pain, and filled up my boot so much that I thought it impossible to get it off. When I showed that I meant to go to bed in all my clothes, the hussars remonstrated, and a woman who seemed to be a kind of house-steward adding her influence to theirs, I allowed them to remove my clothing, and they did it with incredible care, skill, and speed.

After they had put me into my bed they put Le Duc into his, and the next morning they both returned to dress us. This was not accomplished without difficulty and pain, but with as great care as they had used the evening before. I had especial difficulty in putting on my boot again, not liking to part with it, for fear it should be lost. They gave us breakfast and we departed. I was able to see my cuirassiers before I was carried to my sledge, and they told me that they had had enough to eat, and had not suffered from cold. I was uneasy about the wounds of some of them; Le Duc's head was enormously swelled, and he had not slept.

We marched fast without stopping; the hussars' horses did the whole march without refreshment, and without seeming tired. We halted at night at a hamlet of a few houses only, and Le Duc and I were taken to a mill that was probably the best lodging in the place; the sergeant and three hussars came there with us. The miller received us with abuse and threats. He seemed so furious and exasperated that I think he would have killed us had we been alone; but he was strictly restrained by the sergeant and hussars. The man had lost an arm, and had one of the ugliest faces that could be met with.

This evening I undertook to dress Le Duc's wounds. I was afraid that the cold would produce mortification, and begged the quartermaster to get me a little old linen. The miller harshly refused to find any, but he was obliged to yield. He had a daughter of fifteen or sixteen years, whose pretty face expressed the deepest consternation and great interest on our account during the exhibition of her father's violence. Having watched me for a moment attempting to make lint, she came quietly and sat opposite to us, looking at a little that had been brought me, and made some herself. Meanwhile the miller was casting savage and angry glances at us, and in a corner of the room the hussars were drinking beer.

It was not at all easy to dress Le Duc's wounds. The sabre cut that had laid open his head crossed the forehead from top to bottom as far as the left eyebrow, where there was a deep cut; the bone was much injured and inflammation very severe. The whole presented the appearance of a serious wound, but was nothing compared to that in the left hand. Having lost his helmet, he had tried to protect his bare head with this hand, and the arm had been cut an inch deep; his fingers had no power. I summoned up my courage, washed his wounds with warm water, and by means of lint and bandages, with the help of the sergeant and the girl, I succeeded in dressing them tolerably. Le Duc bore the operation without a frown; indeed, he smiled at times, and this increased the respect that the hussars already bore him.

A few minutes afterwards our guardians went to their horses, and the miller, who had gone out during the dressing of the wounds, looking as if he was in a great rage, came back and, seeing us alone, heaped a torrent of abuse upon us. His rage was increased by the carelessness with which we listened, and he rushed upon us with his fist clenched, though we were in such a pitiable condition; but his daughter threw herself between him and us, and spoke to him quietly and strongly. No doubt she had a great deal of influence over him, for he was quieted in a moment, and never renewed the attack. Her mother was dead, and she seemed complete mistress. At the moment I write, her pretty face is as clear before my sight as if I had seen her yesterday, though it is a remembrance of nearly fifty years ago.

Afterwards, when not a prisoner, I saw the miller again, and only the feeling of gratitude that I had for his daughter protected him from the harm I could have done him, not from a revengeful spirit, but because his odious conduct deserved a severe punishment.

We lay down on the straw arranged by the hussars as best they could. Le Duc and I were both feverish and passed a bad night. Next day we started early. It was a remarkable exception to the general course of the weather in this latitude and time of year that no snow fell during our whole journey, and otherwise we should have suffered much more; it was one or two feet thick on the ground, and our sledges moved without shaking us.

About the middle of the day we heard a sharp cannonade, without knowing whether it came from the right or from the left, because the woods reflected the sound in such a way as to make it appear to come from several quarters. It was the action of Haff, which was the forerunner of the Battle of Eylau. At the beginning of the following night we joined the baggage of a Prussian corps that I supposed to be retreating, because it was going in the same direction as ourselves. Our escort caused us to go on the side of the road to get past the convoy, and as it was impossible in the darkness and snow to judge of the breadth of the road, the sledge in which I was with Le Duc turned over into a deep ditch and passed over us, but without doing us any harm, thanks to the thickness of the snow in which we were buried.

Considering our sad state, this accident might have been productive of much mischief. Happily, Le Duc's wounds did not suffer from it, and necessity gave me strength to rise alone and go to help him. His first thought was to ask me if I was hurt and relieve me on his own account. The sledge was brought back, we were replaced in it, and an hour later reached a little village crowded with troops. We made a long halt in the street, by no means a fortunate thing, especially for Le Duc and me, because the snow had got into our clothes when we had our tumble in it, and it was exceedingly cold.

The room that was to serve us for our night's lodging was heated to twenty-five degrees, and the floor was covered with soldiers lying on one another and snoring in competition. We were placed on benches against the wall and given a little bread and beer. Very soon after our arrival Count Moltke came in, and this seemed to me like finding an old friend. He came close to me and spent the rest of the night there. He said he should go to Königsberg next day, and that we should very likely meet there; he seemed very sad. We marched as soon as it was light, always with the same escort.

The cannonade soon recommenced, and seemed nearer. It was the Battle of Eylau. The notion that my regiment might be there vexed me much. The dragoons whom we had fought with joined us during a rather long halt in the middle of the day; but they only passed by. Another detachment of their corps had united with them, for they were in greater force, and I saw officers whom I did not know. During our halt I was witness to a specimen of manners that I cannot help putting down here. A young officer of dragoons was sitting in the general room, near the innkeeper's daughter; he was tranquilly smoking his pipe, with his right hand completely buried in the bosom of this girl of, perhaps, seventeen or eighteen years of age; she was pretty, looked modest, and was diligently working away at a bit of sewing, though thus in contact with her neighbour. This took place quite openly under the eyes of her father and mother, and those of several persons present, and nobody seemed to think it at all extraordinary.

Our entrance into Königsberg was frightful; we reached it at the same time as the wounded; the streets were crowded with sledges on which they were heaped up. Many had died on the road, and lay by the side of the dying. We advanced slowly through this, exposed to the outrages of the people in a state of exasperation at this sight, and of Russian soldiers who had not been present at the battle and wished to revenge their comrades' disasters upon us. Our escort had really to fight for us, and I was several times afraid they would be compelled to yield. In consequence of the crowd, we made a long halt before the house of a little humpbacked apothecary, and he tried like one possessed to stir up the Russian soldiers to cut our throats, and our escort to give up our protection.

I was put alone, without knowing the reason, into a private house standing in a little unfrequented street; I remained there till nightfall without eating, unguarded, and having seen no one but the man who opened the door, and him not again. The time seemed long to me. At last someone came; it was M. de Moltke. He had learnt what took place on our entry, and seemed to feel it very much. He asked me if I could bear a quarter of an hour's walk with the help of his arm. We tried in the room, and I felt that I could. After going along some crooked streets, we reached an open space full of men. Looks were turned on us, and a Russian soldier driving a sledge made a cut at me with his whip, but missed me. M. de Moltke dashed at him, dragged him out of the sledge, and gave him a sound beating with the flat of his sword. Whilst he made this rush I was separated a few paces from him, and enveloped in the crowd; but nothing hostile was done to me, and I even met with more than one kindly look.

We entered a large room that opened directly upon the square, crowded with wounded Russian officers; there was not an empty seat, and they brought me a chair, of which I was in great need. A few moments afterwards Le Duc was brought in, having remained with the soldiers, and thought he was parted from me for the whole time of his captivity; our union again was due to the care of Count von Moltke. The place where we were was crowded with Russian wounded; among them was a colonel with a broken leg, crying out piteously; and two French officers of the 4th Dragoons were also brought in, one of them being Dulac, who, I think, became a lieutenant-general. He was then a sub-lieutenant, of fine figure and bearing; he had a high spirit of defiance, and his entrance gave me a pleasant sensation. He was not wounded, but his comrade had suffered severely with three lance wounds, two of them through the chest.

A Prussian surgeon came to attend us, urged by a young Russian infantry officer, whose coat was riddled by shot-holes received at Eylau two days before. He helped in all the dressings with extreme care and activity, and a fantastic and cheerful air; at last, when he saw that everyone had had his wants attended to, he quickly let down his trousers and showed to the surgeon and the spectators that his back had been pierced by a ball which had made four wounds, that had not been dressed for forty hours. The cold had stopped the blood; but as soon as the surgeon removed the clots in washing the wounds, it flowed in frightful quantities.

Next morning, we were placed on the sledges with a dozen other soldiers who were taken prisoners and had been placed with my *cuirassiers*, and we departed from Königsberg without knowing where we going. The evening before, some kind man had brought a jam tart to the guardroom, and Le Duc and I had each a piece of it, and that was all we got to eat the whole day. For a short time, we skirted the Frische Haff, frozen hard and looking like a sea of ice; for the tongue of land that parts it from the Gulf of Dantzig, and called the Frische-Nehrung, was two leagues off, and so covered with snow as to be indistinguishable from it.

We made our way over the ice, leaving the shore, to proceed to Pillau, our destination, and though we thus pursued a straight line, we got there late from our escort being infantry, as the march had to be regulated by their pace. Before we reached Pillau there had been a mutiny of the new prisoners against the escort, who cocked their guns and took aim at them. A Prussian sergeant in command of the escort showed great calmness and decision. We intervened, and peace was made.

CHAPTER 3

Exchange of Prisoners

When we reached the fort of Pillau, we were surrounded by some thirty officers, who had been prisoners there for a longer or shorter period. There were men of all branches of the service, and they overwhelmed us with questions, everyone entirely in his personal interest; then came the turn of our story, for every newcomer was obliged to tell his. I there learnt that I should have forty shillings a month, but five of them kept back to provide bedding. We were lodged in a room where there were seven beds; one of them occupied by a young prince of the house of Darmstadt, in other respects a very insignificant personage.

Le Duc's bed was near mine; we went to get our meals in a house on the parade of the fort. This parade was set apart for our place of exercise, and the captive sub-officers and soldiers were also brought there, having to march in file by twos, escorted and guarded by Prussian soldiers, who would not let them lose their distance. I had the pleasure of seeing all my cuirassiers in succession come and join the column of men marched out in this way, except those who died of the effects of their wounds, perhaps from want of attention; for the hospitals were crowded, and the surgeons had not the practised skill acquired by ours during the interminable wars that had put their talents to so many proofs.

Among the prisoners who arrived at Pillau after us, I ought to mention Count Kuminski, colonel of a regiment of Polish Light horse; he had been taken in Pomerania by the partisan leader Schill, led to Kolberg, and as he was of the Grand Duchy of Warsaw, and thus a Prussian subject, he was tried there by a council of war and condemned to be shot. The King of Prussia caused an offer of pardon to be made to him, on condition that he would forsake the Polish cause, and use all his influence in his country to stop the insurrection, which was now assuming dimensions that were very alarming to the Prussian rule in Poland. He refused haughtily, and was going to be executed when the Prince of Ponte Corvo (Bernadotte), being within reach of Kolberg, sent in a flag of truce to say that, if this execution took place, he should immediately have General Kalkreuth shot, who was in our hands. This threat saved Count Kuminski, and he was sent by sea to Pillau, and came thither preceded by the fame his magnanimous refusal had acquired; and he was appropriately received there.

The *commandant* of the fort had received orders to exercise the most active vigilance over him, and as this *commandant* was a fool, he put an orderly with the count, with orders not to leave him a moment. So, this orderly sat by his side at table, and marched by him when he moved about in his own room. The horrible nuisance this was to the count may be imagined. At last the orderly one day took upon himself to smoke, and the count told him to leave off; the orderly, who was a tall grenadier, made an impertinent answer; but it had hardly left his lips when his pipe was broken on his bleeding face; he was seized, lifted up like a child, and thrown, quite stunned, across the table where he had been sitting, by Kuminski.

After this exploit, the count immediately went to the *commandant* of Pillau, followed by all the witnesses of the occurrence, myself among them. We arrived tumultuously, and Kuminski angrily complained of the annoyance to which he was subjected; we warmly supported him, causing it to be understood that this annoyance recoiled on all the captive officers, because, being forced to pass the day in one common room, the keeper set on Count Kuminski was a nuisance to all. The *commandant*, who was a tolerably good fellow at heart, gave way, and the orderly was removed.

The count was small, very well made, had a pretty figure, and was excessively powerful. When a general he played an important part in the Polish rising of 1831. In 1807 he was thirty years old, and was a colonel; I was twenty-three, and was a sub-lieutenant; but, notwithstanding these differences of age and rank, he became more intimate with me than with all the other officers there, and when I was exchanged, he showed much regret at our separation, in congratulating me on that event. I never saw him again.

Some weeks after my arrival at Pillau, I received a letter from Count de Moltke, informing me that my exchange with his brother had just been sanctioned by the king, and that I should immediately be conducted to the French advanced posts. He added that, knowing that I had received neither the property nor the money I had asked for from my regiment, he sent three Fredericks with his letter, that I might repay him when I was able. A few days afterwards I was informed that I was going to Königsberg, to be thence despatched to the advanced posts. Four other officers received similar communications, among them were De Castres, an Engineer captain of the Geographical Department, and D'Haubersaërt, son of the President of the Court at Douai. My poor Le Duc remained in captivity till the peace was signed in the month of July following.

We departed in a sledge in twenty degrees of cold; it was the end of March, our sledges were open, but we had straw and our cloaks. Our return was easily accomplished, and it may be said agreeably. At Fischhausen, a little town situated on the road from Pillau to Königsberg, an invitation came to us to breakfast, and we found three ladies in a very comfortable house, one of whom sang to us with the accompaniment of a horrible spinette and in French, of which she did not understand a word "*Femme, voulez-vous éprouver?*"

At Königsberg we were all five quartered together, and given four of the body-guard under the orders of a corporal for our protection; they were very fine men and very polite, being carefully picked soldiers, and better dressed than the others. They had a white uniform, very tight, and very short, a sabretache stuck tight against the left leg, and the enormous hat adorned with a great plume, peculiar to all the Prussian cavalry, except the hussars, who wore the shako.

When I first passed through Königsberg the truncheon of my sword had been taken from me, though it had been courteously left me by the officers I had fought with; and I was much surprised on my return to that city, to see an officer in a uniform I knew not enter the room where I was with my comrades, holding in his hand the remnant of my sword, which, after having asked my name, he restored.

Anyone who can imagine the crowd of troops that were then at Königsberg, and the excitement caused by the presence of the Emperor of Russia, the King of Prussia, and their staffs, will understand how greatly I was touched by this attention. I must own I was very glad to bring back this relic of my defeat to my regiment, as it was not only broken, but bore many marks of the blows it had received.

The Count de Moltke, who came to see me during the day, assured me he had nothing to do with this polite act. He said we should meet again, and, in fact, after two days' march, he came to relieve the officer conducting us, and to deliver us at the advanced posts we were approaching. We both travelled in the same sledge; he slept on straw with us, and next day at nine o'clock in the morning, we reached the banks of the Passarge, opposite to Braunsberg, a place held by the French.

At Königsberg I had observed that M. de Moltke wore the order of military merit, which I had not seen on him seven weeks before. He told me he owed it to our fight, and that the sub-officer who had helped him to save me, and whom I had thrown down at the mouth of the bridge, had also been decorated with the military medal. This sub-officer came to see me, and so great was the distance that separated the Prussian sub-officers from their officers, that this man would not understand that I was holding out my hand to him; and, from respect, he would not put out his own, and had tears in his eyes when he really was convinced that I thus desired to show him my gratitude.

When the Passarges was crossed, I found myself again among the French.

The little town of Braunsberg is situated about three quarters of a mile from the river, and was occupied by General Dupont and his staff. M. de Moltke went with us to the general, and he gave him a capital reception, and invited him and us to breakfast. An hour afterwards we were seated at a table with plates for thirty, economically provided, but with plenty to eat. General Dupont had placed M. de Moltke by his side, and during breakfast asked him in what action he had received the wound in the cheek, as the scar looked fresh.

Count de Moltke answered that I had given him that wound, and this made me the object of general attention, and caused me much embarrassment. I blushed to the white of my eyes, a fault that I have never been able to cure in all these seventy years, and General Dupont having told me to relate the adventure, I had to go through it, and was doubly embarrassed by the presence of M. de Moltke. Not that without his presence I should have had any notion of puffing the matter, but because, conceal it how I might, it had to be told, that with twenty-three men I had fought a hundred and fifty, that the combat had been hand to hand, had lasted half an hour, and that after all my men had been disabled, it appeared that the Prussians had a much larger number of wounded.

Besides, during my relation, which appeared to be very interesting to all my audience, M. de Moltke behaved delightfully, and several times expressed his opinion that I underrate the merit of the action, I also told of his intervention at a moment when but for him and the sergeant, of whom I have spoken, I should infallibly have been killed. Congratulations then poured on Count de Moltke from all sides, and General Dupont spoke to him as if he owed him the life of a relation or friend. Though this scene caused me some embarrassment, it also caused me great delight. I was twenty-three years old, and a crowd of old tried soldiers were giving me approving glances; in the evening one of General Dupont's secretaries told me that the general had several times mentioned my affair during the day, and was much struck with the account of it.

Count de Moltke left us an hour after breakfast; we embraced, and I never saw him again. I heard in 1829 from the Count de la Roche-Aymon, that he had become a general, and was dead. He belonged to an illustrious Danish family, and at the very moment when I am writing this the Danish Ambassador at Paris is a Count de Moltke.

From Braunsberg we were taken to the headquarters of Bernadotte (then Prince of Ponte-Corvo, and afterwards King of Sweden), commanding our first *corps d'armée*, and Dupont's division in it. The prince received us exceedingly well, offered us money and linen, telling us in the kindest way that his purse and baggage were at our service. We did not take advantage of his offers; for my part, I had found an officer on General Dupont's staff, who advanced me the three *Fredericks* which I wished to return to Count de Moltke. I never saw any one that had so much the bearing of a great nobleman as Bernadotte, though he had the far from refined Gascon accent.

My comrades in captivity went in different directions. I proceeded towards the headquarters of the division that my regiment belonged to. I reached it next day at evening, and was coldly received by General Espagne, under whose orders we were. During the dinner he had asked me to, he broke out sharply upon me, accusing me of want of caution, and of being the cause of the loss of my detachment. This took place before twenty witnesses, whose sympathy for me I could easily perceive. I also saw that Commandant Chains had kept silence about the instructions he had given me when sending me out to forage, or rather he had said he gave me different ones from what I have related in the beginning of this account.

I was at first confused by the attack of General Espagne, and the severe looks he cast at me; but I regained my presence of mind enough to repeat the plain facts, and to make it be understood that my orders being to divide my detachment by sending back the men in succession to escort the oats that I was to despatch from five villages named in my orders, it was impossible to suspect that there was any danger at all. If I had been bound to take the military precautions usual in range of the enemy, I should not have had time to search even two villages, the day is so short in that latitude on the 3rd of February. This explanation was successful; but I was grieved to have had to give it. I saw that I had been spoiled by the Prussians, and by the reception I had met with at General Dupont's headquarters, and—due to a circumstance that would not tell in my favour any more—the presence of Count de Moltke.

From the day of my catastrophe, I had heard nothing of my regiment; it is true that some hours after my capture a trumpeter had been sent bearing a letter with a few lines from me to relate what had happened, but it was possible the letter had not been delivered, and I knew not what had been thought of me. In consequence of these thoughts, I moved towards my regiment the next day with some anxiety. Night had fallen when I reached the first village it occupied, and I there found the very troop I belonged to.

I was received with open arms by my old captain, Baudichon, a kind and brave man, with whom I had always been on the best of terms; but I confess that the greeting which affected me most on that evening was from my orderly, my poor Jouette. The captain, in my absence, had kept him in his service, so he heard of my return at once, and followed me into the room where the officers were. While I was embracing them, he took me in his arms from behind, laid his face against my back and began to weep.

Next morning, I proceeded to the colonel, who was living a league away from our village; he gave me such a warm greeting as proved how glad he was to see me again. Major Chalus had not given him an exact account of the instructions I had received; in his presence I proved the facts, and he could not persist in his original assertion.

I was the last sub-lieutenant but one in the regiment. A month later I was made lieutenant, and this promotion did not displease any one of my comrades. The senior sub-lieutenant, Marulaz, behaved perfectly well to me on this occasion; before that I had also received more than one proof of affection from him. He was forty years old, and had no fortune but his sword; he was a strict soldier, performing his duties with scrupulous exactness, seldom smiled, and never laughed, I have preserved the remembrance of him in my mind as a specimen of a rare species. There were three brothers Marulaz in the 6th Cuirassiers.

My regiment was not present at the Battle of Eylau, and subsequently the armies remained facing each other, we holding the left bank of the Passarges and the Prussians the right. This river falls into the Frische Haff, running from south to north; it varies in depth, forming several fords, and is not more than fifty leagues in length. On the right, in front of our line, resting on the Halle, a little river tributary to the Pregel, was the corps of Marshal Ney, with headquarters at Gutstadt.

To give an idea of the miseries that arise from such a misadventure as mine, I must say, that on my return to the regiment I possessed nothing but what I had on and one shirt that I had bought at Pillau, in order to have a change during my captivity. My portmanteau had been sent to the Prussian advanced posts with a sum of twelve pounds, and this I had never received. So, I required an entire new outfit, and had two horses to buy. The regiment advanced me what was necessary, and the colonel himself came to my assistance with all the zeal of friendship. I soon found myself owner of a horse from the Ukraine, as light as a bird and never wearied, and of another that was good but of a more ordinary kind. A little later I purchased for ten *thalers* a Cossack horse that had been left behind sick; he recovered and would have done me good service, but for the little event that deprived me of him, as will be related in its proper place.

The country held by the two armies was soon exhausted, and became the scene of the most terrible misery to be found in history; all the houses were stripped to give the horses the straw of the thatch; there were no oats, and the cavalry regiments received orders to obtain them by any possible means. I was detached with thirty picked men to go on the left bank of the Vistula, with *carte blanche* to seize upon oats wherever I could find any, and also get the vehicles necessary to transport them. I made four days' march without finding any, but in every village, that I passed I requisitioned the best horsed carts and took them with me. I had crossed the Vistula and was following the valley downwards; thus, I drew near to Dantzig, now being besieged.

This operation was entrusted to the *corps d'armée* of Marshal Lefèvre, which was short of cavalry, and what it had were Germans. The valley of the Vistula is very rich, and the villages in it are numerous; those I had passed through had nothing at all left, for the marshal had spared those nearest to him, and had sent to those at a greater distance for his requirements. At last I entered within the circumference of his reserve, and, to begin with, came upon the most beautiful farm I have ever seen in my life. A square court, at least half a mile in circumference, composed of fine buildings, enclosed it entirely.

It was occupied by a detachment of Saxon Dragoons, which was absent when I came, having only left a few men and a son of Marshal Lefèvre, who was put there for some reason I do not know. He was known in the army under the name of Coco; his father had never been able to do anything with him and carried him in his train. He and the Saxons both refused to allow me to take any oats, though there was an enormous quantity in the farm; but having received special orders, I put them aside. The few dragoons that were there mounted their horses, most likely to go for a superior force; but while they were gone I had my sacks filled and loaded my train of vehicles, though Coco opposed me.

The countrymen who drove the carriages helped me as zealously and actively as if they had done it for themselves. When everything was loaded, I speedily got on the road, quite resolved to protect my oats, and yet not caring to have a disturbance with the Saxons, our allies. Happily, I did not meet them. For four days I had been obliged to march slowly, as I was searching the villages that were on my route; but the return was another thing. I had taken care of the peasant-drivers, so that, as we went through each place again, I easily found means to replace the horses that were tired. Having been away a week, I returned to my regiment with a long file of vehicles, and was very well received. My luck had been exceptional, for it appeared that the detachments of other regiments that went at the same time as I did were far from obtaining an equally good result.

During this journey I met with a quite unexpected danger. In one of the villages where I stopped for the night, I was lodged in a house occupied by a widow and her daughter of seventeen or eighteen years of age. It was the beginning of May, and in the evening after dinner I went out for a walk with these ladies; we left the village by a road enclosed on both sides by the palings about four feet high that I described before. When we reached a spot where the road turned, and we could not see far before us, I heard a curious noise like that caused by a storm, while there was not a breath of wind in the air. Then my two companions climbed the palings with symptoms of the greatest fear, without stopping for the precautions that women usually take in the like case, and I followed instinctively.

We had hardly got over when a column of pigs, at least a hundred and fifty feet deep, broke into the road with such an impetus that nothing could have stopped them, and if we had not been sheltered they would have thrown us down and trampled us under their feet; and according to what the ladies told me we should have been taken up dead, or so crippled as to be fit for nothing. These pigs were taken to the woods in the morning, and they got their food in the evening, and this made them so excited that when they got to the village they were like an avalanche, and so compacted together that if anyone had fallen upon them, instead of beneath them, he would not have come to the ground till they stopped and dispersed.

A few days after my return the division to which we belonged was assembled to be reviewed by the Emperor, which had not been done since Monteschiare, that is to say, two years before. I had never seen the Emperor, and arrived at the place in a great state of excitement. At last I was going to have my first sight of the author of the immortal campaigns in Italy and Egypt, the conqueror of Austerlitz. The regiments were drawn up in single line, and had been waiting an hour when a group of horsemen appeared on the horizon and quickly approached us.

At the head, fifty paces in front of a brilliant staff, was in full relief a man of the most martial figure and appearance; he wore a knightly tunic covered with embroidery, white pantaloons, and half high riding boots; a cap of sable with a red busby bag, and bearing a plume of black ostrich feathers shaded his head, an antique sword hung on his left side, suspended slantwise from the shoulder, and its jewelled hilt glittering in the sun.

I thought it was the Emperor, but it was only Murat, the Grand Duke of Berg, who, in his position of Commandant of all the cavalry, came to do the honours of the division to the Emperor. He passed at a gallop from left to right, and then returned at a walk along the whole length of the front, stopped at the left and waited.

The delay was not long; a much more numerous group soon deployed from the end of the plain whence he had come. First there were the Mamelukes, covered with gold, with their splendid horses bounding as if frantic under the rein; then came the *aides-de-camp*, and a hundred paces after them the Emperor, followed by his immense staff; the rear was brought up by the squadron of Chasseurs of the Guard on duty. The Emperor was far from having the martial and terrible appearance of the personage I had at first taken for him.

He wore a grey riding coat of the plainest appearance; a little hat looped with black, with no ornament but the cockade; the riding coat was unbuttoned and just allowed the colonel's epaulettes to be seen on the undress uniform of the Chasseurs of the Guard, the only uniform he ever wore on a campaign after he became Emperor. He had white breeches and waistcoat, and soft riding boots. He was mounted on a beautiful bright grey Arab horse; the housings of the saddle were fringed with a rich trimming of large bullion, and the stirrups were plated with gold, as were the bit and the buckles of the bridle.

He passed across our front to the right at a walk; when he got to the end he ordered the division to form to the light, form troops and dismount. At that time and till the fall of the Empire the regiments were eight troops, forming four squadrons; the officers were also dismounted and took post on the right of their troops, in the order of their rank. As the Emperor came to each regiment he received the written statement, and gave it to the major-general, and then asked the colonel as follows:

What is your effective strength? How many men in hospital, at the small depots, sick in cantonments, or absent from any other cause?

He put the same questions to the captains, and woe to those whose memory or knowledge was at fault; words of reproof and looks that did not bespeak the near approach of favours gave them some cause for unpleasant reflections. This happened to Colonel Merlin, commanding the 8th Cuirassiers; he became so confused in his answers that the result was an immense difference between the total of his effectives, and the amount made by summing up the different heads.

When the Emperor came to my troop, having put his questions to my captain, as I stood on his left, he stopped before me and asked the colonel why my horse's equipment was not in uniform. The colonel replied that I had just come out of the enemy's prison and had had no time to procure the equipment. The Emperor did not like anyone allowing himself to be taken prisoner, especially in the cavalry, and he looked angrily at me and said,

Why your division has never seen the enemy yet.

I did not venture to speak, and his angry eye fixed steadily upon me distressed me much. The colonel was beginning to explain the circumstances, when General Espagne, who had received me so badly on my return from captivity, came forward and passed a great encomium on my conduct on the occasion. During his recital the Emperor's face underwent a complete metamorphosis, and when he had heard it all he made me a low and gracious bow.

We defiled at a trot by squadrons; coming to the Emperor swords were raised in the air with a shout of "Vive l'Empereur." It was a formidable shout, and the review seemed satisfactory to the person in whose honour it had taken place. As he passed our regiment he said to Colonel d'Avenay:

"Colonel, on the first action a bullet or a gneral's stars."

A few days after this review, our division got orders to pass to the left bank of the Vistula and march on Dantzig; the third day we received counter orders, and were told to return with all speed whence we had come. The Russians had attacked Marshal Ney and made an offensive movement on the whole line of the Passarges, and forced it in pursuit of the third corps. The whole army marched against them at once, and forced them to retrace their steps. To conform to this movement, we marched day and night, only taking a couple of hours' rest from time to time, to give our horses green rye, that we cut, to eat, and ourselves devour a little bread.

When we reached the Passarges all the columns were in motion to cross it, the infantry on little trestle bridges, the artillery and cavalry by fords. Never had I beheld such an imposing sight; there were considerable undulations in the ground with a natural slope to the river bank, and the different columns debouching rapidly from all sides, wound round, disappeared and appeared again from the inequality of the ground. We proceeded towards the smoking remnants of a large village that could be seen half a league off. On arrival we were grieved by the sight of the most horrible spectacles of war.

Marshal Ney, retiring before the Russians, had there left all of the wounded he could not transport any further; when the Russians had passed the Passarges they also had there left all of theirs that were in the neighbourhood; when again they in their turn were driven headlong back they set fire to the village, as is their practice in such circumstances. All the wounded were burnt to about the number of eleven hundred, and we passed through the village amid their remains, and a frightful smell of burnt flesh. Shouts of horror and revenge were raised in our ranks, and this was the source of the character of cruelty that on our side was only a reprisal provoked at the first encounter with the Russians. The prisoners were murdered; it was a war of extermination.

On the 9th of June, 1807, the Russians attempted to make a stand in advance of Gutstadt, but they were overthrown. According to their calculations, their halting place ought to have been Heilsberg; they had studied the ground, raised several strong redoubts, and fancied they were in a way to make us suffer a memorable reverse. The night before at Gutstadt no regiment of our division had been in action: only a few bullets had reached us. Here commenced the era of privation that we suffered. We found the villages fearfully devastated, the inhabitants fled or dead in their houses; in one of them there were five corpses side by side, and a child of twelve still breathing. Colonel d'Avenay took him, had him attended to, saved his life, and then kept him as a servant, and left him a sum of sixty pounds by will. I met him at Paris in the Palais Royal many years after his master's death; he was then in the service of the Duke of Reggio.

CHAPTER 4

Battle of Heilsberg

We arrived on the field of Heilsberg on the 10th about ten in the morning; the action had commenced but feebly, and we commanded the position from the height where we were. Below, and between us and such part of the Russian Army as we could see, there was a deep and steep ravine with a stream at the bottom. Before us its direction was parallel to our front, but it turned sharply to the right and extended any distance on our flank, leaving on its left bank a large flat of about three quarters of a mile in extent, bounded on the other side by a wooded hill. Not a single soldier could be seen on this plain, while behind the spot where the ravine turned, twenty thousand Russians were massed in column, with artillery in the intervals and some cavalry.

To the left of this mass, opposite to us, though a little to our right, several lines of cavalry were drawn out, about sixty squadrons, several being regiments of the Imperial Guard. Opposite to us, on the further side of the ravine, was a village held by the enemy, and on one side of the ravine a battalion in line that had probably been forgotten and left there. On our left, from the other side of the wood on the hill, there was a dropping fire of skirmishers, with a few cannon shots. From the point at which we appeared on the scene, looking on every side, nothing could be seen but our division descending at a walk in column of sections to the neighbourhood of the ravine, in the direction of the village and the line of cavalry before mentioned. There were only some Bavarian skirmishers before us not firing.

If the Russian battalion on our side of the ravine had retired two hundred paces, it would have escaped its destined fate, either by resting on the ravine, or, still better, by putting it between them and us; but it was charged by the two first squadrons of my regiment and

56

entirely destroyed. I was not then engaged, as I belonged to the third squadron, and it had been detached to the left a few minutes before to provide against anything apprehended on that side. A few moments later we rejoined the main body of the regiment, thus making three squadrons. The fourth regiment on our right had its right flank about two hundred paces from the bend formed by the ravine that I have mentioned.

This ravine crossed our front at about a hundred paces' distance, and the position rose from right to left, so that the left of the line was fully twenty paces higher than the right. The artillery of our division, two six-inch howitzers and four four-pounder guns, had gone into action a little apart, in advance of our left, and fired uninterruptedly upon the enemy's artillery and the cavalry behind them. The fire in that line was flanking, the enemy receiving it from right to left. The fire we received from them was the same for us. We were within range of grape, and yet our loss was inconsiderable all the time we remained in this position. But one of our guns was dismounted.

Our gunners showed much more skill, and we could clearly see their shot strike in the Russian ranks. Anyone may imagine the hopes that accompany each discharge at such a time, that it may make the greatest number of victims. This can only be understood by those who have felt it; it is natural, though inhuman, and while I experienced it I remembered M. de Moltke, and could not help thinking that those who fell in our sight might perhaps have been our friends if we had known them.

The 7th and 8th Cuirassiers were behind us in the second line. When I had gained more experience in strategy I was confirmed in the opinion I then took up, that we had been placed in a bad position for no useful purpose. Our division was alone on the spot, with no troops in support, and if we had been left a little more to the rear, the undulations of the ground and its great height would have impaired the accuracy of the enemy's fire, and we should have been spared the grape shot, and musketry of the infantry holding the village opposite to us across the ravine.

Some Bavarian hussars who were employed as vedettes for us had been passed across the ravine to reply to this invisible infantry. They performed their duty bravely, with no other result than the loss of men and horses. At last an infantry regiment came up, crossed the ravine with perfect steadiness, and, once on the other side, rushed at the village at the double, entered it by all sorts of openings, even where

Battle of Heilsberg

there was only room for one man to go, and we soon heard nothing but a confused sound of shots and terrible shouts, amid clouds of smoke and bursts of flame from the captured burning village.

At this moment there was another sight for us on the right; the Russian corps that was massed in column there advanced rapidly, separated from us as far as the front of the cavalry was from the artillery. The guns of our division replied with the disadvantage of inferior numbers. There were no French troops to meet this formidable column; as far as sight could reach to the rear of our right, there seemed no obstacle that could stop it, and in watching its progress there was a nice time when we looked to the rear, for it had overlapped us considerably. About a third of a mile from us, facing this column, there was a fold of the ground, making a little valley with its bottom out of sight, and which was scarcely more than an undulation.

The Russians had only just attained the crest of this undulation, when we saw a cloud of smoke arise from the bottom, with a loud explosion that continued without interruption. It was a very well sustained fire, in concert with that of two batteries of artillery which fired with such speed and precision that we could perceive the terrible effect in the enemy's ranks, since we commanded the whole spectacle from a short distance. The head of the column was literally crushed.

We were witnesses to the efforts of those in the rear to penetrate into the valley, whence a thousandfold of thunder seemed to be vomiting forth death; but their attempts failed, and a movement to the rear enabled us to see the brave defenders of the valley, who, with only one to ten, had arrested an advance that would otherwise have decided the fate of the day. They then made their appearance on the ground they had covered with dead, marching steadily in one thin line, and following the movement of the Russians, ceaselessly bearing them down with their fire, to which there was only a disorderly and uncertain reply, doing but little damage. It was the Fusiliers and two batteries of the Guard who had thus covered themselves with glory. Their commander, brave General Roussel, was killed in this action.

Our division was electrified by this sight; faces in which might have been detected apprehension at the imminence of the danger of being turned and taken in flank and rear by a superior force, recovered a courageous expression. At this moment the Grand Duke of Berg (Murat) came up to us; he came from our right rear, followed by his staff, passed at a gallop across our front, bending forward on his horse's neck, and as he passed at full speed by General Espagne he flung at

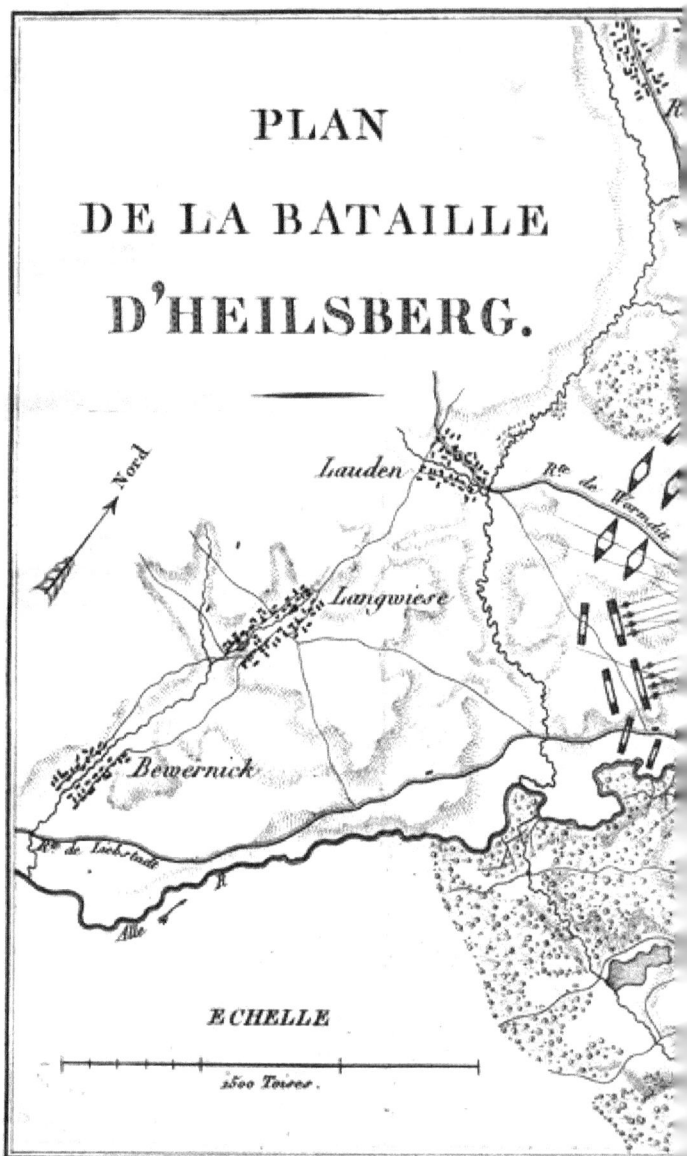

PLAN

DE LA BATAILLE

D'HEILSBERG.

Nord

Lauden

Rte de Warmditt

Langwiese

Bewernick

Rte de Lich. tadt

Alle

ECHELLE

1500 Toises.

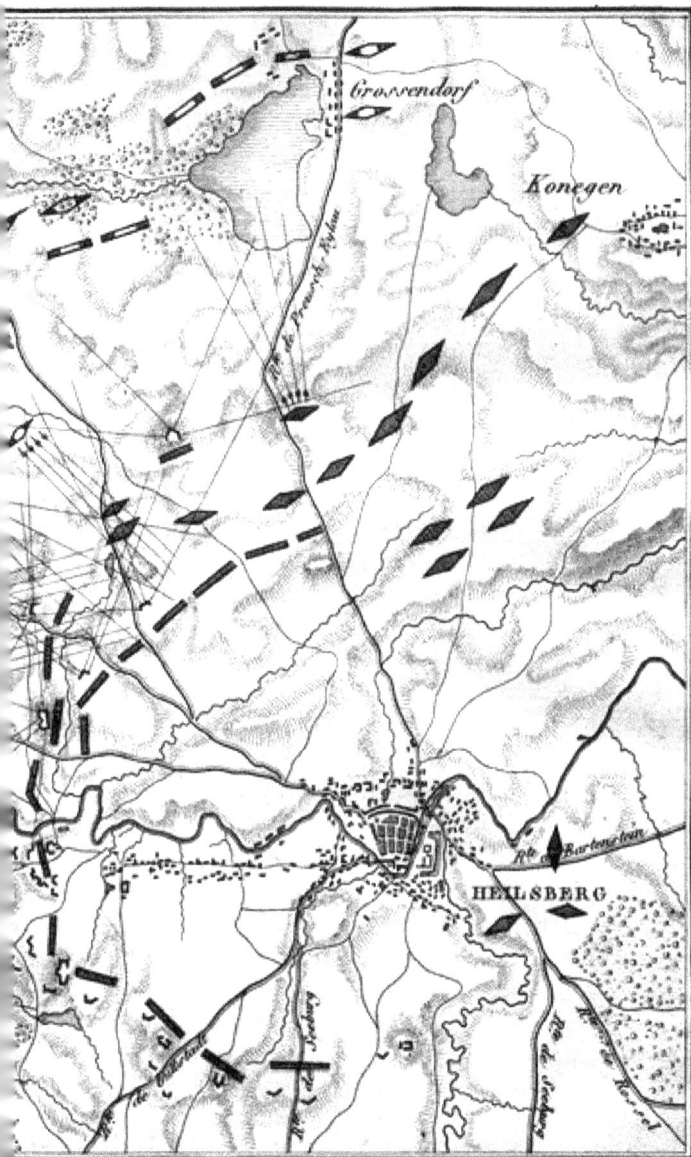

Grossendorf

Konegen

Grossendorf

HEILSBERG

him one word alone which I heard, "Charge!"

This order, given without any further directions for an attack on sixty squadrons of picked men, by fifteen unsupported squadrons, seemed to me the more difficult to understand, since in order to get at the enemy there was a nearly impracticable ravine to be crossed by twos and fours, and it was then necessary to form under the enemy's fire a hundred paces from his first line. In case of a check we had no possible means of retreat, but the order was given and the thing had to be done. The 4th Cuirassiers and ourselves formed sections to the right, and marched to the nearest point of the ravine to the enemy; our battery of light artillery came down at a gallop and took up a position close by, and on the right of the point where we were going to execute our perilous enterprise.

They immediately opened a quick fire of grape to reply to the increase of the enemy's fire at sight of our movement, and to do all possible to stop the first line, now advancing at a walk to meet us. As soon as the 4th Cuirassiers had formed its first squadrons, they rushed upon this line, being overlapped by its right, and repulsed it; but they soon came back in disorder, being in turn repulsed by the first line that had rallied, and the second in support. The artillery on both sides had ceased its fire, and nothing could be heard but the dreadful shouts which the Russians utter on such occasions, mingled with some from our men, though we tried to prevent it. We charged to assist the 4th, and they soon rallied when they reached the brink of the ravine.

I think an incident was of service to us which happened just as our two first squadrons had passed, and when I was coming out of the ravine at the head of the third. The roof of one of the burning buildings of the village I have mentioned being very near the spot where we crossed, fell in, and there arose such a dense cloud of smoke and ashes cast upon us by the wind, that we were covered and enwrapped in it, and probably the enemy's line we were marching on was blinded by it. I cannot understand why but for this at the first moment it did not endeavour to crush us by its numerical superiority, and to throw us back into the ravine which we could never have repassed.

Generally during this day, the Russian troops we had to meet did not display a resolution worthy of their reputation; the check they had received the evening before at Gutstadt was not of sufficient importance to have demoralised them even for the moment; besides, the greater part of those present had taken no part in that action. The next occurrences will be found to support this assertion.

On getting out of the cloud of smoke I have mentioned, and just as I had formed up the section under my command, being the first of the third squadron, I perceived about fifty paces to my left the head of a column of Russian dragoons advancing at a walk upon our flank towards the spot where we had crossed the ravine, the last of the three squadrons following me being hardly clear of it. It seemed clear to me that if I continued to follow the movement of the two squadrons that preceded me we should be turned, flanked in line, and in the worst position cavalry can be placed, and without waiting for orders I turned sharply to the left, quite resolved to be killed rather than that the enemy should accomplish his purpose.

Contrary to my expectation, on seeing me march to meet them, they stopped and began a fire of carbines that hit no one. As I measured the depth of this column, the thought of compelling it to retreat by a charge pressed home seemed to me an absurdity; it was closed in between the ruins of the village and a little marsh, such as there are in all the plains of Eastern Prussia. These marshes are some of them not more than thirty paces in diameter, and present the appearance of fine turf, being not the least dangerous to a man on foot, and quite safely passable by him without being wetted; but a horse sinks in so that he can only be extricated with ropes, and no length of pole will reach the bottom.

I accordingly stopped all the more, because after the example given me the three last sections of my squadron had not followed me, and had gone to join the body of the regiment, its left resting on the little marsh which I had on my right, and on its right the 4th Cuirassiers. There was then a breathing time which can no more be accounted for than a quantity of incidents that take place in war, sometimes to assist, sometimes to overthrow all previous arrangements.

We were hardly fifty paces from the Russians, who were ten times more numerous than ourselves, for, from some reason I have not tried to fathom, the 7th and 8th Cuirassiers had remained on the other side of the ravine, whence our artillery fired on the enemy's left extending far beyond us. In this very critical position only a slight effort was required in order to crush us; but they made no such effort, and for a time, the length of which I can hardly calculate, they contented themselves by firing very wild carbine shots at us, together with volleys of cries and abuse, some of it in very good French, and combined with threatening gestures.

The situation could not last long; a sort of fluctuation having become apparent in the ranks opposed to us, we took advantage of it to charge, and at the moment had a notable success. But it did not continue, and we were driven back to the brink of the ravine. The impossibility of getting across did more to rally our *cuirassiers* than all our efforts could have done; they turned like desperate men, and we soon again saw the enemy who had been in pursuit of us put to flight. This time we gained more ground, probably because orders had been given to the Russians not. to continue to hold the position they were defending. So, their second and third lines, instead of supporting the first, had been executing a retrograde movement, while the first was in pursuit of us, so that they found their supports much further off than they could have expected.

This first line, hotly pursued and losing several men, disappeared between the intervals of the others to rally behind them, and we, in the disorder necessarily consequent on our pursuit, found ourselves in front of a fresh body of troops, in good order, who did not fail to advance to meet us as soon as they were unmasked. Here again they did not display the decision that ought to have been expected of them; we were able to rally and return successfully to the charge, and at last succeeded, after a number of reverses and successes occupying a considerable part of the day, in remaining masters of the ground on which we had fought; but after the last but one of our charges, finding ourselves under fire at short range of the column repulsed by the Fusiliers of the Guard, only a hundred paces from a line of cavalry that was quite fresh, our two regiments, demoralised by their losses, went to the right about without orders, and fled at full speed.

The officers were compelled to follow this movement. Then I turned, finding I was hotly pursued by a dragoon, and saw Colonel d'Avenay alone on foot and already passed by several of the enemy's horsemen. I thought he was lost; threw myself in despair upon the dragoon that had been after me, who, having missed me, was turning back upon the colonel. He fell at the first blow I gave him; but when I looked up again, I was passed by, surrounded, hustled, and my horse carried away by those of the Russians.

The colonel had disappeared in the turmoil, and I thought my fate would be the same, for I was in the enemy's ranks, pressed by them as if I had been one of themselves, and galloping in the same direction. No blow was struck at me for the short time I remained in this position, and I observed on the faces of those in contact with me an expression rather of terror than of animation.

Thanks to the power and speed of my horse, I soon got out of this throng; and tried by inclining to the left to depart from the general direction towards the right; but I had no sooner got a little more at liberty than I became the object of pursuit to several horsemen, and suffered a very disagreeable moment; for three hundred paces in front of me, without a chance of going in any other direction, arose an obstacle of height not to be ascertained at the first glance; it was one of those boundaries of estates like many others in the plain where we were that I have described elsewhere. It was made like the others of two horizontal planks, and was about three feet and a half high; but my horse had for several hours been nearly always at a gallop in a ground covered with furrows, and I was afraid that the effort I was going to require of him might be beyond his strength.

But it did not prove so; at the critical moment I raised him with all the force of the instinct of self-preservation, and in one moment we were over, safe from any risk, for the proceedings on the other side secured me against pursuit. Columns of infantry and cavalry were now really coming to support us. The great Russian mass that had fired on us during its movement in retreat, kept on retiring, and already seemed a long way off. The cavalry that pursued us had been stopped by the height of the obstacle I had been obliged to leap, which did not extend to the place whither the fugitives of my regiment and of the 4th Cuirassiers had betaken themselves.

The rally was sounded on all sides and our men straggling over the plain no longer turned their backs to the enemy. By myself I managed to reform about a strong squadron composed of men of the two regiments, and I brought them as quickly as possible to the spot where I thought they might be useful.

As the Russian cavalry had orders not to prolong the contest, we went in pursuit of them, reinforced by the Saxon Cuirassiers and the 20th Chasseurs, my first regiment. Thus, we arrived beneath the redoubts of Heilsberg, which had been constructed by the Russians long before; for, as I said above, they had selected this position and thought it would be the scene of a conclusive struggle between the armies. We were received by the most frightful fire of guns and musketry possible. The Saxon Cuirassiers, a fine troop composed of old soldiers, could not face it; most part of them gave back. I saw young officers, lads of sixteen, do all they could to rally them, and when they could not, return themselves to the post of danger. Our infantry came late to the field of action, and also abandoned it. The plain was

MURAT AT HEILSBERG

covered with men flying in disorder. Most fortunately night fell, for if the cavalry that had retired by the intervals of the redoubts had been again launched at us, it must have made an immense slaughter without meeting with opposition.

We remained there very uselessly till night fell, and then retired and repassed the famous ravine, establishing our bivouac on the spot we held before we passed it. The roll was called; in the morning the regiment had twenty-two officers present; three had been killed, fourteen more or less seriously wounded. Among the latter was Colonel d'Avenay, whom I had supposed to be killed or taken prisoner. A providential chance together with the devotion of Lieut. Marulaz had extricated him from the cruel situation in which I had seen him. Marulaz in the middle of the struggle had dismounted and compelled him to mount on his horse with his assistance, and it had brought him out with no more wounds than two sabre cuts on the left arm which had been received previously.

As for Marulaz, after this brave action, he had thrown himself on one of the little quagmires I have already mentioned, and stayed there till the retreat of the Russians took place a short time after. We found him safe and sound, and during the rest of the day he was spared, so that he was one of the five officers who alone remained unwounded.

To sum up, the results of this affair were not at first appreciable by us from anything but our enormous loss, but it produced a glorious mention of us in the *Gazette* and a number of decorations, in which I shared. Worn out with fatigue and wetted through by a fine rain that had fallen for several hours, I went to lie down by the colonel under a shelter of pine boughs the *cuirassiers* had made for him. He had seen me coming back towards him at the moment of our retreat, and thought I was killed. He thanked me warmly, and credited me with much more than I deserved in the matter of saving him. I had been half-an-hour with him when I was sent for by Brigadier-General Renault, commanding our division, General Espagne and General Foulers, the senior of the two Generals of Brigade, being wounded. General Renault, having to receive orders from the Grand Duke of Berg, and not knowing where he was, desired me to find him and receive his orders.

Our led horses had not come up; I was obliged to mount again upon the one that had carried me all day, and had scarcely had time to eat a feed of oats. I had to traverse without any direction the whole field of battle, covered with killed and wounded, the latter groaning and crying, and begging for help that no one brought them. I was followed by two *cuirassiers*, and we three could not give these poor wretches the assistance they claimed in this heart-rending manner; nearly all begged for water.

On the skirt of a wood that I entered, the corpses were so heaped up that our horses would not pass, and we were obliged to dismount to find a place where they were not so thick. In this wood I found an infantry brigade commanded by a General whom I knew not. As they were within short range of the enemy's redoubts, strict silence was kept and orders given against lighting any fires. For all my inquiries, I could get no information about the Grand Duke of Berg.

After making a long march in the wood I came out of it and found myself in presence of the first division of heavy cavalry, commanded by General Nansouty, and he began by asking me if I knew where the Grand Duke of Berg could be. General de France, commanding the Carabineer Brigade, and Prince Borghèse, commanding the 1st Regiment, were present and knew me. I conversed with them a, quarter of an hour, telling them what I knew of the affair that had taken place, and the part our division had played. They told me that, having only just reached the spot, they had been unable to take a share in the action, while M. Thiers, in his account of the Battle of Friedland, which took place four days later, makes this first cavalry division cut a figure there, though weakened, as he says, by considerable losses on the day of Heilsberg.

I returned to our bivouac worn out with hunger and fatigue, finding my way through the woods and darkness with very great difficulty. During my absence an officer of Murat's staff had brought an order to remain where we were. The baggage had not come up; we had no bread or anything else to eat. I had a little tea made in a bit of a canister shot case. The ground was covered with pieces of these cases, and shot and muskets. The day was spent in burying our dead, and putting the living in order as far as might be. We made up two weak squadrons; Marulaz had command of the first and I of the second.

The colonel and our other wounded were taken to the rear, and the regiment found itself under the orders of Major Chains. Next day, about five in the morning, the train arrived. We had bread, but very little of it; General Renauld gave me half a bottle of beer, which I shared with Marulaz; since the preceding evening we had been living on the grass which we plucked and chewed.

At ten o'clock the Emperor passed through us, and was saluted by acclamations to which he seemed to pay no attention, appearing gloomy and out of spirits. We learnt later that he had no intention of attacking the Russians so seriously as had been done, and especially had desired not to engage his cavalry. The Grand Duke of Berg had been reprimanded for this, and followed the Emperor with a tolerably sheepish air.

We again passed the night on the field of battle, lying side by side with the dead; then next day we commenced our march, after getting a ration of bread.

CHAPTER 5

Sufferings of the Army

We were a considerable body of heavy cavalry under the orders of Murat, and we had with us two other *corps d'armée*, one being that of Marshal Davoust. So, we proceeded in the direction of Königsberg, while the great part of the army under the Emperor's orders marched upon Friedland. Next day, the 14th of June, we arrived before Königsberg, an unfortified town, with its outskirts covered by some field-works, and by a corps made up of Russians and Prussians.

A pretty sharp cannonade was exchanged, and while we watched our infantry carrying the works and forcing their way into the suburbs with great interest, another cannonade arose at a very small distance to our rear, and we saw the orderly officers hastening from that quarter, looking for the marshals and Prince Murat, to inform them that a force of the enemy of unascertained numbers was coming along the road by the side of the Frische-Haff, in the direction of Königsberg. Our division and two of dragoons then charged front to the rear at a gallop with really admirable precision and unity, and supported by two batteries of artillery, advanced rapidly to meet this new enemy.

There was no encounter; the reconnaissance that had met our people and caused the informant to be sent, fell back slowly without any close pursuit; the corps behind them of five thousand Prussians, nearly all infantry, and with twelve guns, sent a flag of truce as soon as we were in sight and surrendered. The day was very interesting, but it terminated with a disgraceful incident which I choose to relate, in order to tell the truth, and the whole truth, even when not to our advantage.

Towards evening we were directed to the right to ascend the stream of the Pregel; but at a considerable distance from it and on the heights, about one third of a mile from the position that had been our battlefield, the road we followed entered a forest. The 4th Cuirassiers, forming the head of the column, entered into it, followed by the first squadron of my regiment, and they were only just within the wood when a frightful clamour arose in it, amid which might be distinguished cries of "retire, retire," and immediately the *cuirassiers* of the 4th rushed out in terrible disorder, upsetting and entangling in their flight our staff, which was leading, and our first squadron. Expecting to see them followed by a legion of Russians, I at once formed up my squadron to deaden the first shock, if nothing else, and allow the fugitives to rally.

The 7th and 8th Cuirassiers also formed up at a gallop and we waited. Nothing came! It was a panic! The advanced guard had been alarmed, and throwing themselves back on the head of the column had infected it with their terror. Having restored order a little the advanced guard was questioned, and they asserted that they had seen the enemy and that the wood was full of infantry and Cossacks. Information was just being sent to the marshals when four or five carriages were seen quietly issuing from the wood; they were our canteen men who had just come through the whole wood and not met with anything to disturb them in it at all. So, we were obliged to allow that it was a ridiculous mistake.

We resumed our march, and bivouacked in some scattered farms in clearings of the forest that had no resources for us. We had to bear hunger and thirst, for the water was brackish. There was hardly any night at this time of year, and about three in the morning, on coming out of a barn where I had managed to sleep a little, I found myself in the presence of the Grand Duke of Berg on horseback, leaning forward on his horse's neck and entirely alone. He asked me if I had a trumpeter close by, and on my answering in the affirmative, told me to desire him to sound to horse; the call was instantly repeated on all sides, and in half-an-hour we were on the march.

We skirted the Pregel on the heights of the left bank, and I met there one of my friends from Normandy, Le Termellier, commanding a little post of observation of the 20th Chasseurs, my first regiment. He gave me a loaf taken out of a boat they had just seized on the river, as it was making its way upwards with the hope of delivering its cargo of bread to the Russians on the other bank.

During this march we had the first news of the Battle of Friedland, which had taken place the day before, but with no other particulars than those about the retreat of the Russians. We crossed the Pregel below Wehlau; the ford was narrow, and a column of artillery was entangled in it and stopped in the midst; the opposite bank being steep, a slope had been cut in it; the ground was wet, and the march of the train was stopped by a caisson that had stuck in the mud. We had been cautioned to keep close to the carriages while passing below them; but my horse felt the loose traces of a leader between his legs and suddenly turning to the left lost his footing.

The water came up to my neck, but this would not be worth mentioning if I had not promised to record in my tale anything that can give a proper notion of a soldier's career, both physically and morally. My horse reached the other bank by swimming, and I awaited the arrival of the led horses, hoping to be able to get a change of clothes; but there was another misfortune in store for me. In passing a train of artillery in a narrow and hollow road, the horse my servant was riding fell, and the one in hand, carrying my portmanteau, got away. He could not catch it, and I never heard of it again.

At that time the officers had no cloak-case on the horse they rode, so that I was left with nothing but what I wore and that wet through. In this state did I bivouac on a meadow on the bank of the Pregel, covered to the height of six feet with such a thick fog that nothing under it could be seen. As we were all the time without food, it was proposed to slaughter some wounded horses; but night came so late and day so soon, that there would not have been time to cut them up and cook them.

We followed the Russians, foot by foot, as far as Tilsit without encountering a serious resistance at any point. Only once towards evening they seemed to wish to make head, and it astonished us that the Grand Duke of Berg, who was there, was not so enterprising as the commander of the advanced guard should be towards the rear-guard of an army in retreat. At nightfall, without being pressed, he caused us to retire two leagues to take up a position in a large village upon a hill surrounded by several streams of water. Some pigs were found there and killed, but we had no bread or potatoes, and the hot pork without anything to eat with it, had a bad effect upon stomachs that had been empty so long.

At last we arrived before Tilsit, and that was a sight I will endeavour to describe. The valley of the Niemen is commanded by a raised plateau on the side where we arrived. Tilsit was about half a league distant when we first perceived it, and we were formed up in order of battle. In their retreat to this spot the Russian Army had executed converging movements, that had of course been imitated by the different columns detailed went in pursuit of them. They were already on the opposite bank of the river, which is here of considerable size; they could easily be seen, some holding the positions assigned to them, some on the march to take up theirs.

In front of Tilsit on our side, and all against the city, a corps of cavalry, composed of Cossacks, and intended to cover it, waiting till those still left in the town, should have passed the wooden bridge that was already set on fire and had the last of the foot soldiers running over it as fast as they could. This cavalry seemed destined to be sacrificed by remaining behind, and had no course to pursue but to cross the river by swimming, an exercise the Cossacks in general are well accustomed to. All our remaining cavalry was almost on the spot gathered in a mass on the height. The Emperor also was there with his staff, the mounted Chasseurs, and the Horse Grenadiers of the Guard, besides the orderly *gendarmes*, a provisional body composed of young men of family mounted and equipped at their own expense.

Our division on the right received orders to march on the enemy's cavalry before Tilsit. We began to move at a walk, in two lines of but small extent, in consequence of the losses we had experienced on the preceding days, especially the day of Heilsberg. There was something solemn in the movement we were executing.

It was the last blow we were to strike, for the Russian Army, quite disorganised by successive defeats, had lost nearly all its artillery, and could not keep the field any longer, and the Prussians had not ten thousand men left. The last blow was to be delivered under the eyes of the Emperor, as he could overlook the whole position, and under those of all the cavalry of the army, stationed so as not to lose the spectacle we were going to present.

We understood all this; an expression of pride could be seen on the faces of our *cuirassiers*; and though we were all so weak, no one had any doubts of success, as all felt a moral exaltation that supplied the place and more of physical power. We advanced in silence, and had nearly covered a quarter of the distance that divided us from the Russians, when an officer issued from their ranks, passed rapidly towards our ranks with a trumpeter, and raised one of his hands, to show that he was carrying a paper. He made to the spot where the Emperor was easily to be known by his brilliant appearance, and in a few minutes an orderly officer of the Emperor's came to us at full speed bringing an order to halt. It was peace, the peace of Tilsit, that the Emperor of Russia and King of Prussia proposed. An hour later all the troops were moving in different directions to take up various cantonments assigned to them.

Since the morning we had entered upon a zone behind that occupied by the Russian and Prussian Armies. It was a new country, abounding in resources, but wet and unhealthy. I was already consumed by fever, and a violent thirst that had as yet found nothing but bad water to slake it. Being suddenly at rest was far from beneficial and increased my illness; all kinds of food caused me insuperable disgust, and no assistance or medicine was in our reach.

My whole regiment, as well as two companies of infantry, were quartered in the same farm; it is true it was very large, but we all slept upon straw without being able to undress. We remained there a week, and I became frightfully weak; I could not keep on my legs, and peace was concluded without my being even able to go and enjoy the sight that there was at Tilsit, with its meeting of sovereigns and mixture of Russian, Prussian, and French uniforms.

After the signature of this famous treaty, which marked the height of Napoleon's power, all the army retired, and we entered on the land of desolation we had left some weeks before. The horrors of war had never been seen under a more hideous aspect—entire villages, in all directions, depopulated by death; rotten bodies lying in the houses and streets, gardens and yards. There were nine around the house I occupied in the first cantonment where we halted. It was impossible to escape the horrible smell that they exhaled; impossible to think of burying them, as the smell would have suffocated anyone that attempted to remove them.

My illness increased; I had inflammation of the bowels that gave me not a moment's rest; our surgeon-major was an ass, and everything that he gave me produced a contrary effect to what he expected. While this was going on. General d'Avenay was appointed General of Brigade, and asked for me as his *aide-de-camp*. At that time there was no staff corps, and the duties that have been imposed on it since its formation were performed by officers taken from regiments. Thus, it always happened that when a colonel was promoted to be a general, he chose out of the regiment he had commanded the lieutenant or captain whom he thought most fit for the duty, of course with his consent. As for me, it had been arranged between us long before in the prospect of what had occurred.

We set out for Königsberg, where the imperial headquarters were established. General d'Avenay had always taken a travelling carriage with him, and we now made use of it. On our road we found in several places groups of wounded installed in the middle of the fields; they had been there a month without dressings or any means of subsistence but such as was irregularly furnished by the charity of some peasants. There were no French troops in these regions, as they were too completely ruined to provide the necessary subsistence.

It was established by a Prussian Commission, with the Duke of Holstein as president, that the right bank of the Passarges, occupied by the Russians during the four months that had elapsed from the Battle of Eylau to the resumption of hostilities, presented a much greater aspect of devastation than was the case on the left bank that we had occupied. The Russians are allies who do not spare their friends.

At Königsberg our billet was on a rich Jew banker. Our rooms were tidy and we had clean linen. We stayed there a fortnight, to get our new uniforms made and buy what we wanted; then the general received orders to go and give over the command of his regiment to his successor, the Baron d'Haugeranville. We went first to Elbing, travelling the road by which I had been brought to the French advanced posts after my exchange. I had not got well at Königsberg; the fever had increased, and the general was obliged to leave me in a house that had been a portion of the cantonments we had occupied a long time before we marched against the Russians.

An old lady lived in this house with a young one as her companion. They received me with alacrity, and did all they could for me. I looked as if I was dying. Two days after I was installed in this house, our surgeon-major came there, sent to look after me. He began by giving me a drink that threw me into such convulsions that he thought I was going to die; he told my hostesses so, and I heard him. After racking me for what seemed a very long time, the pain abated; but from that time forward I could not take the least thing; a spoonful of *eau sucrée*, or any kind of liquid produced vomiting and convulsions.

I was carried to Marienwerder, and placed under the charge of a surgeon of the 4th Cuirassiers, named Fouillette; and Jouette, my orderly when I was a sub-lieutenant, having requested to be allowed to nurse me, he was sent there. These two men saved my life; the first by attacking the sickness in the proper manner, the second by watching over me night and day with the solicitude of a mother. At last I became convalescent, and when I could eat, Lieutenant-General Espagne, who commanded the division I had belonged to, sent me every day some dishes made up according to the prescriptions of my doctor, and this regime was continued for a long time and cured me.

General d'Avenay had received orders to take the command of the second brigade of the Fourth Division of Dragoons, commanded by General La Houssaye; but he waited till I should be in a condition to travel before going to take up his new duty. We arrived at the *château* of Fürstenberg, where was the staff of the 19th Regiment of Dragoons, composing with the 18th, our brigade. This was a castle of the middle ages, and beneath it was a pretty lake. The owner, a bachelor of about forty, seemed an excellent man and of refined manners.

The colonel of the 19th Dragoons kept on vexing him from morning to night, for the pleasure of playing the despot and conqueror. This colonel, with his splendid and martial aspect, when the enemy appeared did not justify his looks; and yet he died a lieutenant-general, but leaving a very bad reputation. He had no education, but this justice must be done him, he had the art to manage his regiment quite satisfactorily, as it was in capital condition.

The other regiment of our brigade, the 18th Dragoons, was also excellent; it was commanded by Colonel Lafitte, well known to have all the qualities deficient in his comrade. Of tried courage, he was modest and kind; as soon as we knew one another a little intimately he showed that he liked me. He died rather young, a major-general.

We did not remain long at Fürstenberg; it was there that I found the one-armed miller who had received me so badly when a prisoner. I inquired for his daughter, not from him but from the people of the *château*, when I heard that she was no longer at the mill. On leaving Fürstenberg, we took up our quarters near Soldau. The country had suffered much; but as we found ourselves on the left bank of the Passarges, and consequently outside the line occupied by the Russians before the resumption of hostilities, there had been no devastation.

We were lodged in a house belonging to the Baron de Collas, who was there with his wife, his son, and two daughters. The son, a dragoon officer, had been made prisoner at the beginning of the campaign, and released on parole. The family were really very original, and we were much amused at this domestic life of a remarkable kind. Every evening all carried their beds into the garden to escape the heat, and placed themselves a very little way apart. General d'Avenay had a notion of giving a ball.

Mademoiselle Sophie de Collas came and confided to him that she had no dress elegant enough to enable her to be present at this entertainment; and the general at once offered to give her one, which she accepted with delight. Then I permitted myself to present her with a pair of slippers of white satin embroidered with pearls, and a toothbrush, telling her the use she was to make of the latter. Baron de Collas's mansion was very large, modern, and built in French style. Before we came there, we had stayed for some weeks in another mansion at Ludwigdorff, with a charming family, composed of the mother, three daughters, and a governess, all speaking French perfectly.

Towards the month of November, we received orders to recross the Vistula; we dreamed of France and thought we were going to enter it; but the very evening before we were to cross the river, after marching towards it for several days, we received orders to retrace our steps, and to use hostile measures towards the remnants of the Prussian Army, who were following us to resume occupation of the territory that we were leaving, unless they retreated before us. We only found great consternation and passive obedience in reply to the summons we were to our great; regret obliged to make. This offensive movement seemed to us to presage a rupture of the peace, and imagination worked upon this theme till we saw ourselves again parted from France for a long time.

As to the rupture of the peace we were in error, and it was only a question of war contributions that had caused the demonstration that we had been ordered to make. We resumed our cantonments near Soldau, and stayed with Baron de Collas up to the middle of December, at which time we really passed the Vistula on our way to Silesia, the route appointed for our division. When we left our cantonments, the peasants displayed real sorrow at parting with our soldiers, and accompanied them till they joined the body of the regiment, giving them all sorts of marks of affection. General d'Avenay had received orders to bring with him as much live stock as he could, but he caused the inhabitants to be warned, so that they might conceal their cattle in the woods, and he reported that he had found nothing, and this brought a good many blessings upon him.

We crossed the Vistula at Thorn, and leaving Warsaw on the right, we marched on Kalisch to proceed to Breslau by the main road, and thence to the cantonments appointed for us. Those of General d'Avenay's brigade were extended from Landshut, on the Bohemian frontier, to Janre and Strigau, in a beautiful country rich in resources of all kinds. I was lodged with the general in the Château of Rohnstock, one of the princely dwellings of Count de Hochberg, the richest proprietor in Silesia. He lived at Rohnstock with his wife, a princess of Anhalt Pless, and three children, the eldest five years old, and the younger, twins still in the cradle.

The countess was thirty-six, and her first child had been born fourteen years after her marriage. She was a clever woman, and good beyond all expression. The count was a capital man; his character was gay, frank, and of such an equable temper that I never saw it give way. There I also knew the Baroness Richthoffen, born Princess of Holstein, and so of the royal house of Denmark; she was twenty-four, and had just lost her husband, and Count Hochberg had invited her and her four children to spend her time of mourning at his house. This happy family was to us like a bit of home. All the time that we stayed at Rohnstock we received numerous of proofs of the most sincere and vivid sympathy, and at the moment I write this I am still in correspondence with the Baroness Richthoffen.

The eldest of her daughters, Louise, married General de Natzmer, *aide-de-camp* to the King of Prussia; in 1816 the Count de Natzmer commanded the corps of the Prussian Army that invaded France with the other European armies. The second, Agnes, married the Count de Luttichau; the third, Iris, is unmarried, and little Baron Fritz is now the father of two sons who are in the army.

★★★★★★

This was written in 1857, and in 1872, sixty-four years after the time at which M. de Q-Gonneville had known the Princess of Holstein, Baroness Richthoffen, the Countess de Luttichau, her daughter, came to France on purpose to see him, after having sent him, in 1858, her eldest son, the Count Max de Luttichau, Chamberlain to Her Majesty the Queen Dowager of Prussia, and afterwards her second son and nephew Baron Oldwig de Richthoffen.

★★★★★★

In the course of the year 1808 the events that brought on the occupation of Spain by a portion of the forces of France had taken their course. The revolt of Madrid and the Battle of Baylen had taken place. There was also talk of a fresh campaign against Austria; but that power had not recovered the exhaustion of its former war, and being pressed on all sides by the French Army gave way on all the points in question. Our division, as well as several bodies of return troops, received orders to march to Spain, and we quitted Silesia, where we had received so many marks of affection, where we left real friends, where we had lived in luxury and abundance, to proceed to a country that was depicted to us in the darkest colours, where war had become a contest for existence, where assassination and poisoning were publicly inculcated from the pulpit as legitimate methods ordained by God for the extermination everything bearing a French name, without distinction of sex or age.

We had to cross a great piece of Germany and all France, beginning from Mayence, which was then a part of it, to Bayonne. We were royally treated in all Saxony; our reception was beyond imagination; it was no doubt by order, but there was nothing official about it. At Frankfort we were informed that the Emperor being at Mayence would review us next day in front of Cassel, and General d'Avenay's brigade could show sixteen magnificent squadrons in line of battle. The horses were in capital condition, though they had made such a long march. The ten months spent in Silesia had been employed in placing all the resources of the cantons we occupied, as far as was legally possible, at the disposal of our two regiments, and they had been sharp enough to profit by it. By way of showing their respect for the general, they had offered me a horse fully equipped, a present that I had been obliged to accept, and which had gratified me much. It was a charming Mecklenburg mare, very good, and very well drilled.

The Emperor arrived, escorted by all the princes of the Confederation and a crowd of generals. He had reviewed the first brigade of our division on the left bank of the Rhine, and had not been pleased with it, especially with the 27th Regiment under the command of Colonel Lallemand. The sight of our sixteen squadrons, so full of force and power, seemed to surprise him; his face expressed satisfaction and good humour. He was on foot, as usual with him on these sort of occasions, having General d'Avenay with him and talking to him, followed by all his suite.

All at once the general left the Emperor, rushed to me, tore me from my horse rather than let me dismount, dragged me to the Emperor and presented me to him with an emotion I shall never forget, asking for the rank of captain for me. The Emperor remained a moment with his eyes fixed upon me, then he turned to the Prince of Neufchâtel, chief of the staff of the army, who followed him with a note book in his hand, he told him:

Mark M. de Gonneville as captain.

I think that no music ever sounded so pleasant in my ear. I was not twenty-five years old yet, and hardly four years had passed since I had been in the ranks as a private soldier. I gave my name to the Prince de Neufchâtel, and he wrote it down in his notebook, giving me a gracious bow and saying:

Sir, you are a captain.

I was really from that very day borne on the state of staff officers as of that rank and received the appointments. General La Houssaye, commanding our division, a quarter-of-an-hour before had begged for captain's rank for his *aide-de-camp* Millet, a much older lieutenant than I was, and had received a flat refusal. The day was one of the fairest of my life, and all at once I thought of the pleasure that my father, my mother, and my brother would feel when they heard of this my unexpected promotion, such as I had never dreamed of. I had gone away a sub-lieutenant, and it was with the rank of captain and the Cross of the Legion of Honour that I should again come under my father's roof. For when we had placed our regiments beyond the Rhine we were to take post and go to Normandy spend a fortnight there, and rejoin our brigade near Bordeaux.

Another incident took place at the Emperor's review. General d'Avenay required a second *aide-de-camp*. He asked me to help him to choose, and I named to him Saint Victor, a sub-lieutenant in the 19th Regiment of Dragoons, when I had ascertained from himself that he would like the post. The general made the request and it was granted at once, and gave Saint Victor the rank of lieutenant. He was of a good family in Dauphiné; he was clever and had great natural talent. The general was but little acquainted with him, but soon knew how to value him, and we always had to congratulate ourselves on the cordiality that existed between us.

He became a colonel, was second in command at the School at Saumur, then had the 5th Regiment of Mounted Chasseurs; they were sent to Africa, but he had fallen into bad health and had retired. His second marriage was with a niece of his own; much younger than himself, and she made him the father of a numerous family. This digression is foreign to my military history; but I shall at times have to mention persons whose memory remains dear to me.

When we had spent a fortnight in Normandy, we joined our division at Ruffec, between Poitiers and Bordeaux, the same day that the Emperor went by there on his way from Erfurth. We waited for him at the post-house, and while changing horses he questioned General d'Avenay respecting the amount of fatigue of men and horses who had just made a march of four hundred leagues. He appeared satisfied with the account given. While we were there an infantry colonel, in a uniform of a former period, drew near the carriage door, for the Emperor had not dismounted, and in an agitated voice begged to be allowed the honour of going to Spain to share the honours and dangers of the army. The Emperor answered:

"And if I give you employment, will you be wrong-headed again?"

The poor colonel lost his head in a moment, being quite embarrassed by this question, and he stammered out:

"Sire, I will do everything that is in my power to serve as *agreeably* as possible."

"If that is the case," said the Emperor, with a smile, "come to me at Bayonne."

He went there, was appointed to a regiment, and three years afterwards was General of Division. I have forgotten his name. He had been turned out of the army because he had written the word *No* on the voting lists opened for the acceptance of the Empire by the French nation. We learnt this that evening at Ruffec at a party that we had been invited to join.

We marched to Bayonne without halting and rested there. We found Eugène d'Hautefeuille there, one of the companions of my youth. He had spent all his property and separated from his wife, and then by the interest of his name obtained a sub-lieutenancy in the 5th Regiment of Dragoons, and was going to join it in Spain. The general was also acquainted with d'Hautefeuille, and permitted him to march with us, and thenceforward he became our messmate.

This was of great service to him, for, with his inexperience of military matters, and in an enemy's country up in arms like Spain, I do not know how he would have managed. Certainly he had no want of intelligence and assurance, but physical obstacles would have risen before him at every step; for there is no more miserable plight than that of an isolated soldier marching with an army in an invaded country, where there is in consequence no regular authority established, and lodging and food are questions every moment of difficult solution, Eugène d'Hautefeuille was the third son of the Marquis d'Hautefeuille, a lieutenant-general before the revolution, and holding an elevated rank in Normandy, more from his position than his character.

Eugène had plenty of ability and imagination, but a vanity that induced him to revolt against anything that might display any superiority to him of any kind, and to himself he never allowed that he was excelled. This disposition had made him cast himself recklessly into science, art, and exercises of all kinds, and the result was that, having attempted everything, he had only skimmed it all, except fencing, in which he had gone pretty far. He was possessed of remarkable muscular power, though slender and weak in appearance; and the desire of exhibiting this advantage had forced him into immoderate enterprises that had greatly shaken his constitution. Otherwise he was amiable, of a joyous temper, and sometimes quite charming. General Laroche said to him one day before a battle:

"Take care of yourself, for if your wife were a widow I would marry her."

He answered, "I should be very glad, General, if it could be managed without my being killed!"

CHAPTER 6

Entry into Spain, 1808

We made our entrance into Spain. Nothing looks more gloomy or sad than Irun, the first town entered a quarter-of-a-league from the frontier; the houses of dark coloured granite, windows barred up to the third story, the streets narrow and dirty, such was Irun. The headquarters of our division stopped there, the regiments were crammed into it or in bivouac around. We saw hateful countenances all round, but our march passed without incident quite to the neighbourhood of Burgos. There was a sort of shadow of resistance, that was honoured with the name of the Battle of Burgos; it was on the 10th of November, 1808, Marshal Soult was in command, and the Emperor still at Bayonne.

The defeat of the Spaniards was so speedy that it was all over when our division came up, and we entered Burgos the same day. Almost all the inhabitants had fled, and as we took our lodgings in military fashion, that is to say, as we could, and without billets from the local authorities, who had disappeared, the result was a detestable waste that destroyed the greatest part of the resources that might have been obtained in the city, and exasperated the inhabitants in the highest degree. Assassinations multiplied, and it was not safe to leave the assemblage of the troops.

This war now assumed a character of reciprocal animosity, which took its origin from the events that happened in Madrid in the previous month of May; animosity that kept on increasing and was a presage of atrocities quite beyond any before committed. These presages were realised, and the traditional tortures of the Inquisition were often put in practice upon the wretched Frenchmen who fell into the hands of their pitiless adversaries; they were crucified and sawn in two between planks.

We saw a dragoon officer nailed against a door, having between his teeth the proof of the previous mutilation he had been subjected to. A few leagues beyond Burgos we found on the road a civilian cantineer and a child of twelve with their throats cut; they were *artistically* disposed to display the barbarity that accompanied the act, and similar examples were repeated every moment.

The passage of the Ebro was not disputed, and we arrived at the foot of Somo Sierra on the 30th of November. It seemed a difficult obstacle to pass; the mountain chain shows pointed rocks at a great height; the road ascends by zigzags in a narrow gorge, and is cut by a torrent every moment; this was now quite dry, but all the bridges had been cut. This road was the only possible approach to this position, considered impregnable by the Spaniards. They had crowded it with batteries at successive elevations commanding all the portions of the road that could be traversed; clouds of skirmishers lay in wait to right and left of the ravine, and masses of infantry covered the accessible spots of the heights.

As soon as an advance along the road was attempted, the fire of guns and musketry commenced, then there was a profound silence as soon as a movement in retreat had placed the assailants in shelter.

The Emperor was at the foot of the mountain at the entrance of the gorge; a hundred paces further and he would have been under the fire of the first battery, which was covered by an *épaulement* and flanked by sharpshooters, and had two of the broken bridges I have mentioned before it. The Emperor ordered bridges of planks and beams to be immediately thrown across these cuts.

The sappers performed the duty, but with heavy loss. Then he ordered Colonel Piré, *aide-de-camp* to the Prince of Neufchâtel, to go and reconnoitre if there was any possibility of flinging a charge of cavalry upon the first battery. Piré went off at a gallop, was received by musketry, and returned with a rather too much scared appearance telling him aloud that it was impossible. The speech and manner of saying it put the Emperor in such a rage that he struck at M. de Piré with his whip, and the blow was only escaped by a quick movement in retreat.

There were no troops on the spot but the Chasseurs of the Guard, the Polish Lancers of the Guard, two regiments of infantry, one or two of the batteries of the Guard, and our division. The Emperor ordered the Chasseurs of the Guard to charge the first battery. They went off at a gallop in column of fours with their usual determination; but the moment they were unmasked by turning the flank of the mountain that covered us, the gun and musketry fire recommenced with such violence that they retired in great disorder, thus confirming Colonel Piré's information. Then the colonel of the Polish Lancers came to the Emperor and applied to him for permission to attempt a charge; this was granted, and in a few minutes the battery was carried, but with sensible loss. M. de Ségur, who had joined the charge as an amateur, fell pierced with five balls; the neighbourhood of the battery was strewn with horses and lancers. There was one horse with his forequarters within the battery, while his hind legs hung without; his rider was stretched dead in the middle of the battery.

We received orders to support the movement of the Poles, and to take the head of the column as soon as it had dislodged the enemy from the heights. By one of those chances that occur in war sometimes through strokes of audacity, three other batteries better placed than the first to dispute the pass, had been abandoned by their defenders on seeing the success of the Poles. The guns remained there unfired, and not a single musket shot was sent at us while crossing the mountain, though at least an hour's work.

After issuing from the gorge, at a distance of a mile we found Buitrago, a nasty, dirty little town. We reached it at night; our first brigade remained there with the guard and the general headquarters. We received orders to continue our march for two hours cautiously, because we had an enemy before us; but in what direction was not known. Madrid was our aim, not more than two days' march distant. The night was beautiful, and the light of the moon was almost as bright as day.

We arrived at a large village deserted by the inhabitants, and found supplies of all kinds there; the two regiments made their bivouac in front with the requisite precautions, and the general established himself in the best-looking house. Fowls were killed, our cook set to work, and in a couple of hours we had plenty of opportunity of satiating an appetite sharpened by having fasted the whole day.

We were just beginning to do honour to the repast when General La Houssaye, whom we had left at Buitrago with the first brigade, came up with his three *aides-de-camp* and the whole staff of the division. General d'Avenay received them all with perfect grace, had every possible addition made to the meal, and the newcomers seemed delighted to have nothing to do but to sit down to table on their arrival. After supper General d'Avenay offered a share of his room to General La Houssaye, while the *aides-de-camp* settled themselves in a neighbouring room.

It was nothing but just lying down on mattresses on the floor, as, holding the position of extreme advanced guard, we could not even take off our boots. The chief of the staff and his officers went to find other lodgings, for the house we occupied was much too small to accommodate everyone. On hearing General d'Avenay's proposal General La Houssaye burst into a rage, and told him that he had been neglectful in not offering him the exclusive possession of the house as soon as he arrived, as was his due, since it was the best in the place. General d'Avenay replied that however unsuitable the claim might have seemed to him before supper, he would however at that time have allowed it, but that having performed the duties of hospitality in that house, he considered himself at home in it and would not go.

Both were pretty warm, and at last General d'Avenay, driven to extremity, told the other he might go and walk about, and added that if he was not contented there was plenty of moonlight for them to go down into the courtyard that moment and settle their difference. This proposition quieted General La Houssaye immediately, and he answered, reasonably enough this time, that at the advanced posts, even putting aside his superior rank, they would both of them be acting essentially in contravention of their duty by concluding their dispute in such a manner.

At the same time, he held out his hand to General d'Avenay, who took it, and we went to rest. But we *aides-de-camp* were no sooner alone together than those of General La Houssaye allowed their indignation against him to break forth, and they told us:

> Do not let your general trust him. He makes semblance of wishing to forget this scene altogether, but he would remember it a hundred years if he were to live so long. He was afraid, like a coward as he is (it was quite true that he was a coward), and he will never forgive your general.

A few days afterwards we had a proof that the *aides-de-camp* were not mistaken.

In two days we were at Madrid, on an elevation commanding the city at a distance of half a league in the direction of our advance. All the bells, and heaven knows how many there were, sounded the tocsin; guns fired ceaselessly, and there was musketry at the gate of Alcala and the two openings at its right and left. The Emperor's tent was pitched on the left of the road where it begins to go downhill. I saw him surrounded by a ring of sentries, walking about with his arms crossed on his breast, and seeming lost in deep thought. It was during a halt that we made on the height that we could see him in this attitude, and it continued all the time we remained there.

Our brigade received orders to turn Madrid by the right, and attack any reinforcements that might make their appearance coming by the roads that opened on the left bank of the Manzanares. We executed this movement without any further opposition than was caused by park walls and palings that had to be removed by the sappers; these parks were full of stags, deer, and roes, which seemed quite tame as they came up, just as if they were curious to look at us going by. A large body of Spanish cavalry, coming by the road from Aranjuez, retired the moment they saw us in the distance, and we saw bands of armed peasants, who had come to defend the city, now flying in all directions.

We had been joined by Colonel de Piré and he told us that the Emperor had just given him orders to go round Madrid alone. This was probably on purpose to have him killed. It would have been a kind of miracle if he had accomplished his mission without hindrance; for, notwithstanding the movement in retreat that we had caused, there was considerable excitement *extra muros* among the Spaniards on the side where we were, the opposite one to the attack; so that it was an impossibility for a man alone to pass the Manzanares to the east of Madrid without falling either by their blows or into their hands, which would have come to the same thing.

About three in the afternoon we got orders to march upon the Escurial, to halt at the fork of the roads leading there and to the Guadarrama, to send out a strong reconnaissance in the latter direction, to ascertain what had become of the force that was marching on Madrid by Valladolid and Segovia, and if we met the advanced guard of this force, immediately to go and occupy the Escurial.

After halting two hours, we saw our reconnaissance returning, they had met the 5th Regiment of Dragoons, forming the extreme advanced guard of the body we desired to hear of. Then we marched on the Escurial: but during our halt an incident took place that deserves mention as a proof of the fanaticism of the Spaniards. The plateau we occupied is covered with pyramidal stones of a height of from seven to nine yards; almost all of these pyramids are crowned by a stone placed there by the hand of man.

At a distance of twenty-five paces a shot was fired upon us, but the ball passed high above our heads. The sappers of the 18th Dragoons hastened to the point the shot came from, and found behind one of the stones an old man in such a state of prostration from terror that not a word could be got out of him; he was trembling all over, and had to be held up or he would have fallen to the ground.

The poor wretch had stirred himself up to deserve martyrdom by killing one of us, and when he tried to accomplish his intention he did to without having any notion of the direction of his shot, for the ball passed more than five-and-twenty feet over our heads, while if he had aimed at the group of a dozen officers composing the staff, he would have been sure of one victim at least. They brought him to us and made him sit on the side of the road, where it overhung a ravine too dark for the bottom to be visible.

After a time no more attention was paid to this man, and he all at once jumped up and cast himself into the chasm. No one risked going after him; but when I afterwards had an opportunity of examining the spot by daylight, I came to the conclusion that with his knowledge of the spot, our prisoner might have escaped without much danger. The relation of this circumstance, among many others of the same kind, may give a still imperfect notion what feelings of hatred towards us the Spaniards had religiously taken up.

As I have said, we marched upon the Escurial, entering the park with caution, as we had no infantry with us. From the entrance on this side there is a distance of a league to the lower town, and there we were received with some musket-shots, to which our skirmishers replied; while in less than an hour both defenders and inhabitants had disappeared.

It was still night. The lower town is separated from the upper by an escarpment, occupied by the terraced gardens of the palace, and a magnificent slope as a means of communication. At its foot we waited for day, to allow us to reconnoitre—a long time at this season.

At first break of day our reconnoiterers advanced, and had to exchange a few shots. There was firing from the windows of the convent—an actual fortress, an immense mass of stone, and like no other building in the world. We began to parley with the monks; and at last, about mid-day, they opened their gates. There were only five monks left in the convent, the youngest of them seeming a hundred years old, and some serving brothers. All the rest had escaped by the caverns, which were said to issue at a distance of more than a league among the mountains, amid rocks of great height that command the convent and higher town on the west.

We found all the French milliners and cooks of Madrid shut up in the convent: they had been sent there for protection from the fury of the populace of Madrid—the worst populace in the world; and as the Governor of the Escurial was not a bit more able to confide in the disposition of his own people, he had placed our fellow-countrymen in prison, till we delivered them and were called their liberators.

I went over the royal apartments and the convent; the first is in no way remarkable; it would take months to see the latter properly.

The same day we were joined by General La Houssaye and the second brigade of our division. General La Houssaye held out his hand to General d'Avenay, who gave him his very willingly; so, everything seemed to be put to rights; but next day General d'Avenay received orders to proceed to the Imperial headquarters, to receive another appointment and to give over the command of his brigade to General de Caulincourt. Suspecting that this originated with General La Houssaye, who had the reputation of not being straightforward, General d'Avenay hastened to him, accompanied by me. General La Houssaye defended himself vigorously, and swore that he had nothing to do with the measure, declaring it was quite contrary to his wishes. While upon this, he made very fine protestations of friendship.

We departed for Madrid, and remained there a fortnight, when General d'Avenay, who had been excellently received by the Prince of Neufchâtel, Major-General of the Army, received the command of a detached brigade, composed of the third regiment of Dutch hussars and five squadrons of dragoons of different regiments.

The English Army had landed at Corunna, under the orders of General Hill, and was advancing on Madrid, menacing our communications with France, and giving a moral support to the Spanish insurgents, in addition to that derived from a profusion of arms and ammunition being placed at their service. The Emperor having rushed in pursuit of this army with his Guard and the corps of Marshal Ney, we received orders to protect the flank of this column at the distance of two or three leagues; and to halt every evening, as well as possible, opposite the Imperial headquarters, sending thither every morning for orders for the operations of the day.

The English Army commenced their retreat as soon as we marched against it. We passed the mountains of Guadarrama in a frightful hurricane; the snow was driven by whirlwinds and fell with extreme violence, enveloping and covering us with a thick coating that made its way through our cloaks. Several men perished during the passage; it lasted a whole day, and there was incredible difficulty in taking the artillery over.

While we were climbing the Guadarrama with such difficulty, we were on the flank of the infantry division commanded by General Lapisse, and a few steps in rear of the Emperor, who was marching on foot, like ourselves; for no precaution had been taken in shoeing, and the horses fell every moment. The soldiers of Lapisse's division gave loud expression to the most sinister designs against the Emperor's person, stirring up each other to fire a shot at him, and bandying accusations of cowardice for not doing it. He heard it all as plainly as we did, and seemed as if he did not care a bit for it; but when he reached the highest point of the ridge, where a colossal lion marks the boundary of the two Castiles, he stopped, sent for General Lapisse, and told him to proceed to the right to the mountains' foot, and go and take up his quarters with his division in the villages he would find there, and which would afford him supplies.

Next day I was sent very early to the Imperial headquarters, to receive the orders for the day's march from the Prince of Neufchâtel, as had been directed. I had to wait on the ground floor of a little house where the Emperor and the prince had spent the night. I found myself there in company with some generals and officers, besides five fat monks, who had probably come on a deputation, for their faces expressed the greatest anxiety. After waiting half-an-hour, I saw the Emperor issue from a little staircase that led into the room where we were.

On the commotion that his presence excited, the monks, seeing who he was, flung themselves at his feet, murmuring some words I did not understand. The Emperor seemed in very good humour—raised them and tapped them on the shoulder with a smile, telling his interpreter to inform them that they might reckon upon his protection, and desiring them to prevail on the inhabitants to remain quiet and not intermeddle with the fighting, for their own good. This advice was repeated at all points in Spain without being productive of any good.

The Emperor's horse had just been brought, but seeing the thick coating of hoar frost covering the ground, he said he would walk on foot to the place where the plain became more pronounced and there seemed to be no more rime. The Prince of Neufchâtel gave me a sign to attend them; and I soon found myself alone with the Emperor, the Prince of Neufchâtel and General de Montholon, as the difficulties arising from the hoar frost and the crowd of horses had delayed the escort and the mass of the general staff at a pretty good distance.

In a quarter of an hour the Emperor turned, and, seeing me, cast an inquiring look on the Prince of Neufchâtel, which I could easily interpret. The prince had probably forgotten me, and then he gave me the orders I had come for; adding, "Tell General d'Avenay that the Emperor requires the maintenance of the most rigid discipline, and that no sort of pillage is to be tolerated."

The Emperor nodded his head, as much as to say, "Yes, that is my intention."

I turned back to meet the two hussars that came with me and had charge of my horse; and in crossing the space between us was witness to a fact that deserves to be related. At a short distance from the spot where I had left the Emperor, there was an infantry division that must have been at least eight thousand strong, posted on the right of the road, in column, by regiments. I turned sharply at the unanimous acclamations with which this body saluted the Emperor on his appearance at the point they occupied. Enthusiasm was at its height! It was Lapisse's division! the same that the evening before in crossing the Guadarrama had used the seditious language I have mentioned. In the villages where they spent the night, they had found food and wine— and this was the explanation of this sudden change, as the Emperor doubtless had foreseen.

We were soon upon the heels of the English, who had begun to retreat as soon as they were certainly informed that we were marching against them. We crossed the Douro at Tordesillas, and marched upon Benavente. The rain fell without interruption for several days; the roads were broken up; and yet the English left neither gun nor carriage behind them. All the horses were killed that were too much worn out to march, and the men who rode them were obliged to bring in the foot that had the number of the horse and regiment marked on it, as was then the English custom.

The Esla, a pretty considerable river coming down from the Asturias, falls into the Douro; Benavente is on the right bank, at the distance of a mile and a half. We arrived on the left bank. The Emperor, annoyed at seeing no prisoners, was making complaints of the want of energy of the pursuit, so much that General Lefebvre Desnouettes, commander of the Chasseurs of the Guard, when he reached the bank of the river, swam across, though it was excessively swollen by the rains, with his *Chasseurs* and Mamelukes, and charged the English cavalry that was on the opposite bank; they retired on Benavente at a gallop, drawing the *Chasseurs* and Mamelukes after them.

When they reached the walls of Benavente they came to the right about, and with the support of several squadrons charged in their turn. The troop of select men whom they met supported the shock splendidly; but while contending against forces already superior in number, four regiments of English cavalry, favoured by the accidents of the ground, turned their left and came upon their rear, cutting off any means of retreat.

★★★★★★

Napier, in his *Peninsular War,* Vol. 1, states that the pickets and a part of the 3rd German Hussars only were engaged at first against six hundred French, and disputed the ground so firmly as to allow of the retreat of the baggage and camp followers, and that one regiment only, the 10th Hussars, was brought up by Lord Paget to repulse the French.—*Note by Trans.*

★★★★★★

In order to escape, they flung themselves headlong upon these new enemies, while still pursued with all vigour by the first. The whole mass reached the banks of the Esla mingled in a terrible conflict, when the survivors that remained threw themselves in independently. Many were drowned, and hardly a third of the *Chasseurs* and Mamelukes that had crossed the river regained the left bank. This occurred on the 31st of December, 1808.

★★★★★★

Napier gives the number of French engaged at six hundred; the English loss was fifty killed and wounded, the French left fifty-five killed and wounded on the field and seventy prisoners; and Baron Larrey says seventy more wounded escaped. Lefeb-vre-Desnouettes was taken prisoner, and became notorious for having broken his parole and escaped to France, a proceeding justified by the Emperor.—*Note by Trans.*

★★★★★★

The rain had ceased and was succeeded by intense frost. The same day at evening, just at nightfall, we received orders to cross the Esla opposite to Benavente, and to take the orders of Marshal Bessières for the crossing, so I was sent to him. I found him on the bank of the river, with two pieces of cannon which he ordered to be laid for something that seemed to him to be a troop in line on the other side. One of the pieces was fired, and as no movement could be seen to show that they had fired upon anything living, nothing more was done. The marshal gave me orders for the brigade to retire to a large village we had passed, and to wait there. In it we found several of the wounded of the day, and heard from them the particulars related above. They told us that the English did not fire on the *Chasseurs* and Mamelukes who escaped by swimming; and that they even had drawn several out of the water just as they were going to be drowned.

We were prostrate with weariness and hunger. We found sustenance for ourselves and our horses and capital mattresses to lie on; but we had hardly been an hour in a deep sleep when an officer of the general staff brought us an order to resume our march instantly, cross the Esla, and advance on Benavente. He told us that there was a ford that would be shown us when we reached the place where I had found Marshal Bessières. We reached the spot, and found no one waiting to give us the promised information.

Saint-Victor and I entered the water to try the depth; and the dread of finding ourselves below the ford and being carried away by the current without being able to touch the bottom, caused us to bear as much as we could against the rapid stream. The opposite bank of the large river could only just be seen, and it seemed very high and steep. Saint-Victor's horse lost footing and was carried away so quickly that I lost sight of him and his rider in a few seconds.

That very moment my turn came, and I felt a cruel anxiety—not on account of the imminence of danger, as I knew from experience that I could count on my horse—but in thinking of Saint-Victor and of the struggle that must occur between my horse and myself if he did not find footing at the base of the steep bank, that seemed higher and higher as we neared it. Happily, though the water washed the base of the steep, we touched bottom more than twenty paces from it. A last I met with Saint-Victor; he had landed lower down than I did, and by a spontaneous movement we embraced each other.

But we were alone on this river that had received us so inhospitably, and had to consider the means of getting over the brigade which still remained on the other side. The English had left the bank on which we were. We shouted in vain, doing all we could to say that the bank was accessible; the size of the river, and the noise it made, would not allow our voices to be clearly audible, and we only got inarticulate sounds in reply. It seemed absolutely necessary for one of us to recross, and this had to be myself, for Saint-Victor was already suffering from an illness that soon attacked him with great severity.

I found the general very uncertain what he was to do; he disliked the water, and justly, considering that out of the nine hundred horses composing his brigade there would probably be some bad swimmers that would bear their riders to certain destruction. However, as the crossing had to be done, the column entered the river, led by a section of dragoons that were sent in front. But when they came to the spot where the horses lost footing, and were carried off and out of sight in the darkness, the general became alarmed for the consequences that might ensue for the rest of his force were they thus carried down, and he stopped. As my two former passages had hardened me against this kind of danger, I wished to show him that it was not so bad as he thought, and with that purpose I went on again, and succeeded as happily as on the first occasion.

Meanwhile, the general had held to the left, following the stream, and advanced as he found the bottom rise. At last he found the ford, and crossed with the whole column without losing a single man, and without the riders even getting water into their boots. As for Saint-Victor and me, we were as wet as one is when a horse swims, that is to say, to the shoulders, and so up to the throat, because the portion of our clothes that had not been under water had imbibed the wet from the lower portions. I have said that it was freezing, and we marched at a walk till day, which is long in coming on the first of January.

At Benavente we found the infantry division, that had crossed on a bridge of boats, and left it there. I would have given a great deal to be able to warm myself a little at the bivouac fires that were lighted in the streets, but we had to march. It was really a cruel night! At last day broke; we stopped to rest and feed our horses, and I was able to dry myself. When we got near Astorga, where the Imperial headquarters had just arrived, we learnt that General Lefebvre-Desnouettes had been made prisoner the day before.

Our brigade was encamped in a village situated near a brook, and we sent our horses down to it by small detachments, when all at once the English cavalry came to do the same on their side. Two-thirds of the horses were in their watering bridles and the men without arms, so that, after looking one another in the face, both went to the right about and set off at a gallop to report the unexpected meeting that had just taken place. The result to us was an immediate reconnaissance in the direction we had seen the English take, and for them an acceleration of their movement in retreat. This incident showed us that when we halted all military precautions for our protection from an unexpected attack had not been taken, and that if, instead of a small unarmed detachment, the corps it belonged to had made an offensive movement against us, we should have been taken by surprise.

When they came to tell me, I was shaving a beard of fully a week's growth. And before undertaking this operation I had been presiding at the distribution among the officers of forty-three turkeys, which we had found in the house we occupied, all plucked and trussed ready for roasting. This grand treasure-trove was the store of a brother caterer of a convent who had made this provision for the monks to have a proper feast on the approaching feast day of the Three Kings. (The Epiphany.)

He told us this himself with several groans, when he saw how generously we dispensed his treasures, but as may be well imagined we kept our own share. They had for a long time managed to avoid opening the door of the room, but when it was done at last, what a splendid sight for hungry men appeared before our eyes! Forty-three white and plump turkeys with pendent necks and breasts upwards, ranged on the benches around the room. I see them now.

Next night we heard that the Emperor was returning in all haste to Valladolid, and that in all probability Austria was going to declare war against us. At the same time as this information came, we received orders to retire and to march on Toro, a town situated on the Douro that had not yet submitted, with the country which it commands. Coming from Madrid to Astorga, we had left the provinces of Toro and Zamora to our left; no French troops had been directed on that quarter, but it was probable that in occupying Toro we should not have any resistance to overcome, as the movement of the army and the retreat of the English had made the inhabitants understand that submission was the wisest course, indeed the only one to take.

It took us two days to reach Toro; we recrossed the Esla a good three leagues below the place where we had passed the first time. It was written that the river was to be a mine of adventures for me. After crossing it, I remained upon the bank to see the column pass, and this was done without accident. But at the moment when the led horses in the rear were making their way across, the mule bearing our provisions, and the general's cook was carried away by the stream.

The poor cook was just drowning when I caught him by the collar of his coat. I had, of course, been obliged to go into the water, and leave the ford that he had been carried from, and as I was wet through I wished also to save the mule, as his burden was of great value to us.

I managed to get hold of the bridle and to bring him near enough to the bank for the men to drag him out; he was insensible and it was a long time before he regained his feet. It was not a frost that day; indeed, the sun was tolerably warm, so that the bath was infinitely less disagreeable than that I had taken a few days before in the same waters.

A short distance from the river was a large village, and its inhabitants fled at our approach. I hastened after them with Saint-Victor who had learnt Spanish with surprising quickness, and already made himself very well understood; he explained that we would do them no harm if they would return home, whereas if they would not come back, their houses would probably be pillaged. At last we convinced them; our soldiers would have been glad enough to do without their hosts, but nevertheless the promise we had made to the inhabitants was scrupulously kept. We had a good night's rest there. The village was large, no troops had passed before, and it was abundantly supplied with all requisites for man and horse.

The Dutch Hussars, that now formed part of our brigade, were under the command of an old colonel of seventy, named Van House, who had previously been in the service of Austria and Russia; he had fought against the Turks and the Poles. I may here mention a fact that may perhaps seem a bit of vanity. I must relate that the behaviour of Saint-Victor and myself, at the first passage of the Esla, had excited a kind of admiration in him that was very flattering to me, for the old veteran had a long experience in fighting, and he had spent the greatest part of his life in countries where bridges and other means for crossing rivers are not common.

It is quite true that the Esla is large and rapid, and that without any knowledge of it at all, we had plunged into it on a dark night and at a venture, which certainly was a considerable risk. We had become much attached to the old man, from the warm affection he showed to us, and General d'Avenay valued him highly, thinking him wise and capable. He now ordered him to precede us to Toro, in order to take the necessary steps for billeting the troops in concert with the local authorities. The colonel started two hours before the time fixed for the general departure; Saint-Victor went with him to see after our especial lodging. Their escort was composed of twenty-five hussars; an adjutant, major, and surgeon-major also made part of the detachment, the latter at his own request. We allowed the appointed time to elapse and then in our turn took to the road.

Before reaching Toro, we had a long hill to mount. On reaching the summit of this hill the town is in sight and the valley in which it is situated, extending as far as the eye can reach on the left bank of the Douro, and forming the province of Salamanca. The right bank on which we found ourselves, and on which Toro is built, is almost vertical and nearly two hundred feet higher than the opposite bank. When we came to the crest of the eminence I have described, we were surprised to see before us on the horizon a little troop of cavalry halted and guarded by vedettes. I went off at a gallop to see what it was; a horseman came to meet me, and I recognised Saint-Victor. The general followed me closely, and came up to hear what he told us.

They had found a rather numerous armed crowd in front of the gates of Toro; some uniforms could be seen among peasants' and townspeople's dresses. These men approached cautiously, stopping at a little distance; but some of them, who seemed to exercise authority over the others, having advanced and asserted that their intentions were pacific, Colonel Van House, after making known the object of his appearance, and his intention to come to an understanding with the local authorities, thought he could make his entrance into the town, and went on with confidence. No sooner had he got near the gate than a discharge of firearms from the entrance and the houses near it stretched him and his surgeon-major on the ground, and wounded several hussars and horses.

Saint-Victor, not being able to punish this felonious act as it deserved, retired to the height where we saw him, and towards which the Spaniards advanced slowly. The general halted his troops to conceal them; and then gave the orders to go down to meet the enemy with the hussars that had been in sight and to engage in a fire of skirmishers, then to retire so as to draw him away from the town, as he would take refuge in it at once if he got wind of the force before him. The Spaniards were about a thousand in number; they marched in a sort of order that was not fit for defence, as their column was the same in depth as it was in width.

The twenty hussars I had with me roared, that is the word; they had seen the fall of their colonel, whom they quite worshipped, and who had been the victim of a special act of treachery. When they saw that the moment for revenge was come, there was no possibility of restraining them; and against all the efforts of the officer in command and of myself, they threw themselves upon the Spaniards, and sent them flying on all sides, probably more scared by the sight of the column that the general brought up at full speed, on seeing what passed, than by our presence and blows. We reached the town gates before the first fugitives; and they, scattered about the fields, were hunted to death and massacred without pity.

I saved some; and a good many saved themselves; but the lesson was severe, and the recollection must have been preserved at Toro for a long period of years. In this action I saw old hussars weeping and foaming with rage, and uttering nothing but their colonel's name as an excuse for their cruelty when I interfered to snatch a few victims from them. As I pursued the fugitives, they threw away their arms at my mere command, and I reached the two most distant without anyone being with me; one was an absolute Hercules, with enormous black whiskers that could be seen from behind him, the other a lad.

I spoke to the former, with considerable want of confidence in the submission I should find in him; but there was no hesitation—he dropped his gun. As to the boy, when he found me close to him, and heard me call to him "*Basco las armas!*" he turned, took aim at me with most perfect composure, and pulled the trigger at the very moment when I struck his bayonet with my sword, to try and turn away the shot which would certainly have struck me had it been fired, but, happily for me, the piece missed fire. I did not kill the boy.

Toro, though not a fortified town, is surrounded, like almost all Spanish towns, by a wall that secures it from sudden assault, but those who ought to have defended it were the very persons we had just dispersed. A large village, called Morales, that we had on our left at a little distance, had served for a refuge to a great many fugitives from Toro. The general sent me there with a section of hussars. Fearing that they might be endangered, I left them at the entrance of the village, and went in alone with two orderlies. The most perfect silence reigned in it; all the houses were closed, and not a living soul could be seen. I came to the principal part of it, and knocked at a house of tolerably good appearance; I was obliged to reiterate my knock many times till a little wicket above the door opened and allowed the head of a priest to appear, saying to me, "*Pace.*"

On my answering in the affirmative, he came himself to open the door for me. I dismounted from my horse and went in, leaving my two hussars in the street. I made use of the little Spanish I knew, to prove to the priest that he ought to preach to his parishioners in the spirit of the first word he had addressed to me. The good man seemed to me convinced he had nothing better to do; and, raising his hands and eyes to heaven, he made me understand that if they had listened to him, not one of the inhabitants of his village would have taken part in the affray which had just provoked so severe a punishment, though he only suspected the sanguinary result.

When I issued from the presbytery, having hardly been ten minutes there, the village green, which just before had been as deserted as the streets, presented a very unexpected sight to me; it was covered with people, among whom could be seen the fugitives that had taken refuge there. It was easy to recognise them by their shoes and legs being covered with mud. Before the frost, which never lasts long in this country, the ground had been soaked by heavy rain, and the fields that our enemies had crossed in their flight had set a mark on them to betray them. I mounted my horse in the midst of this crowd; and their behaviour would, no doubt, have been most hostile had they not been restrained by fear.

I left the village by the same road as I had entered, and did not find the outside section of hussars that I had left, with orders to wait for me. Not knowing what had become of them, I proceeded towards Toro and crossed our field of battle, covered with dead and dying; amid them more than six hundred muskets had been flung away. On coming near the gate, I saw no vestige of our column, but as it could not possibly have gone in any other direction than the town, I entered and followed a narrow and deserted street with houses close shut.

I had a moment of uneasiness but was relieved on coming to the principal square, where I found our dragoons and hussars drawn up. I there learnt that Colonel Van House was not dead, and that none of the three wounds in his head were considered mortal, but he had not yet recovered his senses. The Spaniards had carried him into a comfortable house. As for the poor surgeon, he died on the spot.

General d'Avenay, at the moment I returned, was in conversation with a priest who spoke French very well, and was deputed by the authorities to appease the anger of the victors, and protest that they were strangers to the odious action that had aroused our vengeance. This priest was an Irishman; he seemed to be an excellent fellow, and told us he believed what the authorities said. We made a show of doing the same, and promised the inhabitants oblivion and safety in a proclamation issued the same evening, and composed by Saint-Victor. Everything connected with the food and lodging of the troops was arranged, and matters resumed their usual order. Though the *corregidor* and *alcalde* had been sent for and had promised submission and obedience, yet we took all the military precautions that prudence dictated before we went to rest.

Repose was not to be my lot, for Saint-Victor, whose turn it was to go a journey, had been compelled to take to his bed for the severe illness he was suffering from; and so, the general told me that the next day I must carry the report of the occupation of Toro to the general headquarters at Valladolid.

Two days before we arrived at this town, a battery of artillery of the Guard had been carried off two leagues away on the territory of a commune called Penilla. We found the six guns at Toro with their caissons; the gunners that managed to escape had taken away their horses: the information we could obtain, showed that the whole country round us was insurgent and in arms. So, my mission to proceed to Valladolid, twenty leagues from Toro, was most perilous; not merely in respect of the danger of death, but chiefly on account of the tortures that the Spaniards, with their natural ferocity exalted by religious and political passion, used to inflict on the French who fell into their hands.

We had fresh proofs of it every day, and the notion of being sawn asunder between two planks, and crucified after mutilation, was not pleasant. It was the peasants, especially, who committed these atrocities when a solitary Frenchman found himself in their hands; they then stirred up one another, and tried who could display the greatest invention—the women especially signalised themselves by their ingenuity.

So, the next day I left Toro on a dark night, with a guide whose wife and five children were taken as hostages, with the information that if he did not lead me faithfully they should all be shot, while if I did get back he was to receive fifty *piastres*. These precautions had a somewhat gloomy aspect, and I confess I could not see them taken without emotion. Saint-Victor was in despair; and the general embraced me and recommended the greatest care. The Irish priest told me he knew my guide, and that he might be trusted. Lastly, I put my confidence in God, and mounted Palaker, my Ukraine horse, to carry me to Tordesillas, twelve leagues from Toro, where there was a post of dragoons in a fortified house outside the town.

When the gate of Toro was closed behind me, and I found myself alone with my guide in perfect darkness, abroad in a country where every inhabitant was an infuriated and ferocious enemy, full of cunning and only thinking how to cause the death of everything appertaining to the French Army, my arrival at Valladolid and my return to Toro seemed to me very problematical things; and one of the best chances that came before my mind was to get myself killed in a desperate defence, so as not to fall alive into the hands of our cannibal enemies. It is at such a time that the peace of home, and the dear remembrance of our native country comes to mind. It was by giving myself up to these recollections, and carrying all my thoughts to Normandy that my dark misgivings were somewhat lessened.

We neared a large village that I had been informed was of bad reputation, and had seen when we left Toro though at a distance of two leagues, for a bright light was burning on the top of the church tower. My guide stopped and whispered to me to listen. We heard voices at a short distance, and soon perceived that we were near a post-house and that the inhabitants of the village were on foot. We left the road and struck to the right among the vines, where it is very difficult for horses to get along, especially at night, though no props are used in Spain. We managed to get through, and recovered the road after a time that seemed long enough to me; the village was turned, and my confidence in my guide increased by this slight incident. He told me that we should not find any more villages before we came to Tordesillas, a place of safety.

Day began to break when I reached the fortified house, the post of thirty dragoons of the twelfth regiment, commanded by a Piedmontese officer named Scarampi. I mention this name with a purpose that will appear afterwards. The fortified houses where detachments were lodged to forward communications were generally isolated from other habitations. They were surrounded with a ditch and palisade; a traverse was placed before the door; they were loopholed from the ground floor to the higher stories, and supplied with provisions and ammunition for a fortnight at least; so, they were perfectly secure from surprise. Indeed, there were cannon in some of them; besides, houses in Spain are built in such a solid manner as is seldom found in other countries.

I left my horse and guide under the charge of M. Scarampi; he gave me a troop horse and an orderly dragoon, and I proceeded on my way. I passed through Tordesillas, the inhabitants were just beginning to appear in the streets; their countenances assumed a sinister aspect, and they cast looks of hatred at me. The road to Valladolid was called a highroad, but that only meant that it was marked clearly enough for persons passing along it for the first time to find it without hesitation. There is only one inhabited spot on this road between Tordesillas and

Valladolid, Simancas, a town or rather village that has a certain celebrity in Spain because the archives of the kingdom are deposited there. This spot was not occupied by our troops, and I had been warned that it might be dangerous; so, I was not free from anxiety when I reached it.

A bridge on the Pisuerga, with a canal by the side also passing under it, is commanded by Simancas. I had to go the whole length of this very narrow and very long bridge; on my arrival it was obstructed by a file of loaded mules. I was obliged to stop at the entrance, and found myself confined between the edge of the road and a steep bank overhanging the river; the mules came towards us, and meant to come up to our horses with hostile intentions, as they are very apt to do, and having no whip, I was obliged to take my sword and strike them on the nose with the flat of it.

Now this might have brought on a disastrous encounter, for the *arrieros* have a well-deserved reputation of being the most quarrelsome people in all Spain, and I leave to the imagination the result for me of a quarrel with a dozen of these fine fellows, each armed by toleration with a long musket. The position would have been ridiculous and dangerous—happily, it did not arise. The mules crossed, and then I crossed in my turn, in sight of the whole population of Simancas, collected on the height to watch me.

I reached Valladolid at midday, and having secured a lodging for my dragoon and the two horses, I waited on the Prince of Neufchâtel, the major-general of the army. He was with the Emperor, and when I wished to give my despatches to the *aide-de-camp* on duty to take them in, he told me that according to the orders now in force, I must deliver them myself, and so wait till I was informed when it should be done. I waited alone in a handsome room, half reclining on a nice sofa covered with sky blue damask, trying to sleep to escape the hunger that began to torment me, and not being able to do so, though I had spent the night without sleep, and had ridden twenty leagues of which the last eight were much the most tiring from the bad paces of my troop horse.

I was invited to dinner at the staff table, and strictly charged not to be absent a moment, as from one minute to another I might be called to the prince, who had been informed of my arrival. I remained there from noon to eight in the evening, and then was informed that dinner was ready. I had eaten nothing for more than twenty-four hours but a little bit of bread and a little chocolate. Under these circumstances the dinner seemed to me magnificent; all the headquarter staff were present, there were several generals and officers of all ranks, and all covered with gold.

After dinner, M. de Flahault, who was then a major and *aide-de-camp* to the major-general, came to conduct me to the Emperor's quarters, the Prince of Neufchâtel received me in a private room. I gave him my despatches, and the paragraph that gave information of the recapture of the six guns of the Guard, pleased him so much that he stopped to go and inform the Emperor, and as he went, said he might probably wish to see me. I was much delighted at this prospect, and prepared in my head the replies I should make to the questions that would probably be addressed to me by the Emperor. I even believe that I made a little repetition of them out loud to judge of the language. I waited more than an hour in impatience and anxiety.

At the end of that time the prince returned carrying a large sealed packet, and another larger, unsealed. The first was addressed to General d'Avenay; the second contained proclamations to the people of Spain. He gave them both to me, and resumed the reading of the despatch; asked me some questions about our affair, and told me that I might wait till the next day to return to Tordesillas, or if I preferred it, go the same evening. I preferred the latter. It rained very hard, the night was very dark, and so if I met with anything dangerous I had a better chance of getting out of it in the dark, because no one could make preparations for my reception, not being able to see me approaching from a distance.

I left Valladolid at midnight, I had placed the proclamation round my body as a protection against balls. I reached Tordesillas without difficulty, and there recovered my horse Palaker and my guide, and when I felt the former under me after his twenty-four hours rest, I seemed to be already out of danger. But I had now to pass by daylight near the great village my guide had avoided with so much care two nights before. They were again in arms there, as I easily saw on observing advanced posts and sentries stationed on the side towards Toro, whence danger might come to them.

This village was called Pedrosa, and had a population of three thousand souls, and the houses were crowded together as they are in all the villages in Spain. The inhabitants of Pedrosa were considered quarrelsome, and were not liked in the country. They saw me quite plainly, but did not make any demonstrations of hostility.

It was night when I reached Toro, there had been great uneasiness on my account all the time I had been away, and I was therefore received as may be supposed. My poor guide was considered an angel and received a gratuity besides his fifty *piastres*. The despatches I handed to General d'Avenay ordered him to strike a war contribution on the province of Toro of a million *reals*—one thousand pounds, to give up the village of Penilla to plunder, as the attack on the battery of the artillery of the Guard, we had recaptured, had taken place in its territory, and then to burn it so as not to leave one stone upon another. The Emperor expressed to the general his satisfaction at the manner in which the operations had been conducted, and made him a present of three hundred and twenty pounds to be deducted from the contribution he was to levy.

We were in consternation at the order to destroy Penilla. During the forty-eight hours of my absence a great part of the country had submitted; by the general's orders the arms had been brought in a mass, and there was every indication that the punishment inflicted under the walls of Toro on its treacherous inhabitants had produced a salutary effect, and there was some apprehension that the destruction of a fine village might drive the inhabitants to despair and exasperate those who might dread a similar fate; but the order was formal and military obedience does not allow of the least objection. The general sent for the Irish priest I have spoken of, and told him to cause secret information to be sent to the inhabitants of Penilla that they might have three days to remove their valuables. They did not waste time, and when the village was set on fire and completely burnt there was nothing in it.

A few days afterwards a deputation from the village came to thank the general for the humanity he had displayed, and expressed the deepest gratitude in good terms. The word pillage in the sense it carries in such a case, implies not only spoliation, but also violation and murder; in a word, all the excesses that men released from discipline can commit in rivalry with each other as invariably takes place.

The Emperor quitted Spain a few days later to go to Germany, and oppose the march of the Austrians who had marched upon Bavaria, our ally, without previous declaration. He left Marshal Bessières at Valladolid, giving him chief command of the North West of Spain, that is to say, the Asturias, Galicia, Old Castile, the kingdom of Leon and Salamanca. General d'Avenay received orders to send a report on the condition of the country he held, as well as any information he could obtain about the orders of the Marquis de la Romana, who, with English assistance, had brought back the corps of fifteen thousand men under his command into Spain, that should have joined our army in Germany as auxiliaries. After the events that had occurred, his defection was quite to be expected, the English had taken them on board near Hamburg, and landed them at Ferrol, whence he advanced towards Leon, but timidly and feeling his way.

Saint-Victor continued ill, and so I had to go again. As relays of post horses had been established, I made my journey at full speed. All went well as far as Tordesillas. There I had a postillion whose countenance displeased me much, and a horse that was not much better. On the road the first kept changing from the gallop to the trot and the second did the same, and his paces were infernal. I called to the postillion to stop this performance, but he paid no attention, and I thought I heard him laugh at the vain efforts I made to come up with him, when he slackened his pace my horrible horse absolutely refused to reduce the distance in front.

A quarter of a league from Valladolid, just in the middle of the road I was on, I saw a large tree that extended its branches horizontally and covered it all. It was now night. Just as we came near the tree, a voice came from the foot of it, and called to the postillion, saying, "Is that you, Manuelo?"

On his answering in the affirmative, he was asked with whom he was. "With a Frenchman," said he, and at the same instant went under the tree into the deepest shade.

A conversation in half tones passed there without my being able to distinguish the purport of it; I only perceived that the number of speakers must be five or six at least. It was impossible to turn back, equally so to turn my horse elsewhere. I stopped at twenty paces from my guide, and tried to take the side furthest from the centre of the tree but could not.

It seemed clear that there were persons lying in wait for some prey, and that the postillion was an accomplice. I also calculated that I should not fall till I was under the tree, and that I should probably be stabbed to avoid giving the alarm by a shot that might be heard at the advanced posts of Valladolid. I gently drew my sabre and let it hang by the sword knot. I took a pistol in my right hand and another in the bridle hand, and prepared to defend myself as best I could, quite expecting that the time was come. I should have a quantity to write were I obliged to relate all the flying thoughts that passed through my head at the moment.

At last Manuelo set off at a gallop, and I did the same, with the feelings a man might have in jumping over a precipice. I passed a group of Spaniards without counting them, and they said not a word; I could not see if they had any weapons, and in ten minutes I was in Valladolid in a French garrison, and in the same room where I had experienced hunger and impatience.

On dismounting, I paid the postillion the price of the stage, but when he asked me for something for himself in a somewhat peremptory tone, I refused, saying that I never gave the postillion anything unless he had behaved well. I had on my mind the repeated halts against my orders, and more than this, his conversation with the men posted under the great tree. He went away grumbling.

Marshal Bessières kept me all the next day, and only gave me my despatches on the morning of the day after. He gave me besides a commission for Prince Mazzaredo, King Joseph's Minister of Marine, who was to stop at Tordesillas that day on a journey from Madrid to Corunna. The Marshal ordered me to follow the prince to the next stage if he had started, and if I did not come up with him within that distance, to return to Toro.

When I reached the gate of Tordesillas I learnt that he had been gone some hours, and they thought he would stop at the first stage, but that the postillion that had gone with him had just come back, and would give me better information. My arrival had collected an assemblage at the post-house that did not seem at all well-disposed. I was in a large room on the ground-floor, which served as a vestibule to the rooms of the house and the stable door. My saddle had just been laid on a bench, and I was expecting the horse to carry it and the postillion to go with me.

At this moment the man who had gone with Prince Mazzaredo came in. It was the Manuelo that had given me so much cause of complaint two nights before. I put my question to him about the prince; but instead of answering, he came towards me and applied a horribly abusive word to me, that was received with a loud laugh of approbation from the assemblage at the door. The word was hardly spoken when a good blow with my fist on the breast drove Manuelo away from me. Then he caught up a heavy wooden bar, the fastening of the door leading to the narrow and retired street where the post-house was, and raised it against me.

I had drawn my sword at the first movement that showed me what he meant. He threw the bar at me, but I avoided it, and he rushed to the door to get help among the crowd; but before he could bury himself in it I reached him and gave him the point in the loins. He cried out and was surrounded in a moment; so was I, and caught from behind and nearly thrown down, I might even say entirely so, for one of my knees and my right elbow touched the ground.

I fought furiously, and having disengaged my arm, still keeping hold of my sword, struck out without looking where I hit; my first blow was at once followed by a cry and by my deliverance, for they crowded round the wounded man, and I could get at my pistols. As soon as I displayed them, the invaders of the house were in haste to get out, and I advanced with determination into the street. The vagabonds then gave way, leaving an open space before the door; I did not know what to do nor what would become of me. There was a considerable crowd before me, and it seemed impossible to reach the dragoons' fortified house on foot, for it was more than half a mile away and the whole length of the city.

I was delivered from this anxiety by the arrival of a postillion with two horses, mounted on one and with my saddle on the other. I found myself on horseback without well knowing how, for I kept a pistol in each band, and I do not know at all when I returned my sword to the scabbard. As I passed through the crowd at a gallop I could see plenty of symptoms of hostility, but they did not try to stop my passage, and I reached the dragoons. M. Scarampi was a most ridiculous sight, such as unluckily I cannot describe here. When he was a little recovered from the disturbance my untimely arrival had caused him, I related what had passed, and desired him to have Manuelo apprehended, he was taken to Valladolid and condemned to be hanged. I got his pardon from Marshal Bessières by accusing myself of having acted too hastily, and perhaps justly so. Manuelo's father had hastened to Toro on hearing of his son's destined fate; the old man had a venerable face and his sorrow affected me greatly.

When I left the dragoons, I told the postillion to lead me on the track of Prince Mazzaredo, as far as the first stage on the road to Corunna. I had imbibed confidence in this postillion from the air of delight and triumph with which he looked at me when we got out of the crowd. He led me by short cuts across fields for four leagues without my seeing a house or a living soul. At last coming round a hill, I found myself at the end of a very large village, and made my way into it without seeing anyone at first; but when I reached the square I found all the inhabitants assembled there, appearing in a great state of excitement, and conversing with great animation, most likely about the visit of the prince which was quite an event.

My arrival was another, and I was immediately surrounded. For one moment I had an idea of dashing in my spurs, but the thought that it would certainly be a mark of fear to fly in this way stopped me. I quietly dismounted at the door of the post-house; told the postillion to take off my saddle and put it on a stone bench by the side of the door. I sat by it, making no secret of being on the watch, with my hand on the holsters. I paid my bold postillion handsomely, and a great many questions were put to him, and after ascertaining that I had no chance of catching the Prince, I prepared to proceed direct to Toro. I had ordered horses, they were a long time coming, and I was not without anxiety seeing that I had become the subject of rather animated discussion, showing that they were not agreed about me.

But a little incident that had taken place a few minutes earlier was reassuring. When I paid the postillion who brought me from Tordesillas, a man of somewhat higher rank, who I thought was the schoolmaster, begged to be allowed to see my purse, made of silk with steel beads, and a burnished clasp. I handed it to him with a show of perfect confidence. He opened it, turned the contents into his hand, and I saw the purse and a dozen *napoleons* that had been taken out of it, passed from one to the other, and submitted to an examination that was long enough to make me think it would not all come back.

This was not at all the case, and the whole sum, as well as the purse, was faithfully returned. At last the horses were brought; my saddle was put on one that looked very fresh, and I made a brilliant departure, though rather anxious for the effect I should produce as a horseman in the eyes of those whom I left with great delight.

We galloped towards Toro by roads unknown to me; I had only one village to go through, and I think there was a band of guerillas in it, for I saw two that came out to the door of a house at the sound of our horses' gallop, and instantly went in again, either to get their weapons or to hide themselves, and escape if they thought I was followed by any force. At last I got to Toro. The day Marshal Bessières had made me spend at Valladolid had given them reason to suspect that I was killed. The general and Saint-Victor clasped me in their arms. The latter wept, never having ceased to despair and blame himself, thinking of the dangers I ran in his place. A poor sinner never expiated his fault more sincerely and sorrowfully, for it must be owned that it was his own fault that he was unable to do his duty.

A few days afterwards I took the same ride to Valladolid without any notable adventure. Marshal Bessières gave me orders to proceed to Zamora immediately after my return to Toro; but when General d'Avenay heard that I was sent on this, he would not allow this new duty to be thrown on me, and took upon himself to go and examine the citadel of Zamorra. This town had been occupied after our arrival at Toro by a brigade of cavalry, under the orders of General Mancune, and by two battalions of Lapisse's division: and we also had received a battalion from it.

I returned to Valladolid to give an account of the state of the citadel, and was the object of an ovation when I passed the post-house at Tordesillas. It was known that the pardon of Manuelo the postillion, was due to me, he was then with his father, and I was surrounded by a number of people in a very different spirit. The post-mistress had been wounded by me as she was trying to interpose and stop my assailants, and still carried her arm in a sling. She was a good woman, and thanked me with animation for what I had done for her postillion.

On my side I expressed all my regret at having quite involuntarily hurt her, she assured me that it would be nothing, that it was only a flesh wound; I had been told of this on my two previous visits in going and returning, but I had never seen the woman. This halt at Tordesillas procured me an experience I have never forgotten. The habitual expression of Spanish faces in regard to us was hatred and ferocity, and the general character of their physiognomy lends itself to this. Then, on the contrary, I met with kindness and even affection, and the contrast was too exceptional for it not to have made an impression on my memory.

I returned to General d'Avenay with orders to go and establish himself at Zamora; the provinces of Toro, Zamora and Salamanca were put under his command. He was given nearly five thousand infantry, a troop of horse artillery, and five squadrons of dragoons were added to his cavalry. These forces were to be concentrated at Zamora, and our duty was to observe the Spanish corps of Romana, and a Portuguese corps that was formed at Miranda del Douro. Romana had twenty thousand men, and was fifteen leagues from us. We never knew the exact force of the Portuguese corps, it was at a distance of ten leagues, but we had nothing to fear on the left bank of the Douro, and the circuit that they would have been obliged to make to attack us by the right bank, increased their distance by three leagues.

The army of Romana was in great part composed of troops of the line brought back by him from Germany. The Portuguese were nothing but an assemblage of people of all sorts, and among them was a regiment entirely made up of monks.

Zamora, whither we went, is one of the most beautiful cities of Spain; it is surrounded by high walls with flanking towers, all in a good state of preservation. At the western extremity is a citadel fortified in modem style, but so little separated from Zamora, commanded from so near by the cathedral and its bell tower, that it would have been impossible to prevent approaches from that side; yet the defence was quite easy with a siege train.

The general was very active in procuring supplies of all kinds for it, and in providing lodgings for all our force in case of necessity. The clock tower of the cathedral was mined, so that it could be blown up if necessity should occur; and when all was done, the general sent me, for the fifth time, to Valladolid, to inform the marshal of the state of things, and also of all the information we had got touching the corps of Romana and the Portuguese forces.

Three spies that we had sent, had been detected and hanged. They left widows and orphans who excited much compassion, and for whom the general begged assistance, and it was granted. It must be said in justice to the Spaniards, that it was very difficult to find spies among them. The frontier that we occupied offered more resources than usual of this kind from the large number of smugglers to be found there; persons of adventurous character, for whom the word *country* generally has no meaning.

In my last journey from Valladolid to Toro, I had fallen at night into the midst of a band of brigands of this kind, armed to the teeth. I was so tired that I had gone to sleep on my horse, and waked up as he stopped short. Before I had time to take stock of my position they spoke to my postillion, and he went off at a gallop, and as I followed him I heard that I was saluted with a "*Vaya usted con Dios Senor Caballero.*" These comfortable words gave me a great deal of satisfaction.

The journey from Zamora to Valladolid presented a much more unpleasant aspect, in one respect, than that I had taken from Toro; there was a distance of nine leagues more to traverse across a kind of desert, and a wood of two leagues in extent. I had to pass through Toro, and it was no longer held by the French; and all the way to Valladolid I had no assistance to expect but the post at Tordesillas, and this was especially slight, as the dragoons composing it kept quiet in their fortress, and had formal orders never to go fifty paces away from it, unless in case of imperative duty.

A post that we had established between Zamora and Salamanca had been surprised, and all their throats mercilessly cut. So, I may be forgiven for the gloomy ideas that oppressed me in the midst of such dangers. I must regard my escape as a miracle: every day we heard of the disappearance, and sometimes of the cruel death, of some officer who was like me going with despatches. We were allowed very large travelling expenses as some recompense for the dangers that we encountered; thus, for going to Valladolid from Toro and back, twenty pounds, and from Zamora, twenty-four pounds. This was but a small set-off to these gloomy thoughts and to the kind of danger that we ran, but it was a kind of encouragement to some. How many received it and never got any benefit from it!

Two little events happened at Zamora that may give a notion of the kind of life we led. The general gave a ball, and everything presentable at Zamora came there with the greatest delight; among them was a certain Lopez, who had organised and commanded the resistance that we had overcome at Toro. All our military precautions were taken as usual; we had cavalry pickets ready to march night and day. But, lo and behold! just at midnight, when everyone was trying to enjoy himself and make some pleasant acquaintance, information reached us that the Spaniards were attacking the Toro gate.

The general gave me orders to hasten to the infantry quarters, take three companies, and go to the gate with all speed. It seemed probable that the attack could not have taken place without being supported by persons within, for guns would have been wanted to blow open the gates of Zamora.

As soon as I was outside I heard some musketry that was sustained, but it did not seem in great force, and seemed to come from a point to the right of the Toro gate. There were no street lamps at Zamora and the night being very dark, it took me more than ten minutes to get to the infantry quarters. I passed the hospital, containing about three hundred sick and wounded, and saw a very affecting sight. The sick were drawn up along the walls and leaning against them, with their firelocks in hand and packs on. Some wore nothing but their shirts, thinking there was no time to dress. Large fires had been kindled on the open ground before the hospital, and lighted up the pale faces of these poor soldiers, quite determined to defend themselves to the last extremity, for the Spaniards almost always cut the throats of the wounded when they captured a hospital.

The infantry were already under arms in their quarters. I took three companies, as desired by the General, and ran with them towards the Toro gate. But before I got there I perceived that the firing did not come from thence, but from the higher part of the town commanding the Douro; the artillery and cavalry barracks were in that direction. Having visited the Toro gate and ascertained that there was no attack there, but that the guard was very uneasy, I left one of my companies there, and with the other two proceeded in the direction of the fire. Approaching by a street that turned to the right, the sound of the balls striking the walls that we had on our left and in front showed me, without being quite clear, that firing was going on partly from our side and partly from another, for none of the shots struck us.

We were hardly two hundred paces from the spot whence the firing came, and we heard not a shout, not a word. I ordered a call of "Who goes there?" and the answer was "France." Then I gave the order to cease firing, and on coming up, found a sergeant in a most extraordinary state of excitement. He told me that on going towards a market about twenty paces from there, with a roof supported by a great number of posts, he had seen an assemblage of armed Spaniards with fires lighted and warming themselves. He had cried out "Who goes there?" and instead of answering, they had put out the fires and returned musket shots at him; that he had been replying for half an hour, but had really not received any other shots than those that had brought on the affair.

The matter was examined into, and it was ascertained that some twenty oxen had been provisionally lodged with their drivers in the place in question, that the unfortunate sergeant had been struck with hallucination, that no shots had been fired upon his force of fifteen men patrolling the streets, that the drivers of the oxen had been scared by the approach of this troop and the challenge that they did not understand, they had tried to extinguish their fires without reply, and that then firing had begun and killed most of the oxen, happily without hitting the men, who had thrown themselves on the ground at the first shots.

It was a serious matter for the sergeant, and he was immediately put under arrest. Zamora was in a state of siege, and the penalty for a false alarm is death. His crime was ascribed to temporary madness, and his life was saved; but he was condemned to a long imprisonment. I have related this unimportant incident to give a slight notion of the anxious and disturbed life we led during these Spanish campaigns; there would be no resemblance between their history and that of others of the same kind, if it were possible to collect all the circumstances of them. By the side of heroic and sublime actions will be found others that are most atrocious and sometimes most grotesque.

A few days after the adventure I have just related, a guard of four men and a corporal, that we kept a few hundred paces in front of the Toro gate, were surprised during the night, and their throats cut without the least noise to give the alarm. This guard could only have been surprised by some neglect of duty, for it was placed in a little isolated building, very substantial, which should have been kept shut at night, according to the standing orders. Now the door had been found open without any mark of breakage, and the men were probably killed by poniards without making any defence. We supposed that they had made acquaintances among the Spaniards, as was often the case, and fallen victims to treachery.

A corporal of the garrison was also found hung by the feet in the shop of a butcher of Zamora with whom he had made acquaintance. The butcher, assisted no doubt by some accomplice, had opened the corporal as one opens a pig, and removed the whole of his inside; then after the horrible exploit, he made his escape, and on breaking into his house it was found to be stripped.

I made a sixth journey to Valladolid, to give an account of the movements of the corps of Romana, and a reconnaissance General d'Avenay had sent towards the frontier of Portugal. I remained at Valladolid a whole day, and made acquaintance with a young officer, Belgian by birth, De Sevres by name, attached to the staff of Marshal Bessières. A peculiar circumstance of which I was a witness induced him to make a confidant of me, in a way that put us in a few hours on the footing of old friends.

I returned to Zamora without accident, but I cannot conceive how I managed so many times to escape the dangers that lay so thickly around the paths I traversed. At that time the condition of things was such in Spain, that there were orders against any man connected with the army, either officer or soldier, going further than a gun shot from the fortified posts or camps that we occupied; before the doors of these posts were opened in the morning a reconnaissance was sent out to explore the neighbourhood, and they seldom returned without having exchanged shots; every inhabitant was an exasperated enemy and a fanatic against us. Well, there were twenty-five leagues of country to be crossed alone among a population so hostile, that the murder of a Frenchman was considered a meritorious action in the eyes of

God and the country, and all the discourses of the priests from the pulpit tended the same way.

And so, every time in the dark night that I preferred for starting on my journey, when I took my way towards the gates that protected us, when I saw them open and then close behind me, so that I was left to myself, I felt my heart sink. But this disposition of my heart did not last. There was distraction in the sustained attention kept up by the instinct of self-preservation. The ear on the watch, the eyes searching into darkness, I tried to account for the least noise, or the smallest object; at the same time the remembrance of family affection came to my assistance, and caused a distraction from the presence of danger. I knew the horses at the different posthouses where I changed, and they gave me those I liked best; I had to spare them for each of them had a long stage to do. This sixth journey of fifty-six leagues coming and going was my last.

A few days afterwards, at the end of March, 1809, an event happened which caused some trouble among us. The general's brother, M. Adrien de Villaunay, arrived at Zamora quite unexpectedly. He was the husband of a charming wife; had two children, and lived in a mansion six leagues from Caen, in the enjoyment of a sufficient fortune. Unhappily for him, he had been appointed mayor of his commune, and in this capacity, he had, with imprudent kindness, contrary to law, signed a document relating to the conscription, that rendered him liable to a prosecution instituted against him by the public prosecutor, and a conviction might entail the penalty of penal servitude.

In order to avoid this, he had come away from France to get support from his brother. Adrien de Villaunay was a good sort of man, but a great boaster; very full of notions of his own consequence which were really founded upon next to nothing. We had been intimate from childhood. As to the two brothers, they were by any means on such terms; and the general received him coldly enough, though quite inclined to do him any service in his power.

Villaunay had been about three weeks with us, when General d'Avenay received orders to go to Italy to take the command of a brigade of cavalry, being a part of a division under the command of General Sahuc. While we were preparing for our departure, we were joined by Eugène d'Hautefeuille returning invalided to France, and a young Westphalian officer going with him for the same reason. They waited for us, and went with us a few days afterwards. Our troop was composed of the general, his brother, the two officers just named,

Saint-Victor and myself; with four hussars of the 2nd regiment, attached to our staff for several months, a farrier of the 12th regiment of Dragoons, and ten servants with led horses. An escort of twenty-five dragoons went with us as far as Tordesillae, where we arrived on the second day, and on the third we entered Valladolid. Marshal Bessières having been summoned to Germany to take command of the Imperial Guard, was replaced by General Kellermann.

I may say, without the least partiality, that in the important command entrusted to him, General d'Avenay had displayed great capacity, remarkable activity, and, in a word, every quality that marked him to all eyes as fit to perform the highest military services. His foresight extended to the smallest details, and he could not be found at fault in anything. He was placed at Zamora in a dangerous position, in front of forces of the enemy of ten times his strength; but he managed for four months to impose upon them in such a way as to preserve the country entrusted to him intact, and to prevent. any serious attempt being made against him.

The taxes were regularly paid to the Spanish financial officials, and they kept the account; the pay of our little *corps d'armée* was defrayed with exactitude; and the soldier so cared for that he had never been so well off. The Spaniards who had charge of the supplies of food performed their duties to perfection, and so a whole French commissariat staff that was sent us was put aside. The members of it objected and made a great outcry, but in vain—the general was firm.

After our departure, matters did not remain on the same footing in the three provinces of Toro, Zamora and Salamanca. General d'Avenay's successor was hesitating and timid, and the Spaniards regained 'the confidence they had lost with us. Romana and the Portuguese advanced; bands of men were got together; the communications between Zamora and Valladolid were interrupted; and to remedy this state of things required an expenditure of time, men and money.

General Kellermann, son of the marshal of that name, received us very well. I had long been desirous of knowing him, being acquainted with the part he played at the Battle of Marengo, the victory being almost entirely due to him at a moment of despair. He was a little man, of unhealthy and insignificant appearance, with a clever look, but false. During our short stay at Valladolid we heard some things about him that lowered him considerably in our estimation. He was a merciless peculator. Under political pretexts he would bury the most notable inhabitants of places under his control, extending over a fourth part of Spain, in the ancient dungeons of the Inquisition; he would then make a composition with their families and set the prisoners at liberty for a price that he pocketed.

In later days, under the Restoration, he had a great reputation for piety. Without wishing to contest the sincerity of his religious feelings at this later period, I cannot help making the remark that, at the dedication of a church that was built at his expense near Paris, in a commune where he was owner of a house and lands, the Abbé Fraissinous, renowned for his piety and eloquence, preached a sermon in praise of the virtues of the founder. It is very likely that both house and church were the result of exactions committed in Spain.

CHAPTER 7

General D'Avenay's Death

No event marked our return to France; the safety of the road we had to travel was secured by detachments at short distances. On reaching Bayonne we left our travelling companions, our horses, there, and we, the General and I, went off at full speed of post to Bordeaux to fetch the carriage we had left there. One servant alone went with us. We made the sixty-six leagues between Bayonne and Bordeaux in twenty hours, and arrived worn out with fatigue. We spent three days there in getting the things we required for a fresh campaign. Nothing positive was known of the course of events; the only subject of conversation was the rapidity with which the Emperor was marching his troops on Germany to repulse the Austrian invasion of Bavaria without previous declaration.

We started for Italy by post, going northwards as far as Moulins, because of the bad state of the roads in Auvergne. We were impatient to reach new battlefields, to revisit the Italy we had known before, and the Austrians also, old acquaintances with whom we found we had not measured ourselves quite enough. We were almost always conversing about military matters during this long journey almost alone together. We were to form a part of the advanced guard, meeting an army reorganised to great advantage and numerically superior to our own, with the traditions of war weakened by a three years' rest, and we passed in review all kinds of suppositions, being greatly assisted by the knowledge of the ground we already possessed.

In Savoy we met a large number of civil administrators and women escaping from Italy in consequence of a serious reverse we had experienced. Our divisions had been surprised and attacked on a sudden; they had attempted to make head at Sacile between the Tagliamento and the Piave and had been completely defeated. The army had retired in disorder, and only rallied behind the Adige with a loss of ten thousand men. The general was grieved by this information. Was it a presentiment? As far as regards myself I may say in all truth that my desire to be near the enemy was greatly augmented by it.

When we reached Lanslebourg, at the foot of Mont Cenis, we spent the night there, being stopped by a hurricane that rendered the ascent of the mountain impossible. We made the attempt next day, drawn by eight horses and escorted by eight men holding four ropes attached to the corners of the carriage imperial to keep it from falling over. This was a necessary precaution, as we had in some places to pass over fifteen feet of snow, and of unequal solidity, the soft parts being especially dangerous. We only met with one accident that might have had fatal consequences. Coming out of the tunnel that is passed on the descent towards Susa, an avalanche took us by surprise, and would infallibly have cast us into the valley to a depth of more than a thousand feet had it not been divided in two by a mass of rocks above us.

A hired carriage in front of us was not so fortunate, we saw it turning over and over in the gulf for several minutes. The plane on which it rolled was by no means vertical, and the velocity of its motion was delayed by the depth of the snow so much as to make us sometimes think it would not get to the bottom; the desperate efforts of the horses also, which could be seen now buried in the snow and now violently dragged out of it by the weight of the carriage, conduced to break the speed of the fall.

We remained four hours on the spot while the gunners broke a passage for us, and as soon as we were on the way we saw the four horses of the carriage standing with uninjured limbs. It seemed almost a miracle. The two men that drove them had not fallen with them, and had no greater harm done them than being buried a few minutes in the snow, whence they were rescued by our escort.

An hour later we were in full springtime, going along a capital road at full trot, and in sight of the beautiful plain of Piedmont all covered with verdure and flowers. We slept at Turin, and next day arrived at Milan where we wished to buy horses, the circumstances being such that we had not time to wait for our own. The general found one that had belonged an *aide-de-camp* of the viceroy lately killed: but I could not get one at all, for the stables of all the horse-dealers had been emptied to supply the needs of the army. We proceeded in great haste to Placentia, where the general wished to leave his carriage, being the station of the depot of the 6th Cuirassiers.

We thought we should also find a horse for me there, and in reality, the major commanding the depot of the 6th Cuirassiers lent me a troop horse. Thus equipped, we joined the army already across the Adige following a movement of the Austrian Army in retreat, caused by the success of the French Army in Germany under the Emperor's command. We found the viceroy's headquarters at Vicenza, the Prince received General d'Avenay very well, and told him he had been impatiently expecting him, in fact he had not in his whole army a single cavalry general on whom he could depend. They were all old and had not fought since 1806.

Our division, under the command of General Sahuc was composed of four superb regiments of *chasseurs*; the Eighth and Twenty-Fifth formed General d'Avenay's brigade. In a month this brigade had lost two generals, the first killed, the second severely wounded and taken prisoner. This circumstance seemed to me to presage well; it seemed impossible that fatality should brood so much over this fraction of the army as to make it always its turn to furnish Generals for the enemy's shot. It was not long before I was cruelly undeceived.

We made several reconnaissances on the right bank of the Piave, not yet entirely abandoned by the Austrians. In one of these the incapacity of General Sahuc was displayed before our eyes in such a way as to show us that the command of an advanced guard could not be in worse hands. He had entangled his whole division in a narrow road with deep and wide ditches on each side, insurmountable to horsemen. At various places bridges had been thrown across these ditches to communicate with the contiguous fields.

Advantage had been taken of these bridges to throw out skirmishers to right and left, but the ground they had to traverse was planted with mulberry trees tied together by festoons of vines, as is usual in this country; besides, each separate property, and they are very numerous, was parted from its neighbour by a large trench running into the main ditch, and making other obstacles that our skirmishers had to leap without being able to see more than fifteen paces before them, because the mulberries were very near together, and the festoons of vines, so that the chasseurs were obliged to cut them in order to make their way, and so they had to keep their swords drawn in their hands, instead of the carabines that they ought to have had.

As soon as this march began, General d'Avenay had insisted on being allowed to proceed to the front with one regiment alone, and to send it forward in divisions so that the three others might not be entangled before the ground had been sufficiently explored; but General Sahuc refused, and the column with the whole staff at the head was only preceded by a section of twenty-five *chasseurs*.

In this position our skirmishers exchanged fire with an enemy that might be said to be invisible, for there was nothing to be seen but the horses' feet. In this bad position there was only one thing to be done, quite against the rule that forbids troops on a reconnaissance to engage in any serious encounter, but rendered necessary under the circumstances, it was to push whatever was before us vigorously back to the mouth of the defile. Instead of that General Sahuc halted the column, and gave orders to bring up the artillery from the rear of the column, where it was hindered from coming up to us by the two thousand horses before it, in a road where two carriages could hardly go abreast. General d'Avenay showed such good reason against this ill-timed order that General Sahuc deferred its execution.

I was sent to the skirmishers to endeavour to obtain some information, and the officer in command very soon found out that the enemy he thought he had met was only our own 9th Regiment of Chasseurs attached to an infantry division, and they being on a reconnaissance on their own side had taken us for Austrians as we had them. Happily, this meeting resulted in nothing but a few slight wounds to the horses instead of the men. The 9th Chasseurs went in another direction and we continued our exploration, ascertaining that on the portion of the right bank of the Piave that we had been desired to reconnoitre there was not an Austrian left, and this made us suppose that the whole of the enemy's forces had crossed to the other side; and this supposition soon became a certainty.

We established ourselves that night in some villages that had been pointed out to us, and two Hungarian deserters came in, and were sent to the headquarter staff. Next day, towards evening, we received orders immediately to make a demonstration on the left bank, crossing the river by a ford that was pointed out to us. The water is swelled by the melting of the snow, and is always higher in the evening than morning in rivers that descend from the Alps without a long course; and so we had a good deal of trouble in accomplishing our crossing, but it was got through without accident. At this spot the left bank presented a bare space, from two to two hundred feet. wide, and of indefinite length towards our right, while on our left it united with the plain that extends from the banks of the Piave towards Conegliano; we were about two miles distant from this plain.

Parallel with the course of the river and at the distance I have mentioned above, the ground was planted with mulberries and vines, intersected by ditches and drains, and so unsuitable for the action of cavalry. The skirmishers we sent in that direction were received by the fire of infantry and obliged to retire. This, however, was not the case with a section of the 8th Chasseurs that had been sent against two squadrons of the enemy that appeared on our left. These two squadrons halted for a short time, and then began to retire slowly, showing front every three or four hundred paces, and always followed up by our twenty-five chasseurs.

I was expecting every moment to see their complete overthrow, for they were half a league away from us, on the heels of an enemy ten times as numerous, that could easily see there were no supports. Night fell and the skirmish continued. I had twice carried orders to Colonel Curtot to call in his men, had the recall sounded, but it was not heard. An orderly had to be sent after them, and at last to my great astonishment the twenty-five *chasseurs* returned unpursued, without the loss of a man, with a few wounds and nothing more.

We recrossed the Piave without the least hindrance, a great surprise to us; for if the Austrians had only brought two or three field-guns to the mouth of a road that opened on the edge of ground that I have tried to describe, they might have commanded the ford by which we were retiring, and would certainly have caused us considerable loss. Thus, there was no readiness on the part of the Austrian military authorities, and this is a general fault that has been found with them.

We returned at evening to the cantonments we had started from, and rested the next day, but we received orders to hold ourselves in readiness to cross the Piave next morning, as the whole army was to make a movement to the front. This was a signal for a battle, for the Austrians had evidently not had time to pass their luggage beyond the defile that begins at Conegliano and extends almost without interruption to Tagliamento.

The 9th of May, 1809, a day of mournful memory to me, we mounted our horses before daybreak, and marched to the ford we had reconnoitred two days before. We had orders to cross the river at that spot, and try to force the defile opposite, not having been able to penetrate into it before, and then to incline to our left, and disturb the Austrian rear-guard, making head against the mass of our arms about two miles off. This army had come by the high-road from Treviso to Udine, and was coming down upon the Piave where the bridge was

PIAVE RIVER, 1809

destroyed, and just as we crossed the river they threw five battalions of *voltigeurs*, a troop of horse artillery, and the 9th Chasseurs across to the left bank.

We were stopped by Austrian infantry occupying the defile, and while skirmishing with them were joined by a division of dragoons numbering at least four thousand horse. General d'Avenay sent me to ask its commander, General de Pully, to dismount two or three of his squadrons, to try to dislodge the infantry that stopped us— a duty these dragoons might possibly have succeeded in performing, as they were armed with *fusées*, and drilled to fight on foot. I have described this general in my account of the campaign of 1805, and he refused most positively, saying his orders were to support the *chasseurs*, and not open the way for them.

The cannonade was hotly engaged on our left, and General d'Avenay in great doubt as to what to do, when an officer of the general staff, evidently alarmed, came to give us orders to move as quickly as possible to the assistance of the five battalions of *voltigeurs*, as they were threatened by superior forces. We went off at a trot in column of sections, ascending the course of the Piave. It did not take us long to go the distance, and we saw a cloud of dust thrown up by a mass of fugitives running towards the river. This sight made an impression on General d'Avenay, and he said to me:

This is beginning badly, we shall very likely be thrown into the water.

General Sahuc did not seem quite at his ease, and as for the colonels of the two regiments, such complete demoralisation could not have been credited without seeing it. The colonel of the 8th Chasseurs was still trying to put a good face on it, but the other was past giving himself any such trouble, he had become a brute machine, unable to see or hear. The two regiments under their orders did not present the same appearance, officers and soldiers looked calm and intrepid; they were old soldiers of several campaigns, and four years rest in Italy, while fighting was going on in Prussia and Spain, made them feel a desire to measure themselves again with the enemy, and take their revenge for the Battle of Sacile. (Alison's *History of Europe*, vol. vii. The Austrians were defeated.)

On reaching the spot where the action was at its height, we were received with a sharp cannonade that caused us sensible loss, while our division was forming line to the right at full trot. This movement was

Cuirassier with an Austrian banner

executed by the orders of General d'Avenay, for General Sahuc had gone off at a gallop with all his staff to place himself out of the line of fire of the two batteries, one in front of us and the other a little to our left, that were firing uninterruptedly on us and the united battalion of *voltigeurs*, now formed in square, having just repulsed a charge of cavalry. General d'Avenay saw at once that the two batteries of artillery were so little supported, as to give us a chance of taking them before the arrival of reinforcements that were being brought back with all speed by the archduke commanding the Austrian Army, and could now be seen opening out upon the plain.

He hastened to General Sahuc, and asked his permission to charge the batteries at once, as in any case it could not occasion heavier loss than we experienced while doing nothing. General Sahuc refused on the pretext, first that his order only desired him to support the five battalions of *voltigeurs*, secondly because he was of opinion that there was an obstacle between us and those batteries that would stop his cavalry and expose it to a fire of grape at short range. General d'Avenay in vain told him that he knew the ground from having been over it in 1806, that I knew it as well as he did, and that we were certain no such obstacle existed; he would not give up.

General d'Avenay irritated by this obstinacy, and greatly shocked at the ravages that the balls were making in his ranks, was determined to make sure again that there was no obstacle to approaching the batteries in question; and so, we rode towards them followed only by two orderlies. We had a near view of the square of *voltigeurs* surrounded with dead, and with their wounded in the centre; and what wounded! General Desaix, commanding, came out to come and speak to us, and was very nearly carried off by a shot that passed an inch from his shoulder. They literally hailed upon the spot where we were; some could be seen to ricochet, the wind of others could be felt, and there was a continuous hissing that caused very grave reflections.

At last we ascertained that there was no obstacle on the ground to stop a charge of cavalry, and were just fancying ourselves masters of the batteries that had caused us such cruel loss from the commencement of their fire. There was one which was destined to strike me much more directly!

Just as we were turning to go back to our men, a sound that still rings in my ear, together with the whistle of a shot, informed me that either the general or his horse was hit; a hasty movement of the latter gave me hopes for a moment, that he was the only sufferer. To my anxious question the general replied as he let himself fall forward on his horse's neck "My thigh is carried away." I still hoped it was not the case. Seeing him totter, I took him by the arm and tried to keep him in the saddle; but our horses were at a gallop, he could not guide his own, and in a few moments, I could not prevent his falling to the ground. I was on the ground the same moment, and the two orderlies who had followed us to the extreme point of our reconnaissance, with a sergeant of *voltigeurs* came up at my signs and shouts.

We made the general sit upon the sergeant's *fusée*. I supported him behind in my arms, the chasseurs raised him up upon the two ends of the *fusée*, the sergeant supported his leg, which only remained attached by the flesh on each side. The ball had shattered the knee, striking it from below, and had made a diagonal furrow on the horse's neck. We walked for a considerable time, but very slowly, and always under fire; the balls struck the stony ground through which the Piave runs in this place, and the pebbles flew around us. The horse of one of the *chasseurs* who was carrying an end of the *fusée* that supported the general was hit by a shot. The fall of the horse very nearly caused that of the man, as his arm was through the reins.

This accident stopped us, and the general desired to be placed on the other orderly's horse. I had let my own go, and he had run away without my troubling myself about him, as may be well supposed. With great difficulty we put the general on the horse; I walked by his side holding up the poor wounded leg, while he begged me to cut it quite off with my knife.

We were making our way directly for the Piave, but the general desired me to lead him up to General Sahuc, who was standing with his staff out of the full direction of the shot, though this did not prevent a captain of the staff being killed on that very spot. General Sahuc seemed very much affected on receiving our mournful visit. He raised his hands and eyes to Heaven, and wanted to say some words of comfort to General d'Avenay, but could not speak; while the latter, with a voice as firm as if nothing had happened, gave an account of his observations, and advised him not to delay the capture of the guns, assuring him that a single regiment if supported could effect it.

After this, we resumed our way to the river to try and get across it—a very difficult matter. On reaching the bank, I met a *cantineer* who lent me a blanket; we laid the general on it, as he was losing a great quantity of blood which I could not stop by making ligatures of our handkerchiefs. I was all covered with this blood flowing over me as I walked, supporting the leg.

There was neither bridge nor boat to carry the army across, and the passage was accomplished by means of ropes stretched from one bank of the river to the other. The soldiers stripped naked, put their clothes on their necks and heads, as well as their muskets and pouches, and they entered the water holding on to these ropes which were placed parallel to each other, a few yards apart; and in places where the water was deep the rapid stream caused the lower part of the body to float downstream, and kept the heads of those at the greatest distance from the bank above water, when otherwise their weight would have bent the cord. However, notwithstanding all the precautions that were taken, men were swept away and several drowned, in spite of the efforts of a hundred good swimmers posted on the two banks to save them.

I was in difficulties how to get the general across this river a hundred yards wide, when I discovered a little boat at some distance; it was brought up to the spot where I had laid the General, and I found him sound asleep. I thought him unconscious, as was quite likely from the quantity of blood he had lost and continued to lose. He awoke during the crossing, and it caused him considerable suffering; the smallest wrong movement made the dreadful leg swing aside. At last we reached the other side, where an ambulance was established in an abandoned inn.

An amputation was immediately performed, lasting five minutes, and I supported the general in my arms all the time. Several artillerymen, employed as hospital orderlies, were faint at the sight of the operation. I did not give way a moment, though I experienced acute pain at the dreadful sight, and especially from my attachment to the sufferer. Only a few tears fell from my eyes, and the general seeing them, said, "Come, my friend, take heart." These words spoken with a tone of most tender affection provoked an outburst of grief which I could not resist.

When all was over, the surgeon told me that the transport for the wounded had not come; that there was nothing for the use of the ambulance but mattresses and stretchers. The Viceroy of Italy, Eugène de Beauharnais, was a short distance away on the embankment, surrounded by his staff, watching the progress of the action and directing the passage. General Macdonald, not yet a marshal, was in the water on horseback and with his sword drawn. I do not know very well why. The men of all the regiments, officers and soldiers all entirely naked and crowded together, awaited their turn to cross.

I addressed myself directly to the viceroy, and he gave orders to place twenty-five grenadiers at my disposal, to carry the General to Treviso. They were furnished by the 62nd regiment; and I have still in my mind the displeased and sulky looks of the grenadiers at having to dress and lay down their muskets and packs; they followed me in silence. On reaching the ambulance, four of them placed the stretcher with the general on it upon their shoulders, and the melancholy train began its march. The general's servant had found his way to us; the orderlies had managed to catch our horses, and even my sword which I had thrown down in my haste to support the general, was brought back to me.

We had three long leagues to go at mid-day in great heat. The grenadiers relieved one another by turns, marching quietly with the greatest carefulness when carrying their load, making no complaints of the weight, or of the heat of the sun, or of the dust that blinded them. They performed their duty conscientiously; but from their silence and the dejection of their looks, it was easy to see that they regretted the danger from which they were removed.

A league from Treviso I went in advance to secure quarters, and had a quarrel with the *commandant* of the place, an Italian officer, as he showed the greatest ill-will. He wished to have the general taken to the hospital. I treated him so roughly and threatened him so much, that at last he gave me an order for quarters. I ran to the mayor's office, and they gave me a billet that I had not time to visit; I only sent word that a bed must be got ready, and then went to the hospital to request the chief doctor and surgeon to come and see the general as soon as they could, and then I went to meet him and found him just at the entrance of the town. The quarters he was taken to were very gloomy; there was no one but the doorkeeper in the house, there was a fairly comfortable bed for my poor general, and he said in my ear as we were laying him in it, "We must be generous to these good grenadiers who have carried me so carefully."

Though so full of grief, I was deeply affected by the fact I am going to relate; it is so honourable to our soldiers, that I should like to give it publicity, and add it to others of the same kind that are noted in history, and have raised the French soldier to so high a rank.

I followed the grenadiers into the room outside the general's, and giving coins to the amount of sixteen pounds to the man who was pointed out to me as the senior, told him that the general had desired me to thank them, and offer them this little mark of his gratitude to share among them. Their voices were raised unanimously in refusal, and it was not without a long contest, having persuaded them that the general would be pained and wounded by their refusal; having called them my comrades and friends and shaken their hands that I managed to overcome their resistance, and they took it, leaving me with the feeling that it was condescension on their part.

Then I told them that they must be in great want of a dinner, and that I had ordered one for them at an inn opposite. They thanked me very much and went away. A few minutes afterwards I saw them altogether in conversation in the court. I went down to know what they were waiting for, and I learnt that they had considered that honour would not allow them to sit down at table while their comrades were fighting, and that consequently they could not take advantage of the meal I had offered. I could not shake their determination, and with much difficulty persuaded them to take some loaves and bottles of wine that I sent for in haste. They started at once. It was five in the evening, and probably they had not eaten since the night before, as I was fasting myself.

I have lived too long with our soldiers not to know their faults, which are great, but they have also, to a very great extent, honourable feelings in them, simple and sublime.

The days succeeding this mournful one gave us the best hope; suppuration was established without the least inclination to fever; sleep was quiet, there was very little pain, and the dressings were changed without increasing suffering. All went well for a fortnight. Unhappily, stormy weather had a most fatal influence upon the general's nervous system, and at the end of that time a fearful storm broke; every clap of thunder caused a convulsive movement of the patient; his features were drawn up as the detonations continued every moment.

That evening the doctor found there was fever, and the result of his consultation with the surgeon gave me the greatest anxiety. It was a disturbed night, and in the morning some incoherent words made me apprehensive of delirium, and in reality it was not long before it appeared with alarming symptoms. Four days passed without a ray of improvement for our comfort. I had written to Villaunay, and he arrived two days before his brother's death on the 29th of May, 1809.

This glorious but melancholy end of a friend who had given me so many proofs of attachment, and whose interest was displayed in the smallest matters, left me some deep-seated memories that time has left unchanged. The circumstances of this mournful event often recur to my mind, and make me feel the heavy loss that was inflicted upon me, and also, I am convinced, upon the army and the country. General d'Avenay had all the qualities requisite for a great command. He seized at once upon the duties required by the position in which he might be placed, and mastered all the details with readiness and indefatigable activity.

These qualities were peculiarly exhibited during our stay at Zamora. With six thousand men in a most hostile country, he had kept two actual armies in check; and for four months that we remained there within their reach, they dared not make an attempt against this little isolated corps, that had no supports but the troops at Valladolid, at a distance of thirty leagues.

On reaching the army of Italy the position of General d'Avenay, speaking literally, seemed to be inferior; but it was quite evident that he was only brought there to make occasion for his being appointed General of Division; as, in fact, there were no general officers of cavalry of that rank with the army, but perfectly incapable men; and that the first words of the viceroy said to him on his arrival, "Ah, General, I was impatiently expecting you;" as much as to tell him of the influence he would have in the cavalry operations that were to take place.

The days following his death were employed in paying our last duties to him, and putting his papers in order; among them we found one packet with this inscription: "To be opened after my death by M. Aymar de Gonneville, my *aide-de-camp.*" I gave this packet to Adrien de Villaunay, considering that if the general had been able to foresee the presence of his brother at his last moments, he would have addressed it to him. The envelope contained a will, by which the general bequeathed to me the enjoyment of a property in Westphalia which the Emperor had given him as a pension with the title of Baron that he had received after the Prussian campaign of 1807.

In default of this property, and supposing that the bequest should not be carried into execution, he gave me a sum of sixteen hundred pounds from his savings, and any horse I might select from his stable, with its equipment. There were in the will several legacies to his sister, to his young cousins de Caux, and his servants, and I was appointed executor. All these directions were carried out, except that of the sixteen hundred pounds to me; because the general's father, with the intention of contesting my right to this sum, had insisted that M. de Caux, who had charge of it, should place it in the hands of a banker to await the decision of the court. It was given in my favour; but whilst the lawsuit was going on, the banker became insolvent, and the sixteen hundred pounds were lost.

The general's brother and I placed an inscription to mark the spot where his remains were laid, and then we went to Placentia, and I wrote to Saint-Victor to come to us there with the baggage. I sent all the general's property back to France, and I sold his horses, except the one that I was to select, and two that were left to his sister with his carriage. When all was finished we started to join the army, and went as far as Udine, where we were obliged to stop, because the line of operation not being quite established, Carinthia, Styria, and Carniola were in a state of insurrection. A corps was being formed at Udine able to open communications and to impose on the mountaineers of those countries, men of warlike nature and more intolerant of the strangers' yoke than others.

While we waited, General Caffarelli, *aide-de-camp* to the Emperor and War Minister of the Kingdom of Italy, arrived there invested with the powers of the Viceroy to take the command. I had known him a long time; he was intimate with General d'Avenay and had married in Normandy Mademoiselle d'Hecquevilly, niece of the Marquis de Balleroy, an intimate friend of ours. I had known Madame Caffarelli before her marriage; and her husband, coming alone, took Saint-Victor and me to act as *aides-de-camp* to him.

This service lasted six weeks; the duties we performed were most interesting, as they initiated us into the general affairs of the Kingdom of Italy, and especially its military resources. General Caffarelli was very kind to us and showed confidence in us; he had valued and loved General d'Avenay, and understood our regret, especially mine. While we were at Udine, the Battles of Raab, Essling and Wagram took place, and the successive reports were received by the Italians with transports of joy. As for us, while we very sincerely shared in the rejoicing, we were ashamed of the repose we enjoyed while such grand and memorable events were in progress.

At last the communications with the Grand Army were open. The column organised at Udine was put in motion, and Saint Victor, Adrien de Villaunay and I put our servants and horses under the care of an officer of this column, and started for Vienna in a post carriage, having to cross sixty leagues of country where we should not find a Frenchman, and only a day or two before the population had been up against us. I must say in praise of the inhabitants of these mountains, that we had not a single hostile act on their part to encounter, not even a painful word, and we reached Vienna without the slightest hindrance. There was an armistice and treaty for peace; but for all that, armaments were pushed with an activity that caused suspicion that the last words of war had not been spoken.

The Emperor was at Schönbrunn. We had to go there, as there was a standing order to the effect that any officers of the staff who might be without employment by the death of the generals they had been attached to, should proceed to head-quarters for fresh appointment. Saint-Victor and I made promises that we would not part, and that we would request to return to a cavalry regiment, not wishing to serve as *aides-de-camp* any more, especially with a general we did not know. We had, in consequence, to take some precautionary measures. Besides, an audience of the Emperor had to be obtained for Adrien de Villaunay, as the only person who could relieve him from the judicial condemnation that he would certainly have undergone.

I knew General Savary, the Emperor's *aide-de-camp*; we went to see him; he received us very well, promised to present us himself, telling us to be in readiness for the moment he might think most favourable. We spent our time in visiting the curiosities that Vienna contains, and went to Schönbrunn at the time of the parade, when the Emperor always was present. Nothing can give an idea of these parades; they really were reviews, for, besides the troops on duty, all the detachments arriving from France and Italy appeared there, and the regiments in cantonments round Schönbrunn, among them those of the Guard, and that at only two leagues from the battlefields of Essling and Wagram.

The most fortunate chance caused me to meet with Colonel d'Haugeranville who had succeeded General d'Avenay in command of the 6th Cuirassiers. He offered me the place of captain in my old regiment, and of lieutenant for Saint-Victor, knowing that we did not wish to be parted; but a special permission from the Emperor was required on account of the standing order about *aides-de-camp* to deceased generals. I spoke to General Savary and he made an appointment with us for the next day but one, the grand parade day, and promised to present us to the Emperor after it.

I watched this parade from the top of the flight of steps at Schönbrunn. The Emperor at the foot of these steps, surrounded by marshals and general officers of every rank and nation; the Austrians were present in great number, with an appearance of the greatest respect for the Emperor's person, and showing their admiration for the splendid troops then present.

There was a Portuguese division that was not trusted, and not without cause, as Portugal was attacked by us while they were in our ranks. Just as this division was marching past, the Emperor without apparent purpose, as if he was a little absent in mind, took a few steps forwards right into the centre of the column, four files of the first section were broken off to avoid the Emperor, and so in succession with all, quite to the end of the division of four regiments. No doubt this was a calculated move. Was it that the Emperor wished to give a mark of confidence in the Portuguese, or an exhibition before the strangers, especially the Austrians, of the fascination that he exercised over the soldier of any nation whatsoever? I cannot tell at all, but certainly this took place designedly.

There were forty thousand men at this parade, in better form and better drilled than I had ever seen. The Emperor was radiant. The fact is that without such resources as he could dispose of, without immense activity seconded by abilities of the first rank, and by the obedience he had made habitual to all that depended upon him, it would have been impossible, within a month or two of the Battles of Essling and Wagram, to produce such perfect and beautiful regiments as appeared at this review, and with the exception of the Guard, were not superior to the rest of the army.

After the march past, the Emperor went back to the palace and entered the gallery opening on the stairs. We followed the numerous and brilliant group that accompanied him; the time for the presentation had come and my heart beat quick. When once the Emperor had gone into his rooms, he would not entertain general matters, and only received those with whom he wished to converse. He was walking quickly to the door of separation from us. I anxiously questioned General Savary with a look, and he gave me a sign with his hand to address the Emperor, not choosing or not venturing to press the favour he had promised us any further.

There was no flinching. Not only was it necessary for Saint-Victor and myself to obtain permission to re-enter the line, but what was of much more consequence, for Adrian de Villaunay to beg, in consideration of his brother's death, for a promise of amnesty from the consequences of the conviction he could not escape, and if the opportunity was missed on that day, it was adjourned indefinitely. So, I resolutely advanced upon the man who overawed everyone so much, even the marshals and his familiar friends. He stopped and heard me with an air of great kindness, and then turning to the Prince of Neufchâtel, the major-general of the army told him,

You will appoint the *aides-de-camp* of General d'Avenay as they have requested.

He continued his walk. I made despairing signs to Villaunay, for he did not come forward, Saint-Victor took him by the arm and brought him to me just as the Emperor was entering his rooms, followed by three or four persons, and the door was closing. Before it was quite shut we pushed him in by the shoulders, without having time to reflect on the position he was placed in. Thus, he found himself in the presence of the man who was to pronounce judgment upon him in a question as it were of life and death, for he might be convicted of felony. In a few minutes he came out with a joyful face. The Emperor had been surprised and annoyed at his presence in the room, and at first asked him in a severe tone what he wanted, but as soon as he heard the petition, and knew that Adrian de Villaunay was General d'Avenay's brother, he told him,

Return to your home. I cannot stop the course of justice; but I have the right of granting pardon, and in your case, I will not forget it.

A few days later Villaunay left us and returned to Normandy, and obtained his pardon through a general amnesty granted at the time of the marriage of the Emperor to the Archduchess Marie Louise of Austria. He has been dead a long time as well as his wife and son; his daughter married M. de Caumont, well known for his archaeological labours. (And an eminent architect.—Note by Trans.)

A few weeks afterwards we received our appointment; and we spent the time we were waiting in getting our fresh outfit, but it cost three times as much as it would have in Paris. I was particularly well off in horses, having four; my Ukraine horse; the mare that was given me by the 18th Dragoons, an unbroken mare that I had taken in exchange when I was appointed aide-decamp, and lastly the mare that was left me by General d'Avenay. She is worthy of a special description that I could dwell upon with pleasure, but I will only say that she was the best charger I ever saw, and had not a single fault.

When our commissions arrived, we joined the 6th Cuirassiers six leagues from Vienna on the road to Snaim; every person in it had been changed since I was among them. The old captains and the greatest part of the officers had been killed, or invalided, in consequence of wounds. The sub-officers, I knew before, had come in for a good deal of promotion, and I made the acquaintance of officers from the military school, and transferred from other regiments.

Saint-Victor and I were excellently received, and a month had hardly passed since I joined, when Colonel d'Haugeranville told me that the first captain he should recommend for promotion to be major was myself, and that after M. Kauffer, the lieutenant of my troop and the senior in the regiment, Saint-Victor would be the next he should recommend for captain.

The cantonments of the regiment occupied a considerable extent, I had three villages for my company. We were authorised to make requisitions for cloth, leather, and everything necessary to replace the expenditure and losses of war. Without making any abuse of this power, I had the good luck to find a good-will in my three villages, that enabled me to make all the repairs; and I took great interest in watching my artisans at work, and the advance in my men's appearance.

Great pains was also taken with their drill; a great many draughts had been had been sent up from the depot; horses had been purchased in the province we occupied; and the Vienna dealers had furnished others coming from the Danubian provinces and Transylvania. In a very short time we were completely mounted and equipped, and in force. We usually mustered six squadrons on parade. I always was very fond of drill, and as peace was signed, some employment was necessary.

We occupied our cantonments for two months; then we crossed to the right bank of the Danube and made our way slowly towards Salzburg. On our way we had passed some days on the shores of the Gemunden Lake, from which the Traun flows, and had an opportunity of seeing one of the remarkable spots of the Alps where their peaks command, and even overhang, a beautiful expanse of water of enormous depth, and so clear that the bottom can be distinctly seen twenty yards deep. The trout of this lake and of the Traun are famous.

Winter time had come, Kauffer and I were quartered in the abbey of Eiglewerth near Salzburg; this mountain convent is situated on a peninsula in a pretty little lake surrounded on three sides by lofty hills covered with pine trees. There were only the abbot and five monks in it. The abbot was a man of thirty-five, his face, general appearance and manners were very refined. His lodgings were very good, and had only one communication with the abbey; in the lodgings there was established with him a person who was called his cousin, and seemed to be about twenty-six or twenty-eight years old. The abbot informed me that every day a table for six would be laid for me, for both breakfast and dinner. I did not hesitate to accept it, and make the other officers quartered around me partakers of the advantage, as they were generally in peasants' houses,

The lake was frozen and Kauffer and I used to amuse ourselves by taking a sledge up to the top of a bare hill close to it, and sliding down on it with a speed greater than is now obtained on the modern railroads. The sledge was very bright, and whichever of us was in front easily guided it by digging in his heels, while the one in rear held a long pole dragging behind with the effect of a rudder.

One day that the colonel and some officers of the staff had come to ask me for a breakfast, he wanted to make trial of the exercise, and we showed him how; but unfortunately, he had a a notion of trying it on a larger scale, that is to say, by dragging a heavy sledge to the hill-top and then all of us getting on it and coming down together. We pointed out to him that it would be very difficult to guide such a machine with a load of eight persons, and that it was very essential to maintain a proper direction, for there were some trunks of pine trees at the bottom of the slope, rising three or four feet above the snow, and it was necessary to pass between them to escape breakage against them; but he would hear nothing, himself assumed the direction of the sledge, and posted himself in front.

I bestrode a pine plank that projected some feet to the rear, and armed with my pole prepared to do the best in my power to hold our conveyance in the right road, where alone it was safe. I do not know if I should have succeeded; but a short distance from the starting point the plank broke, and I rolled over in the snow behind the sledge, and was much frightened to see it take a slanting course towards one of the formidable trees. If it had struck full against the obstacle, it is most likely that all the passengers would have been killed or seriously injured.

But it was not quite so bad as that; the sledge just grazed it, but enough to break one officer's leg, and give the colonel a contusion of the knee that made him keep his bed three months, and lamed him for life. The surgeon-major was of our party; he set the broken leg, and the two injured men were sent back to their quarters on stretchers.

There was an adventure of another kind in our regiment. A trumpeter in my troop had formed an intimate connection with the daughter of a gentleman in the neighbourhood of Vienna. A few days after our departure, I was informed that the young lady was following my trumpeter and joined him every evening in his quarters. I caused a watch to be set; she was brought to me, and after enumerating all the wretchedness her conduct might bring upon her, I urged on her to return to her father, and threatened that I would arrest her and deliver her over to the Austrian authorities if she continued to follow us. I told her besides, that the trumpeter should be severely punished if he continued to see her after the orders that would be given him. The young lady was thirty, and was not pretty.

Some days passed without any more news about the business, and I thought it was all over, when information came to me that it was not the case, and that the young lady continued with her lover, but very secretly. So, I had him put under arrest, and confined in a dungeon of the abbey, situated in one of the towers commanding the entrance to the court. The dungeon window was closed with iron bars, and was five or six feet from the ditch, now completely frozen over. The second night that he was there the bars were sawn through, and the trumpeter made his escape; most likely with the young lady's assistance, and was never heard of again. He was a splendid man, of bad character, but very brave, an excellent horseman, and a model in appearance.

I left Eiglewerth to enjoy a six months' leave. I visited my family and awaited the return of my regiment to France, as it, with the other forces that composed the grand army were evacuating the Austrian dominions in consequence of the peace, having the marriage of the Emperor Napoleon with the Archduchess Marie Louise for one of its conditions.

As these recollections are of my military life alone, I shall make no mention of events that did not affect my career in the service, though of personal influence on me, and so shall pass over in silence one of the most important events of my life which took place in Normandy while I was on leave. (Monsieur de Gonneville alludes to his marriage to his cousin, Mademoiselle le Pailleur de Langle.)

In the month of August, 1810, my regiment appeared at a grand review, that took place at Paris sometime after the Emperor's marriage. Thirty-two squadrons of *cuirassiers* marched past amid the admiring shouts of a vast multitude. A grander spectacle had never been presented to the eyes of the Parisians. The troops were in splendid condition; a crowd of kings and princes had come from all parts of Europe and formed the Emperor's suite, with the addition of his marshals and all his brilliant staff. Every person present at this review preserves a remembrance of it, as the most astonishing sight that could be imagined. I was there, having been summoned by the colonel to attend on the occasion, although I was not obliged, being on leave.

I returned to Normandy after being absent a fortnight, and took my horses there, as if warned by a presentiment that I was leaving my regiment for good and all. The peace had been made under circumstances that ought to have rendered it permanent on the side of Germany. The Emperor's marriage with the Archduchess of Austria, the terror inspired by his name, an army of almost a million of men, commanded by the most expert generals in Europe, and with the utmost confidence in the military abilities of their supreme head; all this seemed a warrant of security for us after our long and bitter struggles. Besides, the Emperor had himself made the announcement to us on the occasion of his personal inspection, and had told us besides that he expected that the idleness of garrison life, and the distractions it would present to us would not affect our warlike qualities in any way.

But Spain was there to call us to work; and the desperate resistance of its inhabitants continued with its most sanguinary events. The want of unison in the operations of the marshals commanding the various *corps d'armée* entailed frequent losses of men, stores, and horses. Pay and subsistence were far from being everywhere secure, and thence arose relaxation of discipline, exactions, and pillage; and, in consequence, the exasperation of the people was redoubled, and they took their revenge at every opportunity with abominable ferocity. And so, the accounts we received in France represented this war in Spain in the darkest colours, being exaggerated by distance from the scene of action.

A few days after my return to Normandy I learnt that the regiments of cavalry, now six squadrons strong, had been reduced to five, and in a fortnight, by a piece of the greatest injustice, I received orders immediately to join the 13th regiment of Cuirassiers, making part of the army in Spain, under the command of General Suchet. This force occupied Aragon and the Southern part of Catalonia. On the receipt of this order I went to Paris, and remonstrated with the War Minister, pointing out to him that I was not the junior captain of my regiment, and that so, in my case the general rule had not been followed, requiring the juniors of each rank to be the sufferers by any reduction in the number of officers of their rank.

An officer of Cuirassiers

My remonstrance was not attended to, and I had a rather angry scene with the minister about it. At the time I was appointed captain in the 6th Cuirassiers. In consequence of some neglect in the office of the Prince of Neufchâtel, this minister had not chosen to recognise my seniority in that rank, as dating from the time it had been conferred upon me by the Emperor at the review at Cassel, and I had only taken seniority from the date of my last appointment, making me last but one instead of senior captain of the regiment. The last was M. de Brias, of one of the first families in Belgium. His uncle, a senator, applied for him to remain in the regiment, a favour he would never have solicited himself, as he was a man of delicacy and right feeling.

OFFICERS OF CUIRASSIERS AND HUSSARS SHARE A CIGAR

CHAPTER 8

The Siege of Tortosa

I set out for Spain at the end of September, 1810. The grief of my family was distracting at the moment of a parting that they expected would be the last; and I must own that though I pretended to put a good face on it, I was sure enough that there was a considerable probability that these adieux would really be the last.

I took three horses that I could depend on, and my servant Goldfrid, a Silesian, who had been given to General d'Avenay by the Count Hochberg. He had followed us in Spain, Italy and Austria; I had brought him to France to procure payment of a legacy of sixty pounds that had been left him by the general among his other servants, and he begged to go with me again into Spain. He was a strong and clever lad. I made my journey in short stages, alone, and with sorrowful thoughts. Every step that I took seemed to be adding enormously to the distance that already separated me from Normandy. It would be impossible to describe all my miserable feelings during this long journey.

There was another thing, besides, that increased my regret at leaving my delightful 6th Cuirassiers—I had a very bad opinion of the regiment I had to join. I knew that it had been raised from detachments of all the other regiments of the same branch, and I knew the spirit that animated the selection of these detachments well enough to know that they must have been composed of all the worst men and horses the colonels could find. Then, being used to mix only with troops perfect in condition, drill and knowledge, the idea of finding something very different, and besides, having officers with whom I had no sympathy for my comrades was hateful to me.

No just notion of the charm of companionship can be formed by anyone who has not known what it is when springing from fellowship in the dangers, fatigues and privations that are inseparable from any serious war. The character of that now raging in Spain was such as to make the mutual support that is meant by what is termed *esprit de corps* the more necessary, and my conjectures led me to suppose that this feeling was not to be found in my new regiment. I remembered the condition of the 6th Cuirassiers before Colonel d'Avenay took the command, and it seemed to me a very natural supposition that if it had been difficult to compass the fusion of the two parties that made up that corps, there would be many more obstacles to encounter in the formation of the 13th Cuirassiers, composed as it was of detachments from the fourteen regiments of heavy cavalry then in existence; however, submission was a necessity, and I went.

At Tours I found a marching battalion of the 45th regiment of foot on its way to Spain to join the regiment. The battalions that went from the depots to be broken up on arrival, and their men distributed to the companies in proportion to their proper strength, were called marching battalions. As I was proceeding in the same direction, and stopped at the same places, I soon made the acquaintance of the officers of this battalion; a captain was in command, a pleasant companion, and his conversation was a great pleasure to me. He had my billets prepared by his adjutant-major who preceded us, and I joined the officers at their meals; this arrangement, by temporarily breaking my solitude, caused some diversion from my mournful thoughts, and made the way seem shorter to me.

At Bordeaux I found d'Infreville, one of the companions of my youth; he had wasted his whole fortune, and was now awaiting a fair wind to embark for the East Indies, his passage being paid by his family. He died a millionaire.

Ten days after leaving Bordeaux I entered Spain, still with my infantry battalion, deriving the more benefit from their company because it was impossible to travel alone, even a mile from the frontier. I crossed the bridge of the Bidassoa which I had passed eighteen months before in the opposite direction, with my heart full of pleasure and hope, in the midst of friends and attached to the fortunes of General d'Avenay, whose death had more clearly displayed the affection he bore me.

The recollection of that time, as contrasted with the present, made me feel the loss of my dear general and the absence of any friends, with great severity, and cast a mournful shade over the future that I was going alone to meet in this Spain—the scene of a savage warfare, respecting no rights, where every step that was taken brought some fresh atrocity to light. There anything that did not wear the colours of France, or of our allies, was an enemy to be distrusted. We met nothing but looks of hatred, and the most minute precautions for safety had come to be the common rule of life at every moment. At the present time, secure from any risk, I am still under the dominion of the habits of that time, they had taken such hold in consequence of the catastrophes that resulted from their neglect, as taught by continual proofs. (M. de Gonneville when he travelled, and even when he went for a long ride preserved the habit of going armed.)

We went near a barn posted on the highest point of the hills between Iran and Ernani. This barn was held by forty *gendarmes* as a post of communication, and it had been attacked two months before by Mina's band, three thousand men strong. It was only loopholed, and had not even what is called a traverse to protect the door. The defence was such that the Spaniards lost more than two hundred men during the two days their attack lasted, and were forced to retire before the assistance that was sent to the brave *gendarmes* from Irun and Ernani. The whole roof had been burnt; but the fire began at one end, and that fell in before the other end was on fire.

So, the defenders of the barn passed over the burning wood and ashes with their ammunition, so as not to be crushed by the fall of the rest of the roof. The enemy thinking that they must be all burnt, fancied there was nothing more to do but to go into the barn and take possession of the remains, but paid dearly for their belief. Not one of the *gendarmes* had been killed, and there issued from the ruins a fire that caused greater losses than had been incurred before.

Having spent a short time on the scene of this heroic defence we resumed our journey, and next day we reached Tolosa. I there separated from the battalion that I had travelled with for several weeks. I was sorry to part with them for more reasons than one; I had received numerous indications of good will from the officers, especially from the captain in command, and besides being quite alone was a great hindrance to continuing the journey. I had to proceed by Pampeluna and Saragossa to Tortosa, then besieged by the army of General Suchet; but being unable to march alone, I had to face a multitude of difficulties, inconveniences and dangers.

I went to the major commanding the town of Tolosa to ask him to give me the means of proceeding to Pampeluna. I found a man with a mean face, and completely drunk. He had a woman with him of the most suspicious aspect, though far removed from youth, and it might be seen at a glance that she was a worthy associate of her companion in point of intemperance. At seeing two such repulsive beings I felt a rising of anger that I repressed at first, but I broke out when the major, having cast a vague glance on my marching orders, looked me over with a most insolent air, and said that as he could not foresee when he should be able to send a detachment in the direction, I was to start alone the next day. I knew that the way was unsafe for detachments of less than two hundred men, and that three hundred were always sent with the courier carrying despatches.

For fifteen leagues the road skirts a buttress of the Pyrenees, covered with woods, and at that time serving for a refuge for the band of Mina, a celebrated guerilla of that period, who had five or six thousand devoted men under his orders, and intercepted the communications of our army with France by all means in his power. Every day was marked by his expeditions to one point or another. So, the chances were a hundred thousand to one that if I started alone I should not reach my destination, and that I should never be heard of again; for Mina had no single stronghold that could serve him as a depot, so he made no prisoners, and any Frenchmen who fell into his hands were pitilessly shot.

But the *commandant* of Tolosa had some time since come to a resolution, accompanied by a tariff condemning every district where a Frenchman was killed or disappeared, to pay him a sum proportionate to the rank of the victim, and he found that the escorts deprived him of his profits. So, we had a violent dispute, in which he bore a very lame part, especially when I told him that I should immediately go and inform the General commanding at Vittoria of the order to start alone that he was giving me, and his refusal to continue my order for lodging and forage for my horses. It ended in everything being granted to me, and I waited.

Two days afterwards the courier from France arrived, the despatches for Pampeluna were forwarded; I joined the escort and we reached without difficulty Lecombery, a point between Tolosa and Pampeluna. Lecombery was guarded by a battalion shut up in a great fortified house. Strictly speaking I ought to have continued my journey to Pampeluna the same day, being a distance of seven leagues, but I had already come ten at the pace of the infantry, and wished to spare my horses. So, I determined to stop there till the next day, when I should take advantage of the departure of some companies of the garrison, that were to be relieved by others coming from Pampeluna.

I was billeted at the priest's house, and this was separated from that held by the troops by a little open space of about two hundred paces wide. It was scarcely an hour after my arrival and the courier's departure, escorted by half of the garrison under the major's orders, when information was given of the presence of the enemy round the village, and they began to make their way into it by the side opposite to the fortified house.

I was at this moment with the officers, having been invited to dinner by them, and had only time to run to my horses, finding them by good luck ready saddled; my servant was feeding them. I instantly untied one, telling the servant to follow me, and we hurried to our refuge and reached it so exactly in the nick of time, that if the stable had not had an entrance directly from the road, I should certainly have fallen into the hands of Mina, for the priest told me that his men entered the yard as I was leaving the house.

My horses were placed in a ground-floor room where a stall had been fitted for the major's horse, and so I found myself in safety. I ran a much more considerable risk than danger to my person only, as I might have lost my horses, baggage, and servant, and found myself alone in Spain without any equipment but what I had on my body. The day was spent on the alert; some shots without result were fired on our side, and towards night the Spaniards retired. They were about fifteen hundred in number; but, meanwhile, Mina in person had attacked the courier and his escort in a wood two leagues from Lecombery on the road to Pampeluna. The escort suffered severe loss, and all the horses in the column were killed except the major's.

It was a great chance that I was not there, and if I had been, it is most likely that my horses would have perished, being remarkable for their size and beauty. In the course of my military life, I have many times had cause to be thankful to Providence for protection granted to me, and this circumstance is an example, when I escaped two dangers on the same day; for it would have been more natural to have continued my journey with the courier, and on the other hand, by stopping at Lecombery the demonstration the enemy made on this village would have been fatal to me if the information had reached me two minutes later, and if my billet had been anywhere but at the priest's house I must infallibly have perished.

Two days later the major and the men he brought back from Pampeluna came in, and I set out for that town with two or three companies, and we arrived there without misadventure of any kind. There I obtained the first information about the regiment I was going to join. It was such a concert of praises, and marvellous accounts of its exploits, and the terror it caused the enemy, that I felt myself grow taller as I listened to it all, and my thoughts took a different turn, except the sorrow that I felt at leaving Normandy, and the uneasiness that was felt there on my account. So, I became anxious to find myself at my post, and to show that I was worthy to belong to such a corps that was said by all accounts to be so select.

I spent four days at Pampeluna, waiting for the starting, of a train of ammunition that was to be despatched to Tortosa for the siege under General Suchet. The week before a similar train had been attacked a few leagues from Pampeluna, and had lost a great many men before the enemy was driven back. It was very important to the Spaniards to hold Tortosa, as it was their arsenal, and a centre of communication between the insurgents of Catalonia and of Aragon; and this was the reason of the efforts made to impede the despatch of the means of destruction destined for that place.

As an attack was expected on the train that I was to travel with, the escort was raised to fifteen hundred men and two guns. The lancers of Berg were the cavalry. We set off in beautiful weather. The lancers acted as scouts in concert with a company of Miquelets, Spaniards in our pay, and real robbers. When we reached some spot of dangerous repute, their functions as scouts became a dead letter, for they became excessively timid at the risk of falling into the hands of their countrymen, who would have handled them without mercy; but for the three days I marched with them, the lancers performed their duty as scouts with great intelligence and boldness on a country that is very suitable for ambuscades in its whole extent, although but thinly wooded.

We reached Tudela the third day, and the ammunition was stored there; we had not seen so much as an enemy's musket. The escort furnished by the garrison of Pampeluna stopped there. General Reille was in command at Tudela, and report said that his chief of the staff had a Spanish mistress who extracted confidential information from him on the movement of troops, the force and composition of detachments, and then sent it on to Mina. The attack on the preceding ammunition train was laid down to him, and several other misdeeds. I saw the woman one night at an evening party at the *commandant's*; she was playing high, as was also her lover, a man just upon fifty and looking very ill-conditioned. As for her, she might be capable of any wickedness judging by her face and manner.

From Tudela I went towards Saragossa without escort, as the right bank of the Ebro was not very dangerous. Though we had much difficulty in understanding one another, I was not sorry for the company of four Polish soldiers going the same way, to whom I had been of some service in Pampeluna, getting their rations and billets given them; for before I had helped them, they had been long in getting supplied, and sometimes had not succeeded at all. On their side, the poor men displayed their thankfulness by all the little services that they could pay me, they only left me at Mora, near Tortosa where their regiment was.

I took two days in going from Tudela to Saragossa, and was much interested in visiting that city, still half in ruins. All the circumstances of the attack and defence were explained to me on the spot, and this very much modified my views as to the heroism of the defenders, as they were twice as numerous as their assailants; and as they had to fight in the streets from house to house, they should have at last been superior to their adversaries, had they been equally courageous and enduring.

Notwithstanding this observation in the interests of truth, the defence of Saragossa, a town open on all sides, will none the less remain a most memorable fact in history, and it was performed at a time when the Spaniards must have been demoralised by the thought that, their efforts would be powerless against the immense forces that invaded their country by all the passes of the Pyrenees. The fort of Saragossa capitulated on the 2l8t February, 1809, and its commander, Castaños, was carried a prisoner to France and shut up at Vincennes, and was only released in consequence of the events that restored the Bourbons to the throne of France in 1814.

At Saragossa I obtained positive information about the regiment I was going to join. I have already said it was raised by detachments from the twelve regiments of the same arm that were in Germany when it was formed, and two regiments of carabineers; it had acquired an excellent *esprit de corps*, and fabulous stories were told of its exploits. For instance, while General Suchet was besieging that town, it had alone, before there was time to collect the necessary force, attacked and put to flight a force of fifteen thousand Spaniards, commanded by O'Donnel, which was advancing to the assistance of that place, while the besiegers numbered at most ten thousand men.

The march of O'Donnel was so secretly performed that he was only a league from Lerida before his approach was suspected. He was marching in column by divisions in the plain of Martorell, when the 13th Cuirassiers, whose cantonments lay in that direction, flung themselves upon the head of the column, while it endeavoured to deploy at sight of them, and suspecting that they were followed by other troops. The manoeuvre was attempted hastily, caused such confusion that a panic ensued and a general flight, the arms were flung away and the ground strewed with them.

Six hundred prisoners, chiefly officers, were taken; all the guns were captured, and when General Suchet arrived with what troops he could bring without endangering the siege operations, all was over. The loss of the 13th Cuirassiers was very trifling, unless we except that of young d'Houdetot, a pretty sub-lieutenant under twenty, just like a girl. While amusing himself with giving scope to his lightning sword among the flying crowd, he had the misfortune to come across an ill-humoured soldier, who gave him a bayonet wound of which he died next day.

From Saragossa I made my way towards Mora, a large village, and the headquarters of General Suchet, whom I had already seen in Silesia. He received me very well, invited me to dinner and praised my regiment very much to me. General Suchet afterwards became marshal, and his name occupies a brilliant and honourable place in the history of the wars of the Revolution and the Empire; he was then a few years over forty, and only two years before had married Mademoiselle Anthoine de Saint Joseph, a very pretty girl, and daughter of one of the richest merchants in Marseilles.

In the memoirs of Marshal Suchet that she gave me after his death, the account of the action at Martorell is not exactly the same as I have given; but that can be explained by the manner of its commencement, as it was really a surprise by the Spaniards, and that is what the persons who are surprised in war never allow.

There had been no information received of the enemy's march; the 13th Cuirassiers being in the first line on the side of his approach, only received information of his presence from their own vedettes just as two-thirds of the horses had gone to water. These horses were brought back at a gallop, were bridled in haste, without even waiting to put on the cloak-cases, but leaving them on the spot; and with only three squadrons they charged down on fifteen thousand men, regular troops and provided with sufficient artillery, and defeated them utterly.

The fact was known to the whole army, and they professed such admiration for the 13th Cuirassiers that I myself could select many instances. When General Suchet inaugurated his command with the Battle of Moria, this regiment turned the fate of the day in our favour, just as the Spaniards were thinking themselves conquerors and shouting victory, while the French Army was commencing a movement in retreat.

At Mora, I learnt from General Suchet's own lips that the day before a detachment of ten thousand men, stationed at Uldecona as a corps of observation to cover the operations of the siege of Tortosa on the Valentia side, had been attacked by eight thousand men of the army of Valentia; this attack had been repulsed, and the enemy had lost more than two thousand men besides all the guns he had brought. The 13th Cuirassiers were a part of the little force at Uldecona and contributed much to their success. Next day I was to join them, as Uldecona is only seven leagues from Mora, and if I had arrived forty-eight hours sooner I might have shared in this brilliant exploit before I had got off my horse; it would have been a fine beginning.

I started the next day, passing under the guns of Tolosa, and two hours afterwards met the column of prisoners made two days before. They were on their road to France, and were well-equipped and marching in good order. At last I arrived, and was excellently received by Colonel d'Aigremont, the very man who, when he was major, had taken my part at General Espagne's dinner when I had just been released from captivity in Prussia. He introduced me the next day, and I found myself at the head of the finest troop in the regiment, with a strength of a hundred and fifty men and a hundred and twenty horses.

I succeeded Captain Scarampi, brother of the man I had known at the blockhouse of Tordesillas. He had just been appointed major in the regiment, and was on detachment in Aragon. He was a very handsome man, rather slight for his height of six feet, but of good carriage and very martial appearance. He belonged to a noble family of Piedmont; his character was noble, generous, and chivalrous. He was a personification in the highest degree of the legendary figures of ancient champions, at the fairest period of their history. Besides, his temper was charming, and he was a devoted friend. Everyone loved and respected him. He soon returned to the regiment, and I became very intimate with him; his memory is very dear to me.

Two days after I reached Uldecona I was sent to make a reconnaissance towards Vinaros, with fifty *cuirassiers* and fifty hussars of the 4th Regiment. Vinaros is the place where the Duke de Vendôme died during the wars of the succession. He was buried in the church, where his tomb is still to be seen. The Spaniards had evacuated Vinaros, and the hussars pushed on to Benicarlos, four leagues further on the road to Valentia. I waited for them at Vinaros as we had reached it at four in the morning, in splendid moonlight, and on such a night as is only seen in this beautiful climate.

When I had seen to the security of my detachment, making them remain mounted till daylight, I went through the village which is of considerable size, and I came down to the quay just as an English pinnace was putting off to go to a frigate that was to be seen at anchor a short distance out. I was within pistol-shot of the pinnace, and the crew would most likely have given me a very severe salute if I had given them time to pick up their arms: but I prudently re-entered the street and got out of their sight, and went back to my *cuirassiers* in their position in front of the village in an olive grove. The hussars were away for seven or eight hours, meanwhile I obtained food for my men and horses. The hussars found no one at Benicarlos, and we returned at night to Uldecona.

The enemy left us there very quiet for more than a month, up to the 2nd January, 1811, when Tortosa was taken. I went over the siege works in detail, and was much interested, getting a complete idea of the means employed in the attack and defence of fortified places. Tortosa is one of the strongest fortresses in Spain. The breaching battery had been established on the counterscarp of a bastion that served as a counterfort towards the Ebro, and only just thick enough to carry the guns, the gun detachments and the necessary guard.

It seemed to me wonderful that they ever managed to get there. The breach was practicable and the Spaniards made a good defence up to the time when they thought their efforts became useless. At the moment they were capitulating, and General Suchet had mounted the breach to receive their submission, our soldiers on guard in the batteries and trenches, cried out, "Do not surrender, brave Spaniards! your chiefs are betraying you, the breach is not practicable!" The rogues wished, to take the place by storm, that they might pillage it.

A little while after the taking of Tortosa, my regiment received orders to go and hold the post of Daroca, a town in the lower part of Aragon, twenty-five leagues south of Saragossa. We left sixty horses under the command of Major Robichon, and this detachment formed part of the garrison that remained at Uldecona with the object of observing the army of Valentia. Nothing occurred during our march to Valentia, and we reached this town which derives an equal celebrity from the part it played during the occupation of Spain by the Moors, and also by the miracles that are said in story to have taken place there. The ruins of the ancient fortifications still exist, and are of vast extent, much beyond the present proportions of the city containing in 1810 no more than five or six thousand inhabitants. We were then on the advanced posts, having a few leagues in front of us the Count of Villa Campa, more of a partisan than a general, but a person who made it very necessary to keep a sharp look out before him.

We spent two months at Daroca and were as quiet all the time as at Uldecona, although resting a little in the air, for we were alone without infantry, and the troops we had to look to for support were ten leagues in rear. But the regiment had been almost always at the advanced posts, and knew the duty of keeping capital guard, and its formidable reputation also removed any inclination of the Spaniards to trouble its repose.

At Daroca we performed the *Death of Caesar* with some success. The theatre was large and was perfectly crammed. All the ladies of the town were most anxious to be present at this play. During its performance the guards were doubled, and if the enemy had presented himself, the actors, myself among them, must have mounted their horses in the costume of ancient Romans.

We left Daroca to move to the front on the road to Teruel and Albaracin, places occupied by Villa Campa. We were established at Santa Olalla, a large village in the midst of a fertile plain, but perfectly bare of trees. The regiment stayed there several months, and during this time I was detached on many occasions with a squadron on various expeditions, first with the 121st Regiment of Foot, and afterwards with the 44th. I held the post of Origuella in the mountains separating the south of Aragon from Old Castile, we had some alarms there but no serious attack. Afterwards Major Scarampi came to join me with fifty cuirassiers, and took the command of the detachment.

While we were at Santa Olalla, Major Robichon was left at Uldecona and performed a brilliant piece of service. The enemy's outposts held Vinaros, and every morning sent a reconnaissance to Uldecona. This reconnaissance consisted of a squadron, and used to stop a quarter of a league from Uldecona on the bank of the dry bed of a torrent. Major Robichon received orders to post himself in this bed of the torrent to wait for the reconnaissance, and charge the men as soon as they arrived, and pursue them with the object of making prisoners. He exactly performed this duty with fifty-seven horsemen; but having gone eagerly into the pursuit of the fugitives for a league and a half, he reached the borders of the olive wood bounding the plain on that side, and in the disorder, that necessarily ensues upon a pursuit of this kind, he found himself all at once in front of three fresh squadrons coming to meet him with the squadron that had been flying and had quickly rallied behind them.

The situation would have been desperate for men less used to war and less courageous than our *cuirassiers*; but they never gave a thought to a retreat which must have entailed disastrous consequences, and without counting their enemies, who were ten to one, they flung themselves, at their officer's call, upon the mass that was outflanking them on all sides, and after a conflict that lasted half an hour put it completely to flight, leaving forty killed or wounded on the ground, a hundred prisoners picked up after the action, and four hundred weapons of different kinds that were flung down by the fugitives. Major Robichon had only seventeen men disabled, and not one mortally wounded.

The general-in-chief published this action to the army in a special general order, and wrote to the colonel to compliment him on the heroic conduct of the detachment. One specimen may here be given to show the spirit that animated the soldiers of this excellent regiment. A cuirassier of the detachment just mentioned was riding a bad horse, and fell a quarter of a league behind in the pursuit of the reconnaissance. So, from this distance he beheld his comrades surrounded by the four squadrons coming out of the olive wood, and joined by the fugitive squadron, making the number of their opponents more than five hundred.

Certainly, this man could not have been accused of cowardice if he had gone to Uldecona to carry information of the disaster that seemed imminent, and to get support; but he never thought of any such thing. He kept on spurring the jade he was riding, came up at last, flung himself into the fight, and did his part to secure a success that was beyond all probability. He thought he had only done his duty, and seemed much surprised at the praises given to his conduct.

Major Robichon had covered himself with glory on another occasion, several months before my joining the regiment. He was in command of a detachment of forty *cuirassiers* forming, with eight companies of *voltigeurs*, the advanced guard of the division of General Abbé, in charge of the operations on the banks of the Cinca. This advanced guard had just crossed the river by a ford, and was separated from the main body of the division in consequence of a sudden rise of the water, as often takes place in the Cinca, as is noted by Caesar in his *Commentaries* as having caused him to meet with a check. The Spaniards soon saw that Abbé's advanced guard was in a critical position; the tocsin was sounded several leagues around, and more than twenty thousand armed peasants came up to attack this advanced guard, and they, losing confidence from the impossibility of obtaining assistance, entertained proposals for capitulation.

The infantry officers were called together by their commander and agreed to surrender. Robichon alone declared that he would never give up, and was warmly applauded by his *cuirassiers*. So, they had to swim back across the Cinca, and try to join the division, but the division had left the bank of the river opposite to go to a bridge a few leagues higher up, and its place had been taken by the peasants of that side, who had hastened up at the sound of the tocsin to take their share in the hunt.

Under the fire of the peasants they started swimming their horses, landed man by man in the midst of their enemies, flung themselves one by one upon anything that presumed to oppose them, and marched after the division, joining them at night; they lost fourteen men in this glorious retreat. Major Robichon and the two officers under his orders arrived safe and sound.

CHAPTER 9

The Siege of Tarragona

The siege of Tarragona being determined on, General Suchet made the necessary dispositions for securing success in this very difficult enterprise. Tarragona was then considered the strongest place in Spain after Gibraltar and Cadiz. Every addition that could be made by the art of defence to the strength of the position had been made the most of, and the garrison consisted of ten thousand chosen men; so, all the forces of the army of Aragon were directed towards Catalonia, except a small body of which I was a member, left in Lower Aragon to hold the country, to watch the army of Valentia and the different parties acting on various points.

This little corps was composed of the 44th Regiment of the Line, the 3rd Regiment of the Vistula, Poles, of a hundred and fifty *cuirassiers*, a hundred hussars of the 4th Regiment, and a battery of field artillery under the command of General Paris, an excellent man, rather weak in character, but who, nevertheless, during the whole duration of the siege of Tarragona manoeuvred with so much activity and skill that the enemy did not encroach so much as an inch upon our ground. While our little corps being entirely detached, had no support to look to in case of a check, and was in front of forces of twenty times its strength. This position lasted three months, and we hurried, now to this side now to that, to make head against the aggressive movements of the Spaniards.

I was under the immediate orders of Major Robichon, but in several expeditions the whole detachment of *cuirassiers* marched under mine. However, no occasion arose for me to distinguish myself, for whenever we thought we had a chance of meeting the enemy he retired; but during these temporary commands the *cuirassiers* saw that I knew how to throw myself energetically into everything that could contribute to their welfare, and maintain their rights when invaded, as took place, once occasioning an angry scene between the officers of the 44th Regiment and myself, in the presence of the whole regiment and of my detachment, while I got the best of it and the approbation of all.

One thing happened at this time that vexed me very much, and that I should not relate if my ratings were meant to be anything else than an exact picture of a soldier's life. On an expedition to Molina in Aragon, and in bivouac in front of this ruined and deserted town, I had a most severe attack of measles, with violent fever and all its consequences. I was carried into a house which had neither doors nor windows, and placed in a kind of alcove, such as is to be found in almost all the rooms in Spain, very nearly sheltering me from the draughts of air. The illness had declared itself early in the morning, after I had been generally unwell for two or three days.

By evening the eruption was perfect; I was as red as a crayfish and in a burning fever. As the town was perfectly deserted, I was reduced for my only drink to a little tea, which was given me by a major of the 4th Hussars. At one in the morning the drums beat the assembly, and the trumpets sounded to horse. A start became necessary; we were going back; the enemy had quitted the country we had come to in pursuit of him.

We started in one of those fresh nights that follow the hottest days in Spain; an hour after our departure the rash was completely thrown in, and I was in such pain that I could hardly keep on horseback. I had suffered from this illness twice before—a somewhat remarkable circumstance; and I knew perfectly how it ought to be treated, and was fully aware of the consequences of the rash being thrown in. About nine in the morning we reached a large village, and halted there for some hours. A means of transport was contrived for me, by hanging a mattress with cords in a cart, covered with a cloth, and when the march was resumed I found myself comparatively quite easy.

As my cart had make a circuit of two leagues to join the column at the halting place, it was arranged that twenty-five *cuirassiers* should be left as my escort; but after a while I perceived that there were a hundred with me, and was informed that all the men of my troop had requested to march with me, and permission had been given; the more readily because the column had to cross a country of such uneven nature that the advantage of cavalry, in case of action, might have been dubious. I was much affected by this proof of attachment of my men, and at the moment, I fancy I was thankful to the measles, for the rash began to come out again, thanks to the heat and the manner in which I was wrapped up.

When we reached Montreal, a large village on the Xiloca that I had known for some time, I found my lodging prepared in a comfortable house. I had a pleasant room and a good bed; I managed to get some elder flowers, and with my knowledge of the malady, I obtained full benefit from them; and in six weeks the cure was complete, and my health better than before. Happily nothing of importance happened to our detachment while I was inactive.

The battery of artillery with us was commanded by a captain of the name of Hurlaux, a man of the noblest and best disposition I ever met. I became very intimate with him; and, though this friendship was broken by our various movements and mutual silence, it was renewed in 1835, and lasted till his death in 1849.

Tarragona was carried by assault on the 28th of June, 1811, and became the scene of all the horrors that accompany such an event. Neither sex nor age protected the wretched inhabitants. The soldiers were exasperated by a resistance lasting three months that had cost us enormous losses; they respected nothing and massacred without pity, notwithstanding the efforts made by the officers to put a period to the butchery. The garrison had attempted a sortie on the side opposite to the breach; they were surrounded, summoned to lay down their arms, and having surrendered they alone had their lives saved.

The garrison was still eight thousand men strong, and they were led prisoners to France. Twenty-eight French engineer officers were killed in this memorable siege; and it was worth a marshal's *bâton* to General Suchet.

At the conclusion of this important operation, the troops that had been employed in it were taken back to Lower Aragon, and all preparations made for a final conquest of the Kingdom of Valentia; the only part of Spain, besides the Province of Murcia, unoccupied by us. My regiment had resumed its quarters at Santa Olalla; all the inhabitants of this great village came out half-a-league to meet us. We were known there—every person knew us by name; the reception they gave us appeared sincere, and was rather touching. We spent July and August there, pushing on reconnaissances now and then to Teruel, whither the enemy came also from his side, without our ever meeting.

We held Cello, a place that had been the scene of a natural phenomenon in the reign of Charles III. There was a quarry open at half-a-league from the village, furnishing stones of excellent quality and great size; the quarry-men were engaged in detaching a very large stone at the bottom of the quarry, when all at once the stone fell into a cavity and a spring of water gushed out in such abundance as to cast the workmen out of the quarry, and make its way down a valley that had beforetime been very dry, falling into the Ebro and becoming one of its affluents by the name of Rio Xiloca.

Every evening I went and spent some time by this spring, it had been encircled with a wall breast-high by Charles III., and a ring of Canadian poplars. There I used to lie on the grass and watch the famous comet of 1811, thinking that perhaps at the same time in Normandy those whom I loved might also be looking at it, and that the distance that parted us could not impede this means of communication, which, however, it must be confessed, was very indirect.

At last we marched on Valentia by Teruel and Villa Hermosa; and we then entered in the beginning of September upon the chain of mountains that separate Aragon from the Kingdom of Valentia. These mountains show well cultivated valleys, and the appearance of the villages announced easy circumstances, though the tops are bare of vegetation. Our approach put the inhabitants to flight, and we saw them in groups on the slopes opposite to where our road wound its way, no better than a mule path. Our artillery was gone in another direction, as the invasion was conducted in several columns.

No description could give an idea of the sight that this country presents when the plain comes in sight, on issuing from the mountain gorges we traversed. We were leaving Lower Aragon, where any sort of tree is a very rare object, where fruit may be said to be unknown, and all at once, beneath our eyes, there appeared a sort of Eden covered with orange trees, locust trees, and palms, and amid them might be seen beautiful villages, and their churches with domes painted with brilliant colours caught the eye. And then on the horizon was the Mediterranean as blue as the sky, and the Balearic Isles. I beheld all this for the first time on a fine Summer evening, just as the sun was still gilding the summit of the high mountains round Palma. After the lapse of so many years, this fairy panorama is as fresh in my recollection as if I was admiring it at this moment, and the impression it made on me has never grown cold.

We entered on the plain by Villa Hermosa to the north, and on the west of Segorbe and Castillon de la Plana, and made our way towards the second of these cities. The grapes and figs were ripe, and we found these fruits everywhere within our reach; they were delicious, but our men soon learned that they must not be abused. The Kingdom of Valentia is unlike any other part of Spain that I have visited. The towns and villages are clean and charming; the houses of the commonest peasants are lined inside with a dado, shoulder high, of coloured earthenware, and are carefully washed.

The dress of the people is very simple, and extremely elegant. The men wear breeches of white cloth, so wide that the legs cannot be distinguished, a shirt without collar, a bright-coloured sash nearly always and wound several times round the hips, and a kind of woollen Scotch plaid that they throw over their shoulders, and use it as a protection from rain or cold by putting it on the side the wind comes from; they wear the *cothurnus* like the Greeks and Romans.

The women also wear the *cothurnus* and short petticoats; their bodies display the shape perfectly, and are laced in front, being often ornamented with gold or silver embroidery. Their hair is plaited with much grace, and formed into a mass behind the head, secured by long pins with a fall at each end. They are generally well made and walk lightly; almost all of them, in the season for flowers, wear one, a rose by preference, fixed in their hair on one side. It must be well understood that these are the countrymen and women I have been describing; the townspeople there had the same dress as was worn in the other countries of Spain.

The fortress of Murviedro is four leagues to the south of Castillon de la Plana, the ancient Saguntum. It commands the road leading to Valentia, at a point where the mountains come so near the sea that it is impossible to turn the position. It was necessary to gain possession of this fort standing on a high hill, and escarped on every side, before we marched upon Valentia, where the Spanish Army, thirty thousand strong, was concentrated under the command of General Black; being the last resource of Spain, properly so called.

This was our first undertaking, and by flying a sap, a breaching-battery was established only twenty yards from the wall. Twenty-four-pounder guns were dragged up there by manual labour, and in a fortnight, we were ready to open fire. An escalade with ladders was attempted, but without success. Our engineers, generally very correct in their judgment, had calculated the length of the ladders by the height of the wall, without considering the rapid fall of the ground immediately below the wall from its very foot, and so the ladders turned out to be four feet too short. Only three *voltigeurs*, being lifted up by their comrades, got into the fort and were made prisoners in it. This affray cost us nearly a hundred and fifty men.

During these siege operations my regiment was stationed in a village a league to the north of Saguntum, near the marsh that borders the plain on that side. All the inhabitants were agueish, and their pale, thin faces excited compassion. We expected to pay a heavy tribute to the pestilential air of the marshes; but our expectations were only realised in a much smaller proportion, probably from our duty keeping us continually on the move. Every morning at daybreak we mounted our horses, and went to take up a position on the right front of the fort, having to pass under its cannon. We marched in column by twos, and as soon as the head of the regiment came within range, fire upon us began. Shot and shell were poured upon us without interruption all the time we were marching past, and this took nearly a quarter of an hour at a walk, through the folly of Boussard, the General of the Division; for he imagined that if we had passed at a trot the enemy would have thought us afraid.

This general was the most stupid being that I ever met; he could hardly read or write, was incapable of giving an order, or even understanding those he received. I shall soon have to relate a fact that will show what he was.

The breach having been reported practicable, the assault took place, and as a spectator of this grand scene, that made my heart beat a great deal more than if I had taken part in it. A little before nightfall the picked companies that were to take part in the storm were assembled in the places of arms behind the breaching battery. From the place where I stood in perfect safety, I could see these men, many of whom had but a few moments to live even supposing their success to be most speedy, I say I could see them lying on their arms perfectly motionless.

Gradually darkness shrouded everything from view; but I could still just distinguish the two points of such especial interest, the place of arms and the breach. At last night fell. A gun-shot was fired from the breaching-battery. A great shout of "forward" was heard, and immediately a continuous musketry fire, accompanied by the noise of guns and a confused sound of voices. I could not breathe, and more than that, as I write these lines, and remember it, I feel again the emotion that seized me at the time.

Silence succeeded to these formidable sounds, and loud shouts, only broken at intervals by some musket shots. We had been repulsed!

When our soldiers came to tread on the rubbish that composed the breach, it gave way, and on reaching the top the stormers found a piece of wall untouched, and which could not be surmounted but by the help of both hands. And behind this wall and a second higher retrenchment were the besieged, receiving our men with a point-blank fire. The behaviour of our column was excellent; the officers were in front and had the greatest difficulty in making it retreat. But this was necessary, and they fell back with a loss of four hundred men, and several distinguished officers among them—one of whom was Captain Saint-Hilaire, *aide-de-camp* to General Musnier, who had been invested with the command of Aragon by Marshal Suchet, while he was engaged in the conquest of the Kingdom of Valentia.

Saint-Hilaire had requested permission to be present at the siege of Saguntum, and the marshal allowed him to head the storming party. He had a great affection for a young Spaniard of Saragossa, and had a son by her. After his death the child was claimed by his family, taken to France, and in later times I had something to do with his admission to the College of the Dauphiness at Versailles. Saint-Hilaire was not thirty, he was distinguished, clever and amiable; I had known him well on joining the army of Aragon at Uldecona, where General Musnier was in command. He was much regretted, and perhaps more than he would have been but for the romantic circumstances accompanying his death.

We had arrived before Saguntum on the twenty-first of September, 1811. The town of Murviedro is on the north side at the foot of the escarped rock on which the fort is built, it had been immediately occupied by our infantry, and the Spanish troops in it had taken refuge in the fort. At last our morning expedition under the guns of the fort came to an end, we had to leave our agueish village to take up our quarters in bivouac, at first occupying them only by day. I there became acquainted with night-glasses; an engineer officer who had one, lent it to us, and in perfect darkness we could see anything doing onboard an English frigate that was running up and down the coast, and anchoring every night about a league from our observing point. We could make out the uniforms of the officers, soldiers and sailors, and we could also see their faces and what they had in their hands.

Our bivouac was one of the most convenient I ever saw. The *cuirassiers* had made a hut of leafy boughs that sheltered me completely; I shared it with Captain Destombes, and when it rained, we made his young brother, a quartermaster in the same troop, sleep there. Our

Saguntum

Canal

Mortars

Palancia R.

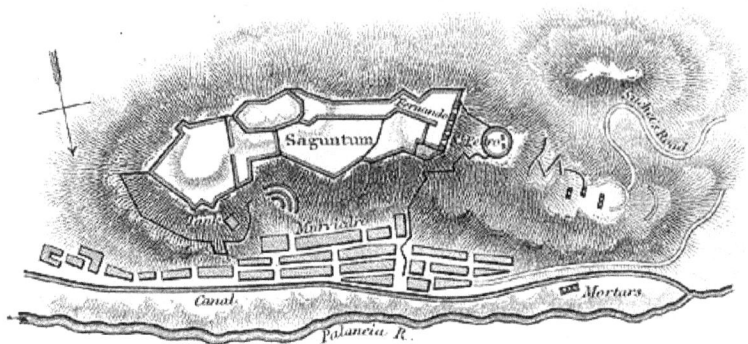

SIEGE & BATTLE OF
SAGUNTUM,
1811.

Gilet

Saguntum

Neapolitan
Div.

Obispo

Robert

Saquers

Chlopiski

Pass of
St Espiritu

Carvagieri

Dragoons

Harispe

Dragoon

Habert

Dragn Napoleon

Beteru

Lardizabal

Zayas

Villacampa

Fuzet

Murcian
Div.

Germands

St Juan

Maya

The Pradon

Elguia

The Carrixes

Canal

3 Miles.

Valencia

Grao

horses were picketted under some large locust trees, with their lower branches nearly horizontal and making a roof of leaves. There was no lack of provisions or forage.

On the first of October, the Spanish general, Obespa, occupied Segorbe on our rear, and was driven from this position, while we on our side made an attack on the left of Black's (better known to English readers as General Blake), army, that was on the left bank of the Guadalaviar and threw it back upon the right bank. My regiment was hardly engaged in this action, but it was bloody. The 70th Regiment of the Line lost several officers there and a hundred men; the Spaniards had five hundred killed, wounded, or prisoners. After the termination of this affair, I was sent out on a reconnaissance on the Guadalaviar with a squadron to ascertain whether the enemy had left any force on the left bank.

I had some very difficult country to cross, some of it being rice-fields, where we had to march in single file on the little narrow banks that divide the portions of ground in which the rice is planted, for as is well known it only grows in the water. The islands intended for threshing-floors for the rice were nearly all covered with people, men, women, and children that had taken refuge there in their flight. Most of the men had arms, and as we very often passed close to these islands, they might have put me in a situation of considerable difficulty by firing on us, because I could not get at them. Fortunately, they did not dare to do so.

Having ascertained that no forces of the enemy remained on the left bank of the Guadalaviar, I proceeded towards Siria, where I was to meet a portion of our army. I got there at two in the morning; we had been twenty-six hours on horseback, having only had half an hour's rest, that we had taken advantage of to give our horses a little barley to eat.

As for ourselves, we may have found a few crusts of bread in our haversacks, I do not recollect, only I remember that when we got to Siria I was dying with fatigue and hunger. There seemed nothing to be got to eat in the town, as it was deserted by all its inhabitants; however, in the house I occupied I found a very large quantity of preserves. I would have given them all with great delight for a little broth, but as there was no choice I was compelled to eat nothing but the jam.

During the whole of the long day's march, every time that we crossed a stream of water we had to encounter a conflict with our horses to prevent them drinking to repletion; we only allowed them to dip their noses in the water and swallow one or two mouthfuls. After a stay of forty-eight hours at Siria, we went back to our bivouac below Saguntum, where the siege was going on.

On the 25th of October, Marshal Suchet received information that General Black had left his position on the Gaudalaviar, and was advancing at the head of thirty thousand men to attack us and raise the siege of Saguntum. We advanced to meet him, turning the fort of Saguntum by our right, and making our way along paths that had certainly never before given passage to any but persons on foot. We led our horses by the bridle at full length, and they would be sometimes five or six feet above us, and could hardly be induced to come down, and then had to scramble like cats. A few guns were passed across to us, and made their way through unheard of difficulties.

At last we found ourselves on a plain full of locust trees where the battle was to take place. We had scarcely twelve thousand men, and our left, when once the obstacle presented by Saguntum was turned, could extend beyond the road leading from Saguntum to Valentia, and rest upon the natural obstacles bordering the sea on that side. Our right crowned the heights that confine the plain near Murviedro.

The Spaniards advanced with resolution, and in capital order. They were confident in their numerical superiority, and besides excited by an energetic proclamation of General Black, giving promise of victory, and telling them that the inhabitants of Valentia and defenders of Saguntum would have their eyes fixed on them during the battle, and would place all their hopes upon their courage and devotion. In reality an army could not be in a better situation to receive such a stimulant. Behind it was a splendid city of a hundred thousand souls with their blessings and cheers to reward a victory, or provide a safe retreat in case of reverse; in front Saguntum to be saved from imminent danger of capture, Saguntum with its walls in sight, and guns continually audible as a call and additional stimulus to conquer.

Our position was not equally good, besides our inferiority in numbers we had the fort of Sarguntum behind us, and defiles that would have made our retreat disastrous in case of a reverse; but we had confidence in the general who commanded us, and in ourselves, and we all advanced without hesitation. The enemy's first efforts were made on the right wing and made it retire. They occupied the village of Pouzol on the main road to Valentia, and in rear of the village was almost all their cavalry under the orders of General Caro, an active and enterprising officer, animated with peculiar hatred against the French.

Battle of Saguntum

My regiment coming up to Pouzol on the right, the 3rd Polish regiment of the Vistula, and a little in front the 4th regiment of Hussars advanced towards the wood of locust trees in front that hid General Caro's cavalry. The first of our three squadrons supported the movement of the hussars, and at the same time orders were sent for the third regiment to go to the other side of Pouzol, as it was supposed they might be wanted there. I remained with the second squadron, almost entirely composed of men of my troop.

A very few minutes had passed after these movements were put into execution when we heard an alarming sound of cries and shouts from the point the 4th Hussars had gone to, and very soon this regiment and our first squadron, flying in the greatest disorder, issued from the wood of locusts pursued by the whole cavalry of General Caro. This force consisting of fifteen hundred horses, was extending on my right, with a front of ten squadrons at least; but it was in disorder, and broken by an advance at full speed through the locust trees, as they are planted in no regular order and are an obstacle to the lines of cavalry.

At first, I feared that my men would be discouraged by the rout of the 4th Hussars and our first squadron; but I was speedily reassured, and experienced the most intoxicating sensation that it is possible to feel on the field of battle. Not having anyone on the spot to give me orders, and perceiving that was coming upon us, I cast a glance upon the squadron behind me with anxiety whether I should find the determination in it that was required under the circumstances. At this glance which was understood, for they were watching me, and looking for the word of command, all the swords were raised and brandished so energetically, and there was something so formidable and intrepid on the bronzed features of the men that I had not a doubt of success, and at the moment I write these lines, fifty years afterwards, I feel my old heart beat again at the remembrance it recalls.

At the signal I gave, the squadron leapt a low wall of dry stone and a ditch before us, and rushed upon the enemy. Everything before us was literally crushed, and for some cause that I never could make out everything that was coming down upon our right began to fly in the oblique direction that we were pursuing, and for half a league we were galloping in the midst of this crowd and decimating it, while they seemed to think of nothing but getting out of a ground that they had been careering over as victors a few minutes before. In this charge we recaptured three of our guns that had fallen into the hands of the enemy, and took five of his that had advanced to support the movement of his cavalry, with the idea that by this movement he would very quickly secure a speedy victory, also rendering the success of his left wing decisive, whereas it also was only temporary. General Caro, commanding the cavalry, received a sword cut on the head, was thrown from his horse and remained in our hands.

After a pursuit of nearly two miles we were obliged to rally, and to stop on the brink of a steep ravine that only permitted of slanting paths, giving room for one horse alone, and that with risk. We watched the fugitives filtering through whom we had passed on our right, without the notion ever coming into the heads of their officers, while moving in the same direction, of attacking us in the rear and surrounding us, though they were ten to one, and they would have found it very easy; for the 4th Hussars and our first squadron, on whom I had counted thinking that as soon as they were rallied they would come to our support, had been despatched in another direction to attack a body of infantry whom they defeated completely, making two thousand prisoners.

So, we were one squadron alone among more than twelve hundred of the enemy's horse, and half a league from any assistance. However, this cavalry had crossed the ravine, had halted, and was keeping up a fire of carbines upon us that might have serious results. Besides, on our left, fifty paces on our side of the ravine, a young lieutenant-colonel of dragoons had collected a hundred men and was preparing to attack. A small hedge of aloes separated us. I thought it wise to be beforehand with him, and we had no trouble in dispersing men demoralised by the former attack.

But to my great regret the young lieutenant-colonel, whose high bred and calm appearance I had admired, remained upon the ground. His efforts to encourage his men had excited my warm sympathy, I went up to him; he had received a severe sword cut on the right side of his head, and that head, a few moments before so full of life and nobility, was lying in a pool of blood with the face three parts hid in it. I asked him in Spanish if he was wounded in the body; he made an effort to raise himself upon one arm, but fell back without being able to answer me.

A shower of bullets which fell around without touching myself or my horse, interrupted me in the midst of my feelings of compassion. The last of the fugitives had got to the other side of the ravine, they had seen me by their lieutenant-colonel, and probably gave the word to fire upon me all together in hopes of laying me beside him. This discharge was followed by that of several pieces of artillery that we did not see, though they were at a very short distance; but as the gunners that served them could not see us, for the trees hid us from each other, they fired by estimation and fired too high; so, though there were several of these discharges of grape, they wounded only one of my men, whom I liked very much, and he died of the wound, his name was Orifel and he came from Provence.

But these discharges of artillery taking place half a league in rear of Pouzol had a great influence on the fate of the day. The enemy's defence on the important line, that had till then been vigorously sustained, ceased all at once, and the three battalions to whom it was confided laid down their arms, being convinced that their retreat was cut off and that no help could come to disengage them. So, the road to Valentia was open, and we saw our 24th Regiment of Dragoons coming in by it followed by infantry. I received orders to go as quickly as possible towards the right to find the 4th Hussars and our first squadron engaged with a column of Spanish infantry that was retiring by the road to Bettera, a large village on the Guadalaviar, a few leagues above Valentia.

I soon joined them, guided by the firing, and had nothing to do there but to be a witness of the most complete rout. More than four thousand muskets lay on the ground, and the prisoners were roughly brought back by the hussars, taking revenge upon them for the disgrace of having fled before Caro's cavalry. However, the head of this column of infantry had managed to get to the continuation of the dry bed of a torrent that had stopped me; had crossed it, and come back to the spot where the high and steep banks of the torrent left no room for anything but the road to Bettera; they formed a line of sharpshooters there, and showed a firm resolution to stop us.

Having no infantry, it was impossible for us to go any further, and very clumsily General Boussard, instead of keeping us at a distance from the ravine, took us quite up to the brink of it, and was kind enough to expose us to a fire that we could not reply to. In this position, which is a good specimen of the aptitude of General Boussard for war, we had an officer and twenty-six men wounded. A ball cut my spur leather on my right instep and gave me a contusion.

Night came at last, and we received orders to return to the bivouac we had left in the morning. All our wounded and those of the enemy had been taken up, as we left them behind us, and thanks to the care of Marshal Suchet, never was battlefield more promptly cleared than

CUIRASSIERS ON THE BATTLEFIELD

that. After this day I understood the part played by chance in battles better than I had done before. It may be said that prudent measures had been taken on both sides. General Black, confident in his superior numbers, had extended his front so as to be able to outflank our wings, and throw forces on our rear, able to seize the defiles that had led us to the plain, and had this manoeuvre been successful, it might have caused anxiety in our ranks and injured the dash of our soldiers.

As our right wing gave way, there was at first some chance of this object being accomplished, and it was probably at that moment that General Black flung all his cavalry upon our centre, hoping rather prematurely that he had gained a success, but his advantage was on the contrary soon changed into a defeat. On our side the general-in-chief, who very well knew the force of the enemy, and also knew what dependence he could put on the valour and devotion of the troops under his orders, had marched on resolutely to the front, without taking much notice of what might be going on upon his right wing—the only one that could be turned, probably knowing very well that when once the Spanish centre was broken, its flight would cause that of all the rest.

And this is exactly what took place, but it must also be said that the success of our centre was due to causes that chance had very much to do with, as I have related above. Besides, the English General Napier, in his *History* of this war in Spain, attributes the victory of Saguntum to the charge of *cuirassiers* I have just described, a charge that he terms furious.

★★★★★★

Napier in his *Peninsular War*, vol. iv. says:—
"Loy's and Caro's horsemen overthrew the French Hussars in a moment, and in the same charge sabred the French gunners and captured their battery. The crisis would have been fatal if Harispe's infantry had not stood firm, while Palombini's division marching on the left under cover of a small rise of the ground, suddenly opened a fire upon the flank of the Spanish cavalry, which was still in pursuit of the Hussars. These last immediately turned, and the Spaniards thus placed between two fires, and thinking the flight of the Hussars had been feigned to draw them into an ambuscade, hesitated, the next moment a tremendous charge of the *cuirassiers* put everything into confusion. Caro was wounded and taken, Loy fled with the remainder of the cavalry over the Piccador, the French guns were

recovered, the Spanish artillery taken, and Lardizabal's infantry being quite broken, laid down their arms, or throwing them away saved themselves as they could."

★★★★★★

In order to fulfil my promise of making known a military career in all its details, I must relate my personal adventures of this day. I hope that no signs of conceit may be perceived in this; for if, on my entrance into the army I had too much admiration for what Madame de Sevigne calls "grand sword strokes," I very soon came to value them at their proper worth, and to understand that they only come within the duty of a cavalry officer in action in the most minute proportion. But this is what took place: when I was engaged in rallying my men on the brink of the ravine and forming them up, a Spanish lancer was crossing our front to join his party who were rallying very near us, and he cast a threatening look at us that angered me.

I was heated and over-excited by the action; I dashed at him, parried the lance thrust he aimed at me with my sabre, and ran him completely through. He fell; and this took place at an equal distance between the two bodies of troops that were there.

The fame of this "sword stroke" cannot be imagined, though so many more were given during the day. The *cuirassiers* talked of it in the evening at their bivouac; and having occasion to go to headquarters next day, it was the first thing the officers of the headquarter staff spoke to me about. At last, in 1833, and so twenty-two years afterwards, an officer of the depot for remounts at Alençon that I was then commanding, going his round, met an old quartermaster of the 13th Cuirassiers, who, knowing him to be under my command, had nothing better to do than to tell him the story of the "sword stroke."

I must also say that on the evening after this business, I was surrounded and warmly congratulated by the officers of the 3rd Regiment of the Vistula, who were on my right just as I gave orders for the charge. I felt this testimony very much. It was one of the flowers of the profession.

We returned to our bivouac, and next day the garrison of the fort of Saguntum, eighteen hundred men strong, capitulated, and went to swell the column of prisoners on the road to France.

During the continuance of the siege of this fort, the wife of Marshal Suchet was living in an isolated tower built by the Moors, and this tower was within range of the heavy guns of the fort. After the surrender, the marshal asked the commander of the garrison why no shot had been fired in that direction; and the reply was, that, knowing his wife was there, the gunners had received orders not to fire any shot in the direction of the tower. This act of courtesy was a rare exception to the usual practice of this war of extermination.

CHAPTER 10

Expedition and Combat

When the fort was in our power the army advanced and took up a position on the Guadalaviar, with its left resting on the sea, and its right extending to the village of Bettera, which was held by my regiment with two regiments of infantry, one of them being Polish. Our advanced posts were on the banks of the river, which was really only a brook, and fordable everywhere; the Spanish outposts were opposite to us, and we left each other very quiet, as is always the case when enemies' posts are very near together. However, at night the Spaniards would sometimes send a detachment above Bettera, and feign an attack upon our right flank, but it was always limited to the exchange of a few shots without result. Yet we took a young officer who seemed as if he was not very sorry to have fallen into our hands. We treated him well. He was a person of distinction, not very frequently the case in the Spanish Army, as the body of officers was recruited from any sources in those disastrous times.

Our inaction lasted a month; then we received orders to occasionally make expeditions on the right bank, and this gave occasion for several combats, one of them being of some importance, and marked by a very dramatic event. General Boussard was with us at Bettera, and General Robert, commanding the infantry brigade, was under his orders. So, a reconnaissance composed of fifty *cuirassiers* and some *voltigeurs* started and crossed the Guadalaviar.

I was not under orders for this expedition, but wishing to see what came of it I mounted my horse with the artillery captain Hurlaux, commanding the battery we had at Bettera, and both of us, as amateurs, followed the course of the reconnaissance, not intending to go further than just to the river; the passage was not seriously disputed, and we were led on by curiosity, though we always intended not to go too far. In this we had not taken into account either the interesting scenes that followed, or the sense of danger we should have experienced by going back after getting some distance from the ford where we had crossed the Guadalaviar, and thus we became obliged to remain attached to the fortunes of the detachment.

They turned to the left after passing the ford, and went in the direction of Valentia, four leagues distant, having to communicate at half that distance with another reconnaissance under the orders of General Harispe, afterwards Marshal of France. When we approached the spot where the two reconnaissances were to meet, we had to climb a rising ground whose direction was at right angles to the course of the Guadalaviar, joining it, and stretching to some unknown distance on our right. Spanish vedettes were posted on the crest of it.

The *cuirassiers* were divided into two sections, one under the orders of the captain commanding the whole, was intended to proceed along the hill for an hour, and then join the reconnaissance. The enemy's vedettes were driven off by the twenty-five *cuirassiers* who remained with us, and we became masters of the height.

It entirely commanded a little plain, surrounded on three sides by a wood of olives and locust trees, the road leading to it, that we had followed since we crossed the river, went down a very steep and stony slope. Before us was a squadron of Spanish hussars with a line of skirmishers. Just as we showed ourselves, General Harispe came out on our left, with a detachment of the 4th Hussars in front, who at once began skirmishing with the enemy. Our infantry, not marching so quickly as we did, was not yet on the ground.

The twenty-five *cuirassiers* that we had kept were commanded by a lieutenant lately come to us from the Grenadiers of the Imperial Guard who had started not very brilliantly with the regiment, for he had got so drunk on the day of the Battle of Saguntum that he could hardly sit his horse, and did not know what he was about. He received orders to put his detachment in single rank, and to go a few hundred paces from the point where the road towards Valentia entered the wood, and thus to protect the descent into the plain.

The generals with their staff were stationed at about a third of the way down, on the side that General Harispe had come by. General Robert was there also. Hurlaux and I had stopped on the crest, whence we could watch all the events of the adventure we found ourselves engaged in without losing any of them.

The skirmishing continued some time. The Spaniards often had the advantage in this kind of fighting and gained it that day. The officer in command of the skirmishers of the 4th Hussars was killed. The infantry did not come up through some accident that I have forgotten. Very soon a thick cloud of dust that arose in the road attracted Hurlaux's and my attention, it was caused by a column of cavalry advancing rapidly to the support of that engaged with our hussars.

To give full interest to what follows, I must here make a digression. When we had occupied the little town of Uldecona, in the north of the Kingdom of Valentia, before there was any notion of subduing it, several officers, in the numerous excursions we made to Benicarlos had opportunities of knowing a French family that had emigrated and settled there. This family consisted of a widow, her two daughters, and a son, a lieutenant-colonel in the Spanish service; he was in a dragoon regiment forming a part of the army of Valentia.

Now these three ladies were superior persons in all respects; their name was d'Outremont, or d'Apremont, and they had begged of the officers I have mentioned to protect their son and brother if the chance of war should make him fall into their hands as a prisoner. It need not be said that this request was received with pleasure, and the most formal promises were made that he should be treated as a brother if the occasion should arise.

At last, through the cloud of dust I have mentioned and the openings in the wood, which we overlooked, we could perceive that a considerable force of cavalry was just coming upon our hands. The ground that parted us from the generals was such as to prevent our going straight to them to inform them. The utmost speed was necessary. I went down at a gallop towards our *cuirassiers*, who were, as I have mentioned, placed opposite to the opening.

I was on an English saddle and without my *cuirass*. I had only just got to them when a detachment of Spanish infantry came out of the wood and, with their backs against it, fired a volley at us at two hundred paces that hit no one. At the same time the Spanish dragoons came out in fours, but just as they wanted to form up their first squadron and were making the movement in a somewhat disorderly manner, we charged them so sharply that they fell over one another, and then their defence was broken. We entered the wood pell-mell with them, and the rest of the column also took to flight in alarm at the rout of its head. Having pursued them for some time, we came back quietly to the spot whence we started, picking up prisoners.

Then we were witnesses to a dreadful scene that still makes as sharp and painful an impression on me as if it took place yesterday. Bordenave, a major, first *aide-de-camp* to General Boussard, had just been mortally wounded, and lay there on a spot that had not been exposed to fire. Not being able to imagine how this misfortune had arisen, I inquired the cause. This is what had taken place. The lieutenant-colonel of the Spanish dragoons had been struck by a sabre in the head and fallen from his horse; when he recovered consciousness, he was taken before General Boussard; they had forgotten to take his sword, and it hung from his wrist by the sword knot, trailing on the ground.

General Boussard, a dishonourable brute, addressed some vulgar abuse to him, and the prisoner's indignation at this proceeding caused him to make a movement of his arm, that shook the blade of his sword without raising it, for he had not hold of the handle. Then General Boussard cried out that he had meant to assassinate him, and told a *voltigeur*, who came up at the moment, to fire a shot at him. Bordenave hearing this barbarous order, started forward to prevent its being put in execution; but the shot went off, the ball went through the head of the unfortunate lieutenant-colonel, and lodging in Bordenave's breast cast him to the ground.

On learning this catastrophe—this cowardly murder of an officer just made prisoner and wounded, I did not try to restrain the feelings of horror that I experienced for General Boussard, and expressed them to him in very violent language. I should have been glad if he had ordered me under arrest, so that I might have been able to proclaim his infamy aloud before a court-martial. But he heard my invectives like a senseless beast; I thought he had some remorse, but the consequences showed he was incapable of it.

And this lieutenant-colonel, stretched lifeless at our feet, was the very one who had been recommended to us by his mother and sisters, and we had promised to treat well if he should one day become our prisoner.

Bordenave was loved and honoured by all, and I was very intimate with him. In our cantonment we always spent our evenings together, playing for small stakes, making punch when we had the materials. Like the Spanish lieutenant-colonel he had a mother and two sisters, and he was their idol. He often told us about them, sometimes read the letters he received from them, and laughed at the reiterated advice contained in all the epistles. These three women, awaiting his return to France as their only possible recompense for the agonies they suffered, begged of him not to expose himself rashly, only to do his duty, to think of them and be prudent. I went up to him, he had beckoned to me; I took his hand, and he pressed mine feebly, murmuring some words of leave-taking. The hospital orderlies carried him to a kind of pretence at a hospital at headquarters, and he died there next day.

However, night approached, and we had to think how we were to get back. As soon as the Spaniards perceived our retrograde movement, their skirmishers pressed us close, and Hurlaux and I had considerable difficulty in rescuing Major Duchamp, seriously wounded, out of their hands. This Duchamp, a kind of Alcibiades, a bad person to have to do with, had, I do not know the least why, taken a great fancy to me. He died lieutenant-general commanding the artillery at Vincennes. Hurlaux and I ran considerable risk in extricating him that day.

We recrossed the Guadalaviar in General Harispe's line, and that diminished the length of our retreat before the enemy to three quarters of a league, as it may well be supposed they did not attempt to pursue us on the other side. I was not acquainted with General Harispe, but I received an invitation from him to follow him to headquarters and dine with him. A few minutes before I had received one from General Robert that I had accepted; and it seemed to me curious enough that when I got back to Bettera, General Boussard sent his remaining *aide-de-camp* to engage me to dinner, and he never invited anyone, not even the commanders of corps under his orders. The result of all this was a conviction that I had been noticed, and considered to have done some service on this occasion; but I may say in all conscience that the notion of attracting attention never came into my mind for a moment.

From the height where I was posted with Hurlaux, I had seen the danger of permitting a force to open out upon the little plain where the contest took place, sufficient to incline the balance to the side of our enemies, and make our retreat disastrous in case of a reverse. And then I was uneasy as to the appearance that might be presented by the officer in command of the detachment of *cuirassiers*, an anxiety that was completely justified as I found him quite drunk, with a gourd of brandy in his hand that he had already dipped into pretty freely, and was making the *cuirassiers* share with him. I abused him considerably, and ordered him to the rear, whither he retired at once.

One circumstance, perhaps, had a considerable bearing on the rout of the Spanish cavalry; just as we were charging the head of the column, the detachment of *cuirassiers* that had been sent on reconnaissance before we came on the ground, made their appearance on the hill, and probably the sight of this reinforcement and the impossibility of conjecturing its strength by the. Spaniards, induced them to make a precipitate retreat.

A few days afterwards General Boussard received orders to send a reconnaissance to a village on the Gualalaviar four leagues from the position we held on the extreme right of the army. The marshal had received information that a corps of six thousand Spaniards had just crossed the river at that point, and so were on the same side with us. The command of this reconnaissance, consisting of a squadron and two companies of Polish *voltigeurs*, was given to me, though it was not my turn for duty. The captain whose turn it was went to the general to put in his claim, and then the general showed us the order he had received, bearing a postscript in the marshal's own hand, "Let Captain de Gonneville command this reconnaissance." I mention this fact to give prominence to some contradictions in the marshal's conduct towards me, which I never could explain.

It was a delicate operation that I had in hand; we had to follow a road along the Guadalaviar for four leagues, two of them being a defile enclosed between a mountain inaccessible to cavalry, and ground cut up by wide and deep ditches. During the whole of this passage we were in sight of the enemy occupying the further bank, and able to communicate with the bank I had to pass along, by several fords. Besides, if the information received by the marshal was accurate, I should find myself in front of six thousand Spaniards, and they would have been sure not to allow me to retire peaceably; and there was also great probability that my retreat might be cut off by troops thrown into the defile from the other side after my passing, as it gave occasion for some movements on the other side, as was shown by orderlies galloping in several directions.

All these contingencies caused me serious consideration during the march I had to make; but on reaching the end I found that there were no enemies, and I only saw three or four thousand inhabitants of the village that I had been directed to examine, flying across the river for safety, bearing their children on their shoulders. The women were crying piteously, no doubt imagining that all their dear household stores would be plundered and that they would find all destroyed on their return. When they did return they ought to have been agreeably surprised, for I had not allowed a single man to enter the village.

It appeared to me so likely that the Spaniards would be lying in wait to attack me in the defile we had passed, that I resolved to return by another road through Livia. It is true this required a long round, but it gave me almost perfect security against attack; in fact, our march took place without interruption. Livia was not held by the French, and my arrival on the side of the town exactly opposite to the positions they knew that we held, caused a sensation, and the greater because I was bringing in a prisoner, an inhabitant of Livia itself and apparently very well known. We had arrested him just as he had come out by a winding path, and was making his way down to the Guadalaviar. He was armed with a bayonet attached to a long stick, and seemed so cast down at falling into the midst of us, that I had no doubt he was a messenger of the enemy's.

After we had gone through Livia, his mother and his wife came up to me, riding excellent mules; they begged of me to set him free, and on my refusal, accompanied him to Bettera. I was naturally obliged to report my expedition to General Boussard, and he, brutally enough, complained of my not having caused the man to be shot on the instant, as he was liable to this penalty for carrying his weapon; but after he had given audience to the mother and wife, the prisoner whom he had at first intended to shoot was set at liberty; and all who knew the General thought that his freedom had been obtained for a bribe of money. This mean general, a man who could do anything, had no doubt frightened the two poor women to get the more.

My prevision of the snare the Spaniards would lay for me was confirmed. We had information that they crossed the Guadalaviar after we had passed by, and took up a position so that they might attack me front and rear when I should be entangled in the defile.

On the 26th of December all the army crossed the Guadalaviar on several points, and attacked the Spaniards with the intention of throwing them back on Valentia, as it was known that General Black intended to retire thither to take up a new position on the Xucar. We with the 4th Hussars, were directed on Torrente, a large village of eight thousand inhabitants that we had to pass to reach the road to Alicante, by which the Spanish Army would probably retire. Before we reached Torrente, General Boussard had advanced with the hussars, and was driven back by a charge of the enemy's cavalry, seriously wounded, and thrown from his horse; he would have been killed but for a charge of ours that rescued him.

His second *aide-de-camp* Robert was killed in his defence. This *aide-de-camp* left a young widow and two children. Some days before his death he had showed me his wife's picture, and as he put it back into the pocket where he always carried it, kissed it with a sorrowful countenance.

We were delayed a moment before Torrento as it was strongly held, but Hurlaux caused its evacuation by throwing shells into it; then we hastened to the Alicante road with the 4th Hussars. General Harispe's infantry division followed us, we reached the road just in time to throw ourselves between the baggage in advance, and the head of the column that was just appearing, and we threw it back upon Valentia. We took possession of the baggage consisting of so many carts and carriages that the road was covered with them for more than a league. All the officers' wives were there, Heaven knows how many.

As we were aware that there was a strong detachment of cavalry at the head of this convoy, we set out in pursuit of them, leaving the hussars behind halted by their colonel, that he might quietly proceed to have something to eat, under the pretext that he had taken nothing the whole day. This colonel, Lamotte Guéry, had but a poor reputation as a soldier, and his two brothers, one of whom was under General d'Avenay's orders when he was struck by a shot at the crossing of the Piave, had no better fame. I can still see the man I speak of sitting on the side of the road eating his meal, while his hussars prepared to pillage the convoy, and did it to the great disgust of the *cuirassiers*, not one of whom quitted the ranks.

While we were passing along this convoy, the ladies in the carriages waved their handkerchiefs at the windows, making feeble shouts of "*Viva la Francia, viva Napoleone!*" We told them as we trotted by not to be alarmed, that nothing should be done to them. At last we reached the head of the convoy, but the cavalry that led it had run away, and as night was approaching, we formed up to call over the roll of the men; only two were absent, one being a farrier who had stopped to put on a horse's shoe. We returned by the way we had come, and very soon found our two men.

As we approached Valentia, we saw only the remains of the convoy; several of the carriages had been overturned, the trunks opened and a quantity of property strewed on the ground. The ladies were taken to a large village situated a league from Valentia, and distributed among all the houses. Attempts were made to help them, but I cannot remember that I saw a single one that seemed to deserve it; they were all talking at once, shouting and disputing, boasting about their husbands' rank against those whose husbands held a lower rank.

One of them, a colonel's wife, wore a riding habit, and had three rows of lace on the sleeve to mark her husband's rank. She crushed her companions in captivity by her lofty airs, and exacted marks of deference and respect. Next day all these ladies were permitted to go where they pleased, and we were relieved of them to our great satisfaction; there were more than a hundred of them, and they had been very troublesome to us.

I was detached with my squadron to the village of Sedovia, a fief of the duchy of that name. This was the nearest point to Valentia. I was quartered in the castle, very large, very ugly, very little furnished, and having not the least bit of a garden. This castle was in charge of an old *major-domo* just like Bartholo, wearing the same dress, and calling me your Excellency. The inhabitants of the village did not run away, and found the benefit of it. I had a main guard in front of the village, on the side towards Valentia, and after a few days I had to get on my horse at midnight with my whole force, and take post at that spot, remaining there till break of day.

From there I beheld the bombardment of the city. I could watch the course of the shells in the air by the light of their fuses, and hear their fall, as well as the cries that always followed their descent; I saw the flames of the fires they lighted, and heard the alarm given by the sound of the tocsin from the innumerable belfries of the churches.

Valentia capitulated on the 9th of January, 1812, and the garrison were made prisoners of war, eighteen thousand men strong. I was stationed with a squadron facing the bridge by which the garrison came forth. The cavalry came out first, sword in hand, their trumpets were sounding a march and mine replied. It was touching. On reaching the drawbridge of the work covering the bridge that they had crossed, the sub-officers and soldiers threw their arms into the ditch, and further on they dismounted and their horses were taken.

Several women followed their husbands. One of them was remarkable for her pretty figure and elegant dress; she wore a black riding-habit, a little Henry IV. hat with a black plume, and was riding a black Andalusian horse with perfect grace. Next day I was much surprised to find her at the cantonments of the regimental headquarters. Her husband was bandmaster of one of the captive regiments, and as my regiment was in want of one, the colonel had obtained permission to keep him, and he was delighted to take this means of escaping a journey to France, and to remain with his wife of whom he seemed very fond.

This capitulation of the army of General Black was a great blow to the Spanish means of resistance, there were no defenders of any consequence left in the Eastern part of the peninsula. Ten thousand men had avoided the fate of the army, making their escape by footpaths, and by the tongue of land that separates Albufera from the sea, but great numbers of them dispersed and were never seen again.

We made a triumphant entry into Valentia, and were able to observe the frightful ravages of the bombardment. Several houses had been entirely overthrown, many others had received severe injury, and in some streets the rubbish reached to the first floor, so that our horses could go up to it. All the population in their best clothes lined the road as we went along. The houses were ornamented outside as I afterwards saw them at Easter. Musicians were stationed here and there upon the balconies, singing songs of victory, and ladies waved their handkerchiefs in our honour; but these demonstrations did not deceive us at all, and left us quite convinced that at the bottom of their hearts they were praying for all manner of evil upon us.

A house in the parade before the citadel was prepared for the marshal; it was dressed with all the colours of the various corps that had composed the garrison. It was splendid, and the marshal must have been proud of his conquest and its fame, extending beyond Europe. All precautions were taken that no disorder or abuse should ensue upon our occupation; and upon this everything returned to its usual order, though intermixed with the destructions and private sorrows that inevitably are the consequences of a siege and bombardment.

I had been sent back to my cantonment at Sedovia, and spent several days there; then I had to go to Torrento, a large village I have already mentioned, before which we were stopped on the day of the investment of Valentia. A company of infantry was given me and put under my orders. I quartered them in a convent deserted by the monks, having fortified it, as was usual, by making loopholes in the surrounding wall, and placing a traverse, with palisades, before the entrance.

My *cuirassiers* were placed in the village, in such a way that I could very speedily have them at hand; and I established myself in a nice little house left by the absent owners under the charge of a family consisting of husband and wife and two young children. There was not an article of furniture in it, as is always the case in Spanish country houses, for they are not occupied for the whole of the year; and I had the greatest difficulty in getting a table, a few chairs, and a bed. My duty was to cover the approaches to Valentia on that side, and to make war upon bands of insurgents that might be attempting to make incursions upon the extensive territory attached to my command.

This charge did not trouble me much, and for several months our quiet was only once disturbed by the arrival of enemy's forces upon my ground, trying to levy contributions and live plenteously there, as the guerrillas never failed to do, and this attracted many young persons to their ranks who enjoyed this kind of life; but the population who suffered from it were much disgusted at these visits, and they were the very people who came to give information of their presence. I marched with all possible speed to the point named, but they had quitted it before I got there, and were too many hours in advance for me to think of pursuit.

An incident happened here that was a lesson to me; the time came for leaving Torrento, and the bread and meat that should have been sent from Valentia the same day had not arrived; so, the men started fasting, and made a march of four leagues as fast as the infantry could go. It was in the early days of June, and when we reached the place where we hoped to find the enemy, the infantry were overcome with heat and hunger. I had them halted upon a height commanding the village, and I sent a requisition for wine in the proportion of a bottle to two men, and for some food.

The inhabitants exerted themselves to satisfy my requirements; but, in two hours' time, a halt that I had thought requisite for my people to rest, when I wanted to make a start there was not one of the infantry that could march. They were so drunk they could not stand, and yet had only got the quantity of wine I had ordered. I was certain of this; it was, in very truth, the action of the wine coming immediately upon a hasty march in such hot weather, for not one of my *cuirassiers* was similarly affected. I was obliged to make a requisition for the number of carriages requisite to carry my whole company of infantry, officers and all; but happily, after being two hours on the road, there were very few traces of this adventure left, and I was able to send back the carriages before we entered Torrente.

Sometime after that I had to join the 14th Regiment of Infantry with my *cuirassiers*, to escort a sum of money that Marshal Suchet was sending to Madrid, as far as Cuença. As usual I found myself under the orders of the colonel of the regiment, whose name was Estève, a man of bad repute, not for his military capacity but in all other respects. I had a real antipathy for him, from the reports I had heard. Cuença is forty-five leagues from Valentia on the track, or rather road to Madrid, for at the time I was in Spain there were only two roads in it, and they, it must be said, were excellent, that from Bayonne to Cadiz going through Madrid, and that from Perpignan to Valentia.

We had to cross a country totally unoccupied by the French, and the nature of our duty gave promise of adventures. The 14th Regiment of Infantry had three battalions, nearly eighteen hundred men, and I had rather more than a hundred horses. First, we crossed the chain of mountains that separate Valentia from Old Castile. It was not very wide and was surmounted on our first day's march. Making eight leagues a day we reached Cuença on the 5th; the advanced troops of the army of Madrid were there.

On leaving the little village of Requena, our first halting place after leaving the mountains, we had crossed an undulating plain, with a few villages in it that should, in ordinary times, have contained large supplies, but at the time in question they were quite stripped through the pressure of the two parties that in turn laid their requisitions on them, and especially I had great difficulty in finding a living for my horses.

General d'Armagnac was in command at Cuença, and the ruin of the country was in a measure laid to his charge, and it was said that this ruin tended neither to the profit of the troops under his orders, nor to that of the King's treasury. I found one of my friends, Suzainecourt, there, who entertained me to the best of his power. He was a captain in the 19th Dragoons, a portion of the brigade that General d'Avenay had commanded after the Prussian war, with which we had entered Spain in 1808. Suzainecourt had been made a captain by the Emperor the same day as myself at Cassel before Mayence. We had a great deal to tell each other about our respective adventures in the four years that we had been separated, so the day's rest I spent with him was well employed.

We started from Cuença on the second day after we got there, and returned by the same road as we had come. I was always on the advanced guard, and the horses became very tired from the continued necessity of keeping scouts upon our flanks, for they were obliged to march in the fields, and leap the obstacles that they encountered. They were quite knocked up when we reached Requena, and I was pleased to see that we were on the eve of a rest after a march of a hundred leagues in eleven days; the work of scouting had been doubly tiring, and I was by no means pleased when Colonel Estève sent for me next morning, and desired me to make a fresh start with a battalion that he was sending to the village of Utiel, that we had passed through the evening before, and was two leagues back from Requena.

I was not informed of the object of this expedition, but the reputation of Colonel Estève and my observations caused me to suspect what it was. With great difficulty I managed to be excused from taking any but the least tired horses with me; I took forty of them and one officer only.

A quarter of a league from Utiel my advanced guard exchanged some shots with Spanish horsemen, who were the main guard of a body that was to occupy Utiel, and they retired upon it. I followed them at full speed, sending information to the leader of the battalion behind me, under whose orders I was. While I was having the village explored before entering it, I saw a troop of horsemen, about a squadron, coming up at a gallop along a road that leads to a height commanding Utiel on the left side.

This cavalry was evidently a troop of guerillas, and I did not hesitate to go in pursuit of them. I passed quickly through the village, being of considerable size and well built; all the houses were shut and not an inhabitant to be seen, but when I came to the principal house I saw several elegant ladies upon the balcony, and three or four men of good appearance. When I was opposite the men bowed to me, and the ladies waved their handkerchiefs, crying "*viva*" while I received some gracious looks. This scene took place at some distance from, but full in view of the Spanish cavalry, as they were drawn up at the top of the road where it was very wide, and shut in on both sides by a boundary wall and some vines.

So, I went up at a walk not to blow the horses, and I received a fire that wounded only one horse. Then I ordered swords to be drawn, but had not the trouble of charging, for this motion was the cause of a disorderly flight. We rushed in pursuit of this miserable troop numbering at least a hundred horses; and these horses being more speedy, and especially less tired than our own, though we were most anxious to catch them, only myself and a few of my men managed to press them close.

After pursuing them for more than half a league, and coming to a hollow in the ground with its bottom out of sight, I observed that the head of the flying column did not reappear on the other side. I thought that they were trying a rally there and that perhaps I should meet with some resistance. I certainly ought to have met some, for this hollow disclosed to view a second troop as strong as the first, round whom the others were circling in disorder. I should have been in difficulty enough if they had all fallen upon me, for I had rushed upon them with only a few of the best mounted men along with me at the first moment; but at the look of us, without trying to see any more, all this whole number took to flight, to my great astonishment, and the pursuit began again in a more orderly and prudent manner, giving time for an infantry adjutant to come up and tell me to return to Utiel, by the major's orders.

As soon as the Spaniards saw that I was going to retire, they sent out skirmishers against me, and I was obliged to meet them at a great disadvantage, for my men had nothing but pistols in the way of fire-arms, while the guerrillas had good carbines, and in general were skilful in the use of them. This was not the case on this day, fortunately for me, for they made me especially their aim, so that five or six balls would come at me at a time. Some *voltigeurs* had come after me at a run, and they fired some musket shots that deterred the Spaniards from the idea of pursuing me, and I went very quietly along the league before we came to Utiel.

If they had chosen to overwhelm me with a cloud of skirmishers, under orders to disperse as soon as I should make any show of turning back and resuming the offensive against them, no doubt they would have caused me considerable loss; the ground was very favourable to them, for all the way from the spot and where they had awaited me near Utiel, to the village of Candite, towards which they retired, there was only one plain uncultivated, for the vines stopped at the end of the plateau where I found them drawn up.

When I reached the house where I had seen the fair Spaniards upon the balcony, I saw the major coming out looking very angry. He tried to quarrel with me in very improper language for having acted as I had done without his orders. I was within my duty as commander of the advanced guard, and I let him know it pretty roundly. I expected to be put under arrest by Colonel Estève, who had a very good understanding with this major, a man of as bad a character as himself, but nothing came of it. I supposed that they had been desirous of levying a contribution upon Utiel, and that the major had met with a refusal when he applied to the chief persons of the place; and I suspected this principally from the ironical manner in which the persons upon the balcony, I have mentioned, looked at him—while, on the contrary, they again saluted me most pleasantly.

We returned to Requena in the evening. I was done up with weariness and hunger. For the first time since I had been in Spain, I asked my hosts to give me some supper, finding them at table. They certainly would not have given me an invitation, but they accepted the infliction with a very good grace, and I did honour to an *olla podrida* sent up in a raised crust. It was the second time that I had been seated at the table of a Spaniard.

The next day was taken up in putting a convent outside the town on the road to Utiel in a provisional state of defence. A company of infantry was left there; Colonel Estève wanted to make me leave twenty *cuirassiers* there with an officer, but I made so many objections that I brought off all my people. It would have been absurd to shut up horses in such a place, without having previously secured a fortnight's subsistence for them at least, and there was not a single ration of forage.

We returned to our cantonments and found everything in the best order. Marshal Suchet had allowed me to take lodgings in Valentia, and I went there from time to time, when my presence at Torrento was not required by the interests of the service. I was well acquainted with Major Bugeaud, afterwards a Marshal of France, who was in command of the town, and he would have informed me immediately in Valentia if my command had required my return to Torrento. My lodging was at the house of an old canon of more than eighty years of age. His name was Muños, and he was brother to the celebrated Don Vincent Muños, author of the *History of the New World*. The latter and his wife had both been dead for many years, leaving a son and three daughters, who lived near their uncle, himself a man of distinction.

The three nieces were charming, perfectly well brought up and very superior to any of the women I had seen in Spain. Though this family was Spanish at heart, they came at last not to look upon me as an enemy, and when I departed never to return, the old canon took me in his arms and embraced me with tears, telling me in a low voice that he felt very plainly that he had but a short time of life remaining.

I also went on a strong reconnaissance under the command of General Delort. All my regiment was there; we marched upon Alzira, a pretty town situated upon the Xucar, held by the advanced guard of the relics of the army of Valentia. The evening of our first day's march we reached a very large village, and this means in the Kingdom of Valentia a collection of six or eight thousand inhabitants. It was night, and we found all the inhabitants before their houses with lights, and as the day had been rainy they kindled large fires in all directions to dry us—a thing that had never been seen in Spain from the very commencement of this war. The report of this reception pleased Marshal Suchet very much; it was a tribute to the discipline of his army. At Alzira we found the inhabitants engaged in repairing the bridge that had been cut by the Spanish troops on their retreat, for they had got wind of our coming.

We made our bivouac on the right bank of the Xucar, and General Delort entered it alone with two or three officers and some horsemen, to communicate with the authorities. Having accomplished the object of our expedition, which was to ascertain the disposition of the inhabitants, we retraced our steps, and I returned to Torrento, where I received several marks of sympathy and confidence from the inhabitants.

The first *alcalde*, Pasquale Mora, was a peasant such as is not now to be met with. He had an income of sixteen hundred pounds a year in lauded property, and managed it himself. He was unmarried, and a legion of nephews and nieces, the offspring of brothers and sisters he had lost, lived with him. He tended and watched over all these orphans as if he had been their father, and they lived in the most perfect unison, respecting him, and obedient to his smallest gesture. His numerous servants, and the whole population of Torrento showed him the same respect and obedience.

The arrangement of work was punctiliously observed, and the start for the fields at appointed hours, as well as the return presented a truly remarkable scene. The numerous and splendid mules, with harness in excellent order, all the servants in silence, with their white breeches looking like tunics, their bare legs and Roman *buskins*, left me a remembrance that combines with that of Pasqual Mora. He was a superior man, of an honesty proverbial in the country, so that they were continually taking him as arbitrator. I often saw him; we were very good friends, and our good understanding, no doubt, contributed to the maintenance of the most perfect harmony between my men and the inhabitants.

At the end of the month of August, 1812, I was at my own request, appointed to conduct a detachment of dismounted men of my regiment into France going for horses to the depot at Niort, whom I was to bring back when remounted. The marshal authorised me to give over the command of this detachment to the senior officer who should be of the party, as soon as I had passed the frontier, and to go to Normandy during the time required for the reorganisation of the detachment, implying a stay of about two months. At that time, a stay of two months in the country at home, was an exceptional piece of good fortune. Life is sufficiently uncertain at all times, and was then more precarious than at any other—war claimed so many victims every day.

The army of Aragon was at rest, and if it should receive orders to march on Murcia, I was certain of being able to return before the opening of this fresh campaign. The expedition to Russia had begun; its success did not give any reason to apprehend the disasters that put an end to it, and exercised such a fatal influence upon the fate of the armies in Spain. Thus, I thought I was departing with the best of hopes.

My detachment was to form a part of a column organised under the command of General Montmarie, who was on his way to the waters of Barége, it was composed of two thousand persons as near as may be. There were a number of invalids, men put on half-pay, children, vehicles, and beasts of burden. My *cuirassiers* had muskets and pouches given them, and sandals to wear on their feet.

The day before we started Marshal Suchet sent for me, and gave me a confidential commission for the *corregidor* of Jaca, a little fortified town at the foot of the Pyrenees, and on the extreme frontier. It would have seemed to me more natural had this proof of confidence been given to General Montmarie, and it again disposed me to make the reflections that some words of the marshal's written with his own hand had first aroused, that I should not have mentioned but for the contradictions in Marshal Suchet's conduct towards me implied by them. Indeed, I had a right to expect that he would take advantage of any opportunity that might present itself of pushing my promotion, or of getting some military reward for me.

After the Battle of Saguntum it had been proposed that I should be appointed an officer of the Legion of Honour, and that my name should be put in the general orders. But it was replied that the major commanding the regiment that day was merely a knight of the order, and he was the right person to be named for officer, and as to putting me in general orders, no answer was made and it was not done.

Without any bitterness, for I can truly say that I felt none, even at the time I speak of, I must point out that Major Saint-Georges, a good and brave officer, had performed but slight service on that day, and that by the force of circumstances; while I with one squadron only had repulsed the charge of the whole of the enemy's column, had rescued the battery they had just taken from us, taken the general in command, and five guns with their caissons.

Now a single one of these captures gave a right to some recompense. I had none, while M. de Saint-Georges was appointed officer in the Legion of Honour. Events of this kind often occur, and my mention of this is chiefly intended to forewarn my readers against the disgust that they may feel in similar cases, either in a military career or in any other. I may say that on this occasion the opinion of the army was expressed in a fashion that flattered me.

Afterwards it came to my knowledge that Marshal Suchet had proposed me for a grant of forty pounds a year, secured upon property seized in Spain, that is to say upon the bogs and marshes of the Kingdom of Valentia, a thing which had it come into operation would have suited me but badly. Still later, when the marshal was dead, and his wife had his *Memoirs* printed, she sent me a copy with the splendid atlas engraved for it.

The contradictions in what passed between the marshal and myself have never been explained to me; but it seems evident that his wife had heard him say something on the matter, since several years after his death she thought of doing me a favour that was not granted to many.

General Boussard had made it a condition of his sending in my request to be dispatched to France, (a necessary form according to the gradations of rank), that I should let him have my Polish horse, as he had admired it very much at a review. I consented, on condition that he would return it to me when I came back; I entrusted my fine Norman mare to my friend Scarampi, and only took with me the wild mare I had had in Poland, and a little Navarrese horse that had been taken, and for which I had paid very dear. They were both good animals, but of much lower stature than is required for the *cuirassier* service.

I parted with the other two with great regret. These excellent horses had done me great service, perhaps had saved my life, and at the time I write this the remembrance of them is as fresh as if they were before my eyes. They knew me and loved me, and when I was riding them they did anything I wanted, without my having to think how to make them know it.

These particulars may seem childish to some, they certainly will not to any who have seen service as mounted men, and shared with their chargers such dangers and fatigues as fell to my lot for several years.

To my great disgust, I had taken charge of a sum of three hundred and twenty pounds for conveyance into France for Colonel Millet of the 121st Regiment of the Line, who was a Norman; also of a sum of ninety-six pounds that was sent by a colonel of artillery to the Marquis de Saillant. So, I had a sum of more than four hundred pounds in gold in the cloak-case upon the horse my servant rode; these two commissions entailed a moral responsibility that did not fail to cause me much anxiety upon the road. This unhappy cloak-case could not always be under my eyes, though its weight betrayed that it contained a considerable sum of money.

There is not a single piece of furniture with a lock to it in Spanish houses, and while I was busy on duty during our march, the cloak-case had to remain alone in a room open to all the world, and be laid on the ground whenever we camped out; and this in the midst of undisciplined elements collected from all sorts of corps, French, Poles, Italians, Neapolitans, and very few officers to control them and keep them in order.

We had a long line of vehicles, and baggage of all sorts, and marched thus to Saragossa quite left to ourselves. I had charge of the advanced guard, and we arrived without impediment. General Rey, commanding at Saragossa, took six thousand men, cavalry and infantry, and escorted us as far as Jaca, without our having to encounter a single attack. We crossed a kind of desert strewed with many hundreds of skeletons. They were Poles who had died there a year before, on their way to join the army. It seemed to us that most of them had been killed after they had surrendered, for almost all had a shot hole in the skull. They were young judging by their teeth, and their want of military experience doubtless had been the principal cause of their defeat.

This melancholy spectacle gave occasion for some displays of rage against the Spaniards by our soldiers, and it was really difficult to restrain a similar feeling on thinking of the scene of murder that had taken place on this spot. All these skeletons were of dazzling whiteness, thanks to the heavy dews and the sun, the crows and the vultures had picked them so clean that an anatomist could not have scraped anything up with his scalpel. What a sad fate for these young men coming from the far end of Poland, to die just as they made their first steps on an enemy's land.

At Jaca I found the colonel of my regiment just coming back from being married. He was bringing a detachment of recruits and new horses with him. I dined with him, and gave him a splendid fish the *corregidor* had presented to me, with a trout pie and a couple of bottles of capital Bordeaux. This was the fruit of the commission the marshal had given me for him. The colonel had also invited Major Deshorties to dinner, commanding the fortress of Jaca and the Chasseurs of the Pyrenees, a bold and indefatigable force that had always kept open the passage of the mountains single-handed.

When the fish made its appearance on the table, it threw Major Deshorties into a state of surprise he did not attempt to conceal. He rather sharply asked the colonel where it came from, and if he knew the *corregidor*, because he was quite sure he had met two of the municipal servants, one carrying in great state a fish like the one before us and the other a basket covered with a napkin. I managed to give the colonel a hint, and he made an evasive reply to the first part of the question, and negative to the second. Commandant Deshorties cast a suspicious glance round the table that rested especially upon me, but I bore it well and that was the end of it.

During the journey we had made, I had become acquainted with a Corsican officer in the Neapolitan service. His name was Pompei, and be was brother-in-law to Marshal Sebastiani, having married his sister. Pompei had received an excellent education at the College of Saint Barbe at Paris; he had distinguished himself considerably, and was a major at thirty, he would have had a brilliant career had his health permitted him to continue in the service; but disease of the chest compelled him to return to France for care, and the Faculty of Paris being consulted, condemned him to retire.

Just after Jaca is the beginning of the rapid ascent for the passage of the Pyrenees, they are very narrow in this spot, as we were able to sleep at Oleron the same day at the foot on the other side. That is about eighteen leagues; we had been informed that a long halt would be made upon the summit, and I was enjoying the notion of getting there; for I had been assured that I should be able to see from there Spain on one side, and France on the other, as far as the eye could reach.

I saw nothing at all; Spain was covered by a warm thick vapour, and France concealed by an interminable succession of hills covered with pine trees. I gave Pompei an agreeable surprise by producing the Corregidor of Jaca's pie and two bottles of Bordeaux. We made an excellent breakfast twelve thousand feet above the sea. General Rey and his escort had left us the evening we arrived at Jaca, and we were then in perfect safety, with our foot already upon the soil of France.

On leaving Valentia, Pompei had received as arrears of pay and allowances to superior officers a sum of two hundred pounds in silver, and had no time or means to change it into gold or bank-notes. He put it into an oat-sack, tied up with nothing but a piece of cord, and cast upon one of the hundred vehicles that composed our train, and had, besides their proper burden, to carry any tired men who might come for a little rest.

Every evening when we came to a halt, in the midst of the inevitable tumult caused by the crowd of persons anxious to obtain accommodation for the night, it took a longer or shorter time to discover the vehicle that carried the sack, and the sack itself had often been unloaded without our knowing how or by whom. I told Pompei every day that it was quite certain he would only find the empty sack at last. He laughed, and said he thought it very likely. Well, at Oleron we counted the money, and to our great astonishment there was not a crown missing.

We parted at Pau—he to proceed to Paris by Toulouse and Limoges, and I to Normandy by Bordeaux and Tours. Taking advantage of the permission given me by Marshal Suchet to spend at my home the time required to organise the draft that I was to take back to Spain from the depot of my regiment, I gave over the command of my dismounted men to the senior of the two officers with me. I wrote to the major commanding the depot, and started off thinking that I was in rule; but I had not taken the War Minister into consideration, nor the timidity of the major. For he, fearing that he might be blamed, without telling me, reported that the detachment from Spain had arrived at Niort, but that the captain commanding it had left it at Pau, and gone to Normandy. Upon this a General Order was sent to the *commandant* of the Department of Calvados, to have me arrested and taken to Niort under the escort of a *gendarme*.

We were all together at Cossesseville at the house of one of my uncles, M. de Sainte-Honorine, my father's brother; and I was enjoying the happiness of being with my family, after an absence of two years, in perfect security, when I received a letter from the general informing me of the order he had received, and advising me to start for Niort without delay. It had to be done. So, I started, and on my arrival, I found an order from the minister placing me under close arrest for a month; and this, with the time consumed in travelling, reduced what I had to spend with my family to nothing.

I wrote to Marshal Suchet and to my colonel; and complained bitterly to the major of his want of tact with regard to me. He was a kind of stupid animal, without education, who was not difficult to take down, though he had an almost ferocious exterior.

Nothing was going on at the depot, because the Russian campaign was absorbing the attention of the War Office and causing the Spanish affairs to be neglected. Time passed and brought us to the month of October, when the twenty-ninth bulletin was received, and gave us information of the most fearful disaster that could crush an army, without the enemy's steel having had much to do with it. Every personal feeling in those who had French hearts was silenced by consternation, at least for the moment. Everyone was desirous of flying to the assistance of the comrades who were known to be encountering calamities that could not fail to fall upon them, in consequence of the damage done in a single night.

A few days after the arrival of this fatal news, a letter from the minister informed me that I had been ordered to be transferred, with my rank, to the 1st Regiment of Cuirassiers, the remains of them returning to the Rhine, and the depot being at Metz. The order was accompanied by leave for three months. This is an instance that displays the difficulties that a cavalry officer may have to meet with, however prudent he is. I had left with Scarampi my mare, on which I had reckoned as much as it is possible to depend upon a charger tried at all points, and he was to give her back to me when I returned to the regiment. I had sold my horse from the Ukraine to General Boussard, to induce him to send in an application for me to be despatched to France; and I had only my Polish mare and my little Navarrese horse, both of them too small for our service.

My *cuirass* and helmet remained in Spain. I required a totally new outfit in all this, just at a time when there was a scarcity of horses in France, and the smallest things in a soldier's equipment were not only of exorbitant cost, but very difficult to be got from the tradesmen, in consequence of the army having to be entirely re-organised.

When I reached Normandy, I searched the country over without finding a horse to suit me, and I was obliged to apply to a horse-dealer at Caen, and he sold me a mare at a very high price that had the qualities requisite in order to make a charger, but which had never been saddled or backed, and was besides very bad-tempered. And so, after having always had just the kind of horses to give the most complete confidence, I was going to find myself at the commencement of a most serious campaign with only one horse to meet the enemy, even when it was drilled, and that would take time. I started off my horses with my servant, and at the end of my leave I went to Paris to buy my outfit.

On reaching Metz, in the month of February, 1813, I found that I was the senior captain, and in command of the depot, as there was no superior officer present. This depot was made up of about five hundred recruits, who had to be dressed and drilled, and a small number of horses past campaigning work, but fit to serve for giving the first riding lessons; and, considering the number of young soldiers, this did not promise very good results. I set to work courageously; and, according to the orders I had received, sent off, in succession, to the army, all the superior and best drilled men of the depot. Horses were given them on their arrival in Germany, when they joined the head-quarters of the regiment, and the remnant that had returned from Russia.

It would be impossible to convey a correct impression of the life I led during these three months. All I can say is that I rose before day; only rested at meal times and at night. I spent all the rest of my time on the parade ground of the fort, or on the Champ de Mars, drilling men on foot and on horseback, and superintending the lessons given on the backs of the poor horses that were tired out, and astonished at being brought out in the ring so continually. A major from the Guards arrived in the month of May, and I gave over the command to him. A few days afterwards he received orders to despatch me to Hamburg, with all the disposable officers and men left at the depot; but as I had already forwarded all the best of them to the service squadrons, what I took with me was not select.

I marched with seven officers, most of them recently appointed from the *gendarmerie*; but there were two Belgians, men of education, Van den Berg and Kniff; both men of fortune, especially the latter, an only son, whose mother had offered a squadron of cavalry if her son might be excused from the sub-lieutenant's commission sent him by the Emperor. Van den Berg and Kniff were cousins. Van den Berg had passed through the Russian campaign and served with zeal and energy, in short, he was a good officer. Kniff had been *aide-de-camp* to the Prince of Orange, become King of the Low Countries, and was on the contrary a bad officer, serving much against the grain.

In order to go to Hamburg, we passed by Cologne and descended the Rhine as far as Wesel; but before we got there, as we started from Blankenheim, an accident happened to me that I may put among the tribulations I have experienced in my military career.

A fortnight after my arrival at Metz, in the previous month of February, I had been informed that my servant was coming in with my three horses, and two were said to be very handsome. Not being able to understand how that should be, I went to my quarters and met my servant coming out to me with a triumphant air, and he gave me a receipt for thirty-two pounds countersigned by the mayor of a commune in the Department de l'Eure, to bear witness that the above-named sum had been placed in the hands of the owner of a mare that was described in the document, as the difference in exchange of this mare against a little horse said to be Navarrese.

I gave a good scolding to the author of the above exchange, but there was no way of getting out of a bargain that was made a hundred leagues off, nor of leaving the mare on the hands of the man who made it—besides he had brought her to me with the best intentions, and I could not have replaced her. Besides, the three horses were in perfect condition after the long journey they had made. The new acquisition had a spavin that would reduce her value considerably in the market, but she was well shaped, and when I got on her back I found she was docile and very swift, and I afterwards ascertained that she had plenty of bottom.

Three months after this I was taking her to Hamburg with my two other horses, and on the road from Blankenheim to Cologne, the Norman mare I had bought at Caen, and was riding every day to complete her education, slipped, and strained herself so that she could not proceed on the journey. So, I was obliged to leave her, with my servant and the Polish mare, in a village in the Department de la Roër, where there was by good luck a veterinary surgeon.

It was necessary to have the position of my servant and two horses established according to law, so that they might come on to me, to arrange for their expenses, and to go on with some uncertainty as to their fate, an uncertainty that was necessarily caused by the prospect of events in preparation; we were going to have a coalition of the forces of Europe upon our hands, and had only an improvised army to oppose to them. With such serious expectations, I found myself deprived of two horses and a clever servant experienced in active service. But it was very necessary to harden myself against this difficulty and continue to march towards the appointed goal.

We took boat on the Rhine at Cologne to drop down to Wesel, and we arrived there the next day after sleeping at Düsseldorff. We had to land on the left shore at the foot of a steep and lofty bank. It

Cuirassiers at Hamburg

was night. There was considerable difficulty in making our horses step ashore from the boats, those of the officers only, as the men had none. In consequence of this landing, another accident happened to me that might have been serious.

I had just mounted, when my mare's hind legs which had become stiff by standing so long in the boat gave way, she fell upon me with all her weight, and rolled all along the bank towards the river, where she would have infallibly been drowned, had she not by good luck been stopped by a large oar that was laid flat and slanting with one end on the boat and the other on shore. It was very difficult to get her out of that position, but in the end neither she nor I was injured. But this did not prevent my reflecting that I was commencing the campaign under mournful auspices. From Wesel we went to Munster, Osnabruck, Bremen, and at last we got to Hamburg.

CHAPTER 11

The Formation of the 15th Cuirassiers

Hamburg was in the district of the *corps d'armée* under the command of Marshal Davoust, and my squadron assisted to make up a fresh regiment of *cuirassiers*—the other bodies for it had already arrived, having been drafted from the 2nd, 3rd, and 4th Cuirassiers. Two other regiments of the same arm made up of squadrons furnished by the other regiments, were also in process of formation at Hamburg.

As there had been no superior officer appointed to command the corps I belonged to, I was put in charge of it as senior captain. The three squadrons that had arrived before me had all this time been acting quite independently, and as a beginning it was necessary to put them in unison. We were under the immediate orders of General Dubois, whose heroic conduct in the Russian retreat had been the cause of a special general order for his appointment as general of brigade. I knew him by repute, he was an upright man, but hard, and generally found difficult to get on with. I went as usual to visit him on my arrival with my officers. He received me coldly.

I expected it, as I knew that he looked unkindly upon everyone connected with the old nobility. He spoke in terms the reverse of flattering of the three squadrons that had arrived before me, and of the necessity of reducing these various elements to a homogeneous whole, for he had been informed that this provisional regiment was to be finally constituted and to take the Number 15.

I set to work, I assembled the officers and addressed them to the best of my ability. I only knew two of them, both captains in the 4th Cuirassiers; they were the best, I gave out a carefully considered order, that I had endeavoured to put into clear language. As each squadron had come separately, and had only its regular number of officers, there was no regimental staff. One had to be made, and any materials suitable for filling the different posts had to be made out of the various elements at my disposal.

Van den Berg was active, clever, and might make a good adjutant-major, but he was only a sub-lieutenant. I procured his promotion to the rank of lieutenant, and the next day requested that he might be adjutant-major, which was granted. This favour made some of the lieutenants open their eyes, but I had asked it from knowing that, with the exception of a lieutenant of the 3rd Regiment named Baudot, whom I also caused to be appointed adjutant-major, there was not one of them who possessed the requisite qualifications. A paymaster had still to be appointed, and the vacancies caused by these nominations filled up; it was all done according to my presentments, and this gave me a good deal of influence.

I was not yet thirty, and the most part of the sub-lieutenants were older than I was, having almost all come from the *gendarmerie*. As for the captains, with the exception of two, they were very near the age for retirement. In the matter of soldiers, we had nothing but recruits, and I have already shown how these could not be by any means the picked men furnished by the last levies. However, the squadron from the 4th was an exception in having some old soldiers, and in almost all the sub-officers and corporals having seen service.

The centralisation of the accounts gave me much trouble; those of each separate squadron were far from being in order. The errors had to be ascertained, and a settlement come to that should prevent the responsibility falling on the new administration. The time that I had spent at Metz as *commandant* of the corps, and thus president of the council of administration, had made me familiar with all there was to do in my present position, and was very useful to me. As there was nothing heard as yet of horses being furnished to us, I pressed on the foot drill and manual exercise, for carbines had been served out to us.

I may here observe that the notion of arming *cuirassiers* with carbines, carried on a hook, with the trappings of light cavalry was quite senseless. On horseback and wearing the *cuirass*, it was quite impossible to make use of them; but the idea of an inventor had been taken up without the precaution of a trial which would have showed its impracticability. At a later time, another inventor, Colonel Voisin, suggested that the lancers should also have carbines given them; his idea was adopted without examination, and after all the expense entailed in carrying it out they were obliged to return the carbines. This sort of thing is always being done in France. Inventors, whoever they may be, are nearly sure of being believed at first on their own word, for there are always some people who make a profit out of change.

But to return to what concerns us; having no horses, and shut up in a place that might be invested and besieged, it was quite possible that the *cuirassiers* might be required to do duty on foot, and this really took place, even after we had received the horses.

In two months' time the regiment was as homogeneous as could be wished. The officers had come to understand that they formed parts of a whole that must never be divided, and *esprit de corps* made daily advances that were easily perceptible. I was scrupulously obeyed, and there were hardly any cases of punishment. The paymaster's office, under the control of the military superintendent, was regular and kept up to the day, foot drill had been so kept up that we could match with the infantry in moving and in the manual exercise.

Matters were in this state, when one fine morning I received orders to attend to receive a hundred and twenty horses in an hour's time, and at the same time to receive the saddlery necessary for the equipment of these horses from the stores, and so to mount the first squadron that they might start next morning at six o'clock, to go and do duty at the advanced posts on the Steckenitz, a little river that separated our army from the Prussian Army, about six leagues from Hamburg, and communicates at one end with the Baltic near Lubeck, and at the other end, with the Elbe. This river has only one name, but it is well entitled to two, for it runs in two quite opposite directions, one to the north-east, the other to the south-west.

On some maps the portion that runs towards the Elbe is given a different name, but I never heard it called anything but the Steckenitz in the neighbourhood. The two arms start from a common source in an impassable marsh; it may be seen from this description that this line of an extent of twenty leagues is easy to be held, and cannot be turned. It was said that the Russian Army was a hundred and twenty thousand men strong; we had forty thousand, including six thousand Danes, at that time our allies.

The strength of the Russian Army may be explained by the great desire of the enemy to get possession of Hamburg, where Napoleon had established his grand magazines, containing an immense store of food and ammunition, as well as a quantity of field artillery, besides the armament of the place, which was very numerous, and that of Harburg, held by us on the left bank of the Elbe.

So, the squadron to be mounted had to proceed to the banks of the Steckenitz, from which I have strayed a little. This squadron was the one I had brought from France, and was numbered the first. The notion of letting it go without me never came into my head, although my position as commanding the regiment and the orders of General Dubois would have justified it. But to remain behind when the squadron went to meet the enemy was unbearable to me, and I insisted so strongly on going that I obtained permission to give over the command of the regiment to the senior captain.

The hundred and twenty horses that had been given to me, after being received by General Dubois, a great connoisseur, and hard to please in such matters, were excellent in all respects; but they had never been ridden or even saddled, and, probably, not one of them had ever had anything but a snaffle in his mouth before. These were the horses we had to get in order in twenty-four hours and march with them, ridden by men, nine-tenths of whom had never touched a horse or worn a *cuirass*, except at the reviews on foot. It was an almost impracticable problem to resolve. Marshal Davoust, who was on the Steckenitz, would not have permitted any remarks; General Vathier was a milksop, always in a fright, and General Dubois himself, though very rough, especially towards his superiors, did not dare to make the least objection.

All the men of the first squadron spent the night in saddling and equipping the horses; that is to say that the officers, sub-officers, and corporals did the work almost entirely themselves, as the soldiers had not any notion of the way to set about it—especially with young horses, scared at the sight of the things placed upon their backs, and frightening the inexperienced men by their rough movements and the vast amount of kicking that took place, particularly when the crupper was put on.

I fancy that there cannot be many responsible cavalry officers who have had similar occasion for the sorrowful thoughts that I had that night, even in a long career. Everything that might produce a disaster before the enemy with such a troop came before my imagination. I could not see any power of attack in it or of defence, and the only means of avoiding disgrace was to get myself killed.

In the morning the bridles were put on the horses, and they were brought out one by one each with the man who was to ride it. He was hoisted up with a good deal of difficulty, as his *cuirass* was most embarrassing to him. At last, after an immense number of adventures, the squadron was drawn up ready to start. We were quartered in the suburb of Saint George, and on our way out we had to pass before the guards of the advanced fortifications, and they had to salute us.

I unfortunately thought of giving the order to draw swords, thinking that my men would do this much better at the halt than on the march. The blades issued from the scabbards fairly well together, but their glitter and the noise, that they made frightened the horses so much that they started off like a flight of pigeons, jumping about in all directions and getting rid of their riders, most of whom threw themselves on the ground, when they might have held on longer. At last nearly all were off, and the horses free to go as they liked, and excited by the banging of the stirrups against their flanks, and by the carbine remaining hung by the butt hook, they ran in all directions about the streets of the suburb of Saint George, where the scene took place, on a large open space planted with several rows of trees.

They could hardly be caught in two hours, but my men were picked up without a single serious injury and placed upon them as they had been some hours before. I sent word to the guards upon our line of march not to turn out for us, and I left Hamburg for the advanced posts. The late events had not been such as to cheer me; I had perceived smiles of derision and pleasure upon the faces of the inhabitants who had seen our misfortune, that had put me in a state of concentrated rage, and I thought of my soldiers of the 13th Cuirassiers, such good riders and so brave.

We marched, the officers, sub-officers, and myself on the flank, and kept explaining to the men how to sit their horses, and make use of the bridle and aids. It was settled that lessons should go on during all the marches, from the moment of mounting the horses till we set foot to ground; there was general willingness, but there was no time, and the consequences that might ensue from this want of time presented a desperate prospect in the immediate future.

We had come nearly two leagues without any fresh accident, when we met an officer of the general staff, bringing an order to countermand our departure for the Steckenitz. I mentally addressed most fervent thanks to Heaven for the evident protection accorded to me. We immediately returned to Hamburg, and in two hours were re-installed there. This short experiment had at least served to show me that though these horses had been so inconveniently frightened, they had no vice about them, and there would be no difficulty in training them. This incident had no further result, and in relating it my only view is to place on record one of the tribulations that may all on a sudden fall on the head of an officer, and cause him the sad thoughts I experienced.

At Hamburg things resumed their ordinary course, as far as concerned ourselves, with the addition of training for the horses, that I caused to be pushed forward actively. During the subsequent fortnight, the three other squadrons also received their horses.

The wide alleys of the Saint George suburb were our riding school, and always the whole day long the classes might be seen at the trot, with all the world looking on. In two months we obtained such a result that the Count de Lowendahl, grandson of the Marshal of France of that name, and Commissioner of the King of Denmark with our *corps d'armée*, came one day to see some combined movements that I was trying outside the fortifications, and seemed quite astonished. He told me that no one but the French could possibly have made such progress in so short a time.

Just now arrived Colonel Saint-Sauveur to take the command of the regiment. I had known him several years; he had entered the 6th Cuirassiers as captain after the Italian campaign of 1805, and had always seemed to like me; on becoming major in the 4th Cuirassiers, during the Prussian campaign, he had tried to get me appointed adjutant-major, and this would have been a good piece of promotion for me. He had a large fortune, and was son-in-law to Prince Masserana, Spanish Ambassador to France; he had served in Austria, and been Prince Schwartzenberg's *aide-de-camp*. He might be about fifty at the time he came to Hamburg, and was a very handsome man; he seemed delighted to find me there.

I made over the command to him, and told him everything that could be of any use to him, as well as my observations upon the officers. He approved of all I had done, and his first proceeding was to request that I should be promoted to the rank of major, this was warmly supported by General Dubois, but General Vathier, Commander-in-chief of the cavalry, received it very coldly and did not forward it.

However, we were at the end of November, the Battle of Leipzig had taken place two months before, and all communication with France was interrupted. Marshal Davoust all this time held the line of the Steckenitz, but it was clear he would soon have to abandon it, and return to France through Holland, if he could, or shut himself up in Hamburg. Each of these two courses presented considerable difficulties; the first would have been practicable with our thirty thousand men but for the great number of water-courses that we should have had to cross, where the passage would certainly have been disputed as well as that of all the other defiles. And then the Russian Army of General Benigsen, now before us, would not have failed to march on our traces.

It is true we might have gained a little distance on them by breaking any bridges we had managed to cross; but nevertheless, they would have caught us up in the end and forced us into action under unfavourable conditions. We were much below them in number, and besides an army that does not choose its ground, that still has the enemy in its rear, knows beforehand that whether victorious or vanquished it will be compelled to abandon its sick and wounded.

The other alternative that of continuing to hold Hamburg presented these difficulties; first the population, a hundred and twenty thousand, ruined by our occupation were in a state of exasperation against us; then the communications with Hamburg had to be kept up, separated from Hamburg by the island of Wilhelmsburg and two branches of the Elbe. A splendid wooden bridge united these two towns, across the whole intervening distance of two leagues, but for its protection it was necessary to hold the island of Wilhelmsburg, separated from other smaller islands, both up stream and down, by very deep branches of the Elbe, though not more than fifty yards wide at most. Now it was impossible to think of holding these secondary islands, and inevitable but that they should be occupied by the enemy, who were continually menacing our communications with Harburg.

Before the marshal abandoned the line of the Steckenitz we received orders to go and join him, and this time we issued from Hamburg with four large squadrons looking well enough, but yet not to be classed as very trustworthy cavalry. On reaching our destination, we were cantoned in villages where we could go on with our drill, which had been entirely left to me by Colonel Saint-Sauveur. It made considerable progress during the fortnight we spent there, thanks to a spacious plain with a soil that enabled me to manoeuvre among artificial obstacles that I had made to force the men to get command over their horses.

One evening we received orders to hold ourselves in readiness to start for Hamburg at a signal that would be given during the night. This signal was to be the firing of muskets all along the line, and the detonations of *fougasses* intended to blow up all the little bridges that united the two banks of the Steckenitz. These signals were made about two in the morning. Then the whole army marched upon Hamburg in various columns and by different roads, in consequence of the different positions held by the different corps. We were the rear guard to the infantry that marched with us, and in the earlier part of the march, this was contrary to the rules of war.

For several leagues the ground we had to pass was a marshy defile, the road was narrow and bordered by wide and deep ditches full of water, and it was often cut by great drains with weak wooden bridges over them. To add to this, we had a night in the beginning broken bridges, the enemy could not commence his pursuit for several hours after our start, and we got out of the place without attack, as we had marched very slowly; because the infantry were in front of us in this bad muddy road, and our horses often sank up to their knees, the day began to break when we came out upon a plain, enclosed by hills upon our right and marshes on our left.

We formed line facing the defile we had passed and waited for the infantry to take up their position on the hills and at the other end of the plain, where there was another body of infantry that had probably had to traverse a shorter road, or a better one than that by which we had come. So, we remained thus in position till the arrival of the first of the enemy's scouts, who showed themselves timidly at the opening of the defile and did not dare to advance. A few moments later we commenced our retreat, and when we had got orders we executed it in echelon, often fronting the squadrons in line, a manoeuvre much admired by the infantry crowning the heights, and able from that position to see a strong body of Russians whose near approach we did not suspect.

At the end of this plain we entered another defile, and went to a large village at a distance of four miles from Hamburg that was pointed out to us as a resting-place. There was a mansion there, the colonel lodged in it, and I went to spend the evening with a very pleasant party. Some very pretty women gave us some music, and a young lady had the politeness to sing in French, without the smallest accent, the romance,

Tu le veux donc, ô peine extrême,
Il faut t'obéir malgré moi.

I returned to my quarters about ten o'clock and went to bed. At eleven I was waked by the trumpets sounding to horse. In half an hour we were on the march to Hamburg. For the first time, snow fell abundantly, and the cold was intense. About one in the morning we reached the advanced works of Hamburg, and we were allowed to penetrate within the line of these works without difficulty; but this was not the case with the second line, and we could only find shelter within it. For military rules forbid the admission of any troops during the night into a place in a state of siege, and these were put in full force against us, though we were fully recognised, and entered into conversation with several staff officers of the place, who were called at our desire. We only got into the city at eight in the morning, after having spent seven hours tramping about in the snow, and with it falling on us without interruption. It was a dreadful night; for thirty-six hours we only had the few moments' rest I have mentioned above.

The promptitude of the Russians in pursuit of us arose from their conviction that we should be obliged to abandon the line of the Steckenitz, and shut ourselves up in Hamburg. After the Battle of Leipzig, the French armies, or rather their remnants, had recrossed the Rhine, and it had become impossible for Marshal Davoust to continue to hold the country. And for this reason, the Russians foreseeing the movement of retreat that we had just accomplished, had prepared all possible means for making this retreat as disastrous as possible. The able dispositions of Marshal Davoust, notwithstanding the partial error I have mentioned, caused their project to fail, and we reached the spot intended without having lost a man, or left a cannon or anything of any kind behind us.

We were again established in the Saint George suburb. I had given up my quarters to Colonel de Saint-Sauveur, and was lodging with a coffee-house keeper named Beher, who, in consequence of the state of affairs, had closed his establishment, and boarded the colonel and me.

The duty roll was set out, and to me was entrusted the defence of a bastion washed by the lake that is the boundary of Hamburg on one side. In case of attack we were to make use of infantry weapons, as on occasion is done. The corps of ten thousand Danes that were with us as auxiliaries, proposed to be shut up with us within the fortifications, but this generous offer was not accepted, and these brave men whose conduct had been always exemplary returned to their country. Afterwards when Denmark was compelled to enter into the coalition of the allied powers, this same contingent of ten thousand men preferred to be sent to the Rhine rather than to be employed against us, after having been our brothers for nearly a year.

The force that shut itself up in Hamburg consisted of thirty thousand men, all French, except the remains of a regiment that had been raised in Lithuania during the Russian campaign. These Lithuanian *chasseurs*, about a hundred in number, almost all belonged to the nobility. After the duty-roll had been set out, which did not take long, as the organisation was in existence before on paper, the first care of Marshal Davoust was to appoint a commission with the duty of examining the supplies.

I was one of the five members of this commission, and it ascertained that for our thirty thousand men there were eighteen months wheat and flour, salt meat for two years, and an enormous quantity of wine, rum, and brandy; all this was of excellent quality and in a perfect state of preservation.

For the four thousand horses of the artillery and cavalry there were oats in similar proportion, but unhappily it was by no means the case with regard to forage. The hay had been badly chosen and stored carelessly, it had become damaged, and the greatest part of it was thrown into the Elbe. As there had been no want of time or money, and there are immense resources of this kind in the country round Hamburg, the marshal held a court of inquiry, and on its report brought the agent before a court-martial that found him guilty, and he was shot. He was the father of a family, and intercession was made to obtain his pardon; the marshal was inexorable, and the poor man was executed. It was only justice, but I considered myself fortunate in not having taken a part in the examination of the forage, since it led to his condemnation.

The abundant supplies of every other kind we found under our hands came from the Emperor's orders to lay in a store of provisions at Hamburg, as in the event of the defeat of the allied armies, he would probably have taken it for one of his bases of operation, in order to march on the Vistula—increasing his forces by the garrisons of the strong places on the Oder, and of Dantzig, that he would also have set free. In such an event the magazines of Hamburg would have provided all possible supplies. There were also medicines of all sorts, and all kinds of dressings required for a large army; the hospitals had been organised with extreme care. In short, in our impending position, we were sure that we should not run short of anything, and that is very unusual in a besieged or even blockaded place.

We were in this latter case, a few days after our return. General Benigsen was then in command of a hundred thousand men, and he threw a corps on the left bank of the Elbe, and took possession of the

Cuirassiers pass Napoleon

islands that both up and downstream flanked the island of Wilhelmsburg, a place that we had to keep in our hands at all cost, as our only
means of communication with Harburg, being placed in a state of
defence and provided with a sufficient garrison.

I was placed on detachment on the island of Wilhelmsburg with a
squadron, and under the orders of the colonel of the 30th Regiment
of Infantry, who occupied the part nearest to the bridge. I was in front
of him, along the northern canal, and separated from the Russians by
this canal, about a hundred yards wide at most, and this ceased to be
a barrier when the frost made the ice bear, as happened almost immediately.

I and my men occupied two or three farms situated at the foot of
the embankment, and I found some forage there, oats and food were
sent me from Hamburg. Our presence was very inconvenient to the
poor inhabitants, but nevertheless we made their acquaintance in a
few days, and harmony was established.

In a position so much in the air as mine, the greatest vigilance, and
the most minute precautions were indispensable to avoid a surprise. It
would not have taken more than a minute for a column of the enemy,
lying in wait on the other side, to reach me. Night and day, and especially at night, was it necessary to be on foot, to be scouting, to see that
the sentries were not going to sleep, that the number of horses with
their bridles off was not beyond the proper number, and to watch that
the men detailed for any service in case of attack were always ready.
From time to time I had the alarm sounded, and had arrived at great
speed in the turnout.

My daily intercourse with the colonel of the 30th Regiment
placed me in a position to appreciate him. He was a capital man,
very brave, with a good knowledge of war, and had received a good
education. His name was Pierre, and he lodged at the house of a ship-
builder who had one of eight hundred tons upon the slips in his yard.
When I could get away from my post without risk for a little time,
I took advantage of it to go and see the colonel, and he on his side
visited me frequently. This was almost the only distraction I had from
the necessary occupations of my post.

One evening, after a stay of a month in the island, my attention
was attracted by an unusual noise among the Russians. This noise kept
on increasing, and soon interpreted itself into irregular songs, hurrahs,
and a most infernal disturbance. It was natural to suppose that this was
a signal for an attack, as the Russians generally had a distribution of

Siege of Hamburg

brandy before an assault, and it made them very cheerful.

I galloped off to Colonel Pierre to inform him of my observations. He was out of doors listening, and also expecting that the night would not be concluded without an attack upon us. When we had agreed what to do if this expectation was realised, I returned speedily to my post, having given orders that everything should be ready by my return. We spent the night with our arms through the bridles, but without any idea that it was likely that the attack would take place before the hour preceding daybreak.

In reality, about six in the morning shots were fired from different points around the island to give the signal; and then, sure of what was going to happen, according to my orders, I began my retreat upon the bridge-head on the Hamburg side. Having remained behind alone to be able to satisfy myself about the march of the column that was evidently coming in my direction, I very soon saw it come out upon the canal almost opposite to the farm I had just left. It could be seen trailing its length along the snow, like a great serpent. It crossed the dike that I was on, between the farm where my servant and two horses still were and my point of observation, and descended on the ground all intersected with drains and ditches, as is the whole surface of the island within the numerous dikes that protect it from the overflowings of the Elbe. I thought that my servant and horses were lost; but he let the column go by—not one man entered the house—came after us, and joined us.

I had quitted my post of observation to go and inform Colonel Pierre what I had seen. I met him advancing along the canal, with three companies of *voltigeurs*. The rest of his regiment had been left by him to take up its position on a spot that would probably place it in front of the column that I had seen; but encountered another marching parallel with the dike to get to the bridge, and in the firing, that ensued, the poor colonel was killed by a ball through his head.

The adjutant-major, who was with him, told me that he had intended to fall on the column in the direction I had told him, in rear or in flank, and this would probably have caused the defeat of this column; for an attack of this kind, especially at night, is just the thing to demoralise the best troops. I regretted the good colonel sincerely; all his words and actions seemed to be pledges of loyalty and honourable feeling. The evening before, he had talked to me of his wife and two daughters with such great tenderness and such a desire to see them again, that I had been deeply moved. This need of sympathy probably resulted from the presentiment that he was going to be for ever lost to those whose remembrance thus filled his heart.

I thought of the sorrow of these three ladies when they should learn the sad and glorious end of the brave colonel, as he seemed to be such a kind husband and father. The time when they could learn their loss was far distant, as for more than two months all communication with France had been stopped, and five more passed before it was resumed after the peace and the restoration of the Bourbons to the throne of France.

I had directed my march towards the bridge, and I found half a battery of artillery in position there, just at the spot where it met the dike I had traversed, and where it was interrupted. At that place there was a sloping way constructed as a descent to the short piece of paved road that separated the two portions of the bridge; which was, as I think I have before said, of peculiar construction, across the marshes of the island, and about six miles long. The battery of artillery that I joined was under the command of a young captain whom I knew a little, and his name was M. de Marcillac.

I made my *cuirassiers* move in file as far as a double dike, and drew them up in line behind it. I was able to bring them down from the bridge by a lateral slope, such as are to be found all along the bridge to give access to any ground that has any chance of being useful for some purpose or another.

When this was done I returned to M. de Marcillac, as his guns had only the gunners and no supports, and I persuaded him to lay one of the guns for the angle of a house about a hundred paces off along the dike that I had come by, masking the prolongation of the dike, for it made a turn there. I was sure that anything coming from that side would be an enemy.

There was firing exchanged in several parts of the island, and it seemed evident that the Russians were making progress on the side opposite to that I had held, where was the fourth squadron of my regiment. Day had not yet broken when a dull sound on the dike revealed to us the approach of a column, and its head soon appeared on the snow at the angle of the house that the gun was laid for and loaded with grape. It was fired at once and had such an effect that the column retired, leaving a considerable number of dead, and probably having a quantity of wounded to judge by the cries of pain that we heard.

If this column had been led with resolution it must have easily taken the battery; in order to do so, it would only have been requisite to rush on at the double after receiving the fire of the gun, and it was so near that there would have been no time to reload or to bring up another instead of it. Some skirmishers were placed behind the house and the dike, and poured an ill-directed fire upon us, but one ball hit M. de Marcillac and carried off a finger of his left hand, forcing him to retire; then the half battery came under the command of a quartermaster, and though in strictness not obliged, I thought it my duty to remain with it at such a moment.

Besides my presence was not without its use, for the day was just beginning to break, and as the quartermaster could just see a grey line at some distance he sent a shot at it and was going on, when I remembered that this must be the position of our 30th Regiment, and would not let him continue. It really was the 30th Regiment, and the shot had struck three men, one of them a sergeant, and mortally wounded all three. Such misadventures occur too often in war.

I received orders to return to Hamburg, and the infantry alone continued the struggle on ground where cavalry could not act; but I was considerably pleased after our retreat was accomplished. I have mentioned that our fourth squadron was on the opposite to that occupied by me, and it had its line of retreat cut off by the Russians in force on that spot. The captain in command, De Bousy, a Belgian, boldly flung himself upon the mass that disputed his passage, and crossed it under a sharp fire that however only killed five of his horses.

This arose from the enemy being surprised at the vigour of the attack, and desirous of escaping from the shock of the horses on the road and the sword cuts, they flung themselves right and left upon the ice of the ditches that lined the road, fired upwards from below, and being much afraid of shooting one another their aim was the more uncertain. Captain De Bousy was splendid, he was a very handsome man, and the animation produced by the action and the feeling of danger gave his countenance a superhuman expression.

He and his squadron reached the place when I was in the greatest disorder, and the *cuirassiers*, proud of their first exploit, might be considered veterans from that day. The fire dismounted men believed to have been lost, found means to get away, and joined us a quarter of an hour later.

Two hours after midday the Russians were repulsed on all points, and the island entirely evacuated by them. Their efforts to take possession of the bridges were renewed several times with great fury, and they even succeeded in setting fire to one of them, but it was quickly put out and the damage barely anything. At the beginning of the attack they had set on fire the fine vessel on the stocks near the house that Colonel Pierre had occupied. Such a blaze cannot be imagined unless it has been seen; the flames seemed to reach to heaven, and the sound of the guns they shed a lurid light over the scene of the conflict.

Next day I returned to see the scene of action. It was a sad sight, but very interesting, as it enabled me to distinguish the means employed for attack and defence. I found my hosts at the farm in great affliction, a young girl of sixteen that took care of their child of a few months' old, had been so scared at the noise of the fight that she lost her head, and ran away carrying off the child, probably without knowing what she was doing or where she was going. They were both found dead a hundred paces from the farm, the same shot had gone through both their breasts.

On our return to Hamburg we were again occupied in instructing the men and horses, as it had been suspended during the time we were in the island, for there was no ground for exercise in it.

The neighbourhood of the fortress on its most exposed side had been inundated, and this had been turned by the frost into a vast plain of ice, and every day this ice was broken for a space of two yards near the most advanced works.

It was immense labour from its great extent, and the cold of each night would have rendered it useless unless repeated every morning. During these interminable Winter nights, the enemy made many attempts to get near us and take us by surprise, but was always repulsed.

These demonstrations compelled us to get under arms in an icy cold; the men were roused from sleep and had to encounter a transition from warmth to a temperature of more than twenty degrees of frost, and so the hospitals were soon crowded, and the mortality became so great that about a hundred men were buried every day. It was a sad sight to see the waggon going its rounds to take up the dead and carry them to the common grave always open, when the corpses were thrown in naked and remained exposed to sight.

This grave was dug in the ditch of the town, and was far from any frequented place; but the soldiers went there from curiosity, and these melancholy walks contributed to bring on the home-sickness that helped typhus fever to decimate us. I have been present at many death-scenes during the visit to the hospitals that was incumbent on us both from duty and humanity.

The Colonel and General Dubois kept on sending up my name

with their recommendations for the rank of major; but Marshal Davoust, who never hesitated to exercise his right of appointment to any office up to and including the rank of captain, did not care to make superior officers, and my nomination remained in suspense. While this was going on, I was given command of an expedition that by the rules of war should have been entrusted to a colonel at least. There was a village between Hamburg and the Russian headquarters, and not far from the latter, that was occupied by a post of Cossacks. The marshal had been informed that this village contained a large quantity of excellent forage, and I received orders to go and bring it away.

It was a service of difficulty, for if the Cossacks who held the village did not make any serious resistance, it seemed likely that when they fell, back upon the headquarters with its great collection of troops, they would very speedily return with forces sufficient to force the foragers to retreat, and that under very dangerous circumstances. A map of the country was given me, and our four squadrons. It was a great mark of confidence reposed in an officer of my age, for the capture of four squadrons in this perilous expedition would have been an irreparable loss to our army from its deficiency in cavalry; so, I very seriously felt the responsibility that would rest on me.

A fog, the thickest I ever saw, filled the air; when I left Hamburg, nothing could be seen three paces off. After marching a quarter of an hour, I found one of our battalions, with two guns, established on the bank of a stream that was large enough and considerably embanked, that I had to cross. A temporary bridge of beams and planks had been constructed. The major in command of the battalion, informed me that if I was driven in and pursued rather sharply the bridge would be taken up, and that he should fire upon me just the same as the enemy. I told him he must not put this threat into execution, and I crossed the bridge with two squadrons leaving two on the other side of the brook, with orders to come and join me in succession when they should see one of those that I had with me return laden with forage. Each horse was to bring as much as he could carry, and be led by the hand by his rider.

The road I followed was edged on both sides by deep ditches, and the ground near it was so much cut up by other ditches, and obstructed by the ice and the snow that was drifted by the wind, as to be impracticable even for infantry. My map showed me that beyond the village where my business lay the ground was quite open, and rising for some distance, then sloping gently down to the Russian headquarters; so, there was no fear of being turned either by the right or by the left during my operation, and all my attention might be concentrated on the only side that the enemy could come by. I had hardly a mile and a half to go to the destined spot, and my advanced guard could not see it till they got to the first houses.

I went sharply through the village, and stationed myself with the first squadron, so as to cover it from the enemy's side, while the second, after ascertaining that there were no more Cossacks left, were to dismount and tie up the forage with cords so that the horses might carry as much as possible.

I reconnoitred the ground for a few hundred paces in front of the spot I occupied, and I placed flying vedettes, for the fog would not have allowed them to see what passed between them if they had been only ten paces apart. I had warned my men that if we were seriously attacked we would charge home, without reckoning the number of the enemy, for the fog would be a perfect concealment to us, and we would stop after going three hundred paces, and return quickly to the village, placing it between the enemy and ourselves. I was certain of the effect that would be produced by this brisk movement, for supposing it to have taken place, in consequence of the fog the enemy could not possibly have perceived its extent all at once; and before he pursued us he would have wanted to reconnoitre the village to make sure that it was not held by infantry, as should in prudence have been done.

The foraging squadrons were to retire if they heard my trumpets sound the charge. After waiting an hour, we thought some force was coming upon us, though the sound was deadened by the snow. In a little while its skirmishers came in contact with my vedettes, and retired swiftly. I and the officers with me supposed that they were forming line at a short distance. Shortly the silence that had been kept till that time gave place to conversation, of a somewhat disputatious character, to judge by the tone. It was clear that they were not agreed, and I think I should have had a good opportunity had I fallen on them at this moment, but I did not want to diminish the success of my foraging, as it was going on admirably, thanks to the zeal displayed by officers, sub-officers, and *cuirassiers*.

At three o'clock in the afternoon three squadrons started for Hamburg with such loads of hay as had never been seen. The horses' heads were the only part of them in sight, and the hay being wound up and made into very tight bundles, was hanging down to the ground and piled up in a mountain on their backs. I successively detached the four sections of the squadron that I had with me that they also might take up their load, and I remained alone with a trumpeter to give a signal if any cause for uneasiness should arise. None came, and when the last section sent to inform me that they were ready, I joined them, and we got into the city by nightfall.

This expedition was much talked of, and Marshal Davoust told General Dubois that he was going to appoint me major, and give me the command of the dragoons, a force of a few more than three hundred men of various regiments. But this promotion to a majority was still delayed.

As a determination had been come to not to place cavalry permanently on the island of Wilhelmsburg, it became the scene of the most painful duty that it had ever been considered necessary to impose on them. The island is irregular in form, and its southern extremity is terminated by a kind of tongue, surrounded by other islands, only separated from it by narrow channels, and these were at this time completely frozen, as I have said before.

The enemy, holding these islands, crossed as he pleased to the part of Wilhelmsburg I have just described. I may add that except the surrounding dike, and a road that led from the church to this dike, not a single horse could go upon the rest of the ground. It was ordered that a main-guard of a hundred horses should hold the tongue of land during the day, with a reserve of fifty horses near the church, and the rest distributed in small posts at the end of the road and along the dike. Now it happened, as was easy to foresee, that the first detachment that undertook this duty lost several men and horses, for the Russians mounted upon the dike cut off the retreat of some of the vedettes and small posts.

It was I, with fifty *cuirassiers* and fifty dragoons, who had to relieve this first attempt, and it was not encouraging. I studied the spot with the most minute attention, in order to arrive at an arrangement that should, as far as possible, secure me from the check experienced by the poor captain I had relieved, whom I had found in a state of great dejection. I retired the posts that had been established at pistol-shot from the Russians, and I ordered my vedettes upon the dike to keep up a continual communication between themselves instead of remaining in one spot, and to retire at a gallop, firing, if there was any serious motive for uneasiness.

The duty of this main guard lasted four days, and there was no chance of closing an eye for a single minute during that time, or of taking off *cuirass* or helmet; only ten horses at once could have their bridles off. It was most horrible weariness and it had to be borne for ninety-six hours. In the evening we left the position and the enemy came to take it up, and at daybreak we came to resume it. At first this gave occasion for some skirmishing in the evening and morning, if the place was not found to be evacuated soon enough; but both sides soon came to see the uselessness of these skirmishes, and time enough was given for retiring.

Every evening we went and took up our position beneath a battery that was established beneath one of the transverse dikes I have mentioned. Then the horses were sheltered in a kind of building open to all the winds, but the men lay in the open where no fire could be lighted, as it would have served as a beacon to the enemy, and the skirmishers sent out by night would have disturbed us considerably if they had been able to ascertain the exact spot where we were. It was already disagreeable enough to hear the whistle of the balls that might chance to hit us. We had to endure this in a cold of more than twenty degrees, with our feet on the hard snow, and sitting on trunks of pines which lay in considerable quantity about there, and which we had cleaned of the covering of snow, but there was enough left to render these uncomfortable seats exceedingly chilly. Four consecutive nights spent thus always sent men to hospital and horses to the infirmary.

We petitioned in vain for the main guard to be relieved every twenty-four hours. General Vathier de Saint-Alphonse, having the whole cavalry under his orders, would never mention it to Marshal Davoust, nor come himself to examine the dangers and fatigues both to man and horse of the situation they made us hold. A person must have felt this weariness and need of sleep to form an idea of it. After so many years the recollection is still painful to me; but it is with quite opposite feelings that I recall the warm room I returned to at Hamburg, and the bed where I could stretch myself and sleep.

General Vathier de Saint-Alphonse, during the seven months that we were shut up in Hamburg, never appeared at the head of any armed force, and never put on his uniform except to wait upon the marshal. He was to be found in his quarters all day long in dressing-gown and slippers, and in the evening, he went to the play in plain clothes. He had been made prisoner by the Russians in the Austerlitz campaign in this manner: he was colonel of the 4th Regiment of Dragoons, being part of the army under the command of Marshal

Mortier, operating during the Austerlitz campaign, in 1805, on the left bank of the Danube, while the mass of the Grand Army was marching on Vienna by the right bank.

Well it happened before Krems, a town on the Danube, that Marshal Mortier met a Russian corps much stronger than his own, which put him for a time in a desperate situation. On seeing this, Colonel Vathier secretly gained the shore of the Danube—left his horse—got into a boat that he found there, and pushed out into the stream to get to the right bank, as he knew it was already in the possession of the French. But he had not taken the strength of the stream into his calculation, nor his own want of knowledge of the art of navigation. He was swept down to the bridge of Krems, into the hands of the Russians, and was made prisoner.

Meanwhile, Marshal Mortier had recovered his position, with the help of a division of infantry that had been behind, and appeared at last on the field of battle; having also found means of bringing his cavalry into action, several charges, in which the 4th Dragoons were distinguished, completed the defeat of the Russians, and they were thoroughly beaten. Colonel Vathier's horse had been found, and he passed for dead for some time, but afterwards the truth was learnt from the Russians. However, as his regiment had been mentioned in the despatch, he was made general of brigade when the exchange of prisoners took place at the peace of Presburg.

I relate this fact to give an idea of the chances attending a military career, like all other careers: not the least from any ill-will that he showed me in respect of my nomination as major. If Colonel Vathier de Saint-Alphonse had not been coward enough to run away from the risks of the action at Krems, he might have been killed at the head of his regiment, while he did die General of Division, and I came under him as inspector in that capacity in 1821.

At Hamburg, he never would come to see the inutility of the position we were ordered to hold on the south of the island, and the species of barbarity that there was in requiring the same troop to hold it more than twenty-four hours—a most unusual course. On service, the frequent relief of the posts imposes on the enemy, through the movements that are caused by it; and a fresh and rested troop can keep a much more active look-out than one that is worn out by continual watching. At last the ice broke up on the Elbe, about the end of April, and the natural defences of the island relieved us from the painful duty that I have endeavoured to describe.

Marshal Davoust then considered it desirable to transfer all his cavalry to the left bank of the river. Before the frosts the two streams were crossed in two large barges that brought up to wooden slopes, so that the embarkation of men and horses was made as easy as if they were marching on the level, but at the time we were sent across it was impossible to make use of this method; the waters were swollen by the melting of the snow, and the Elbe was covered with drifting masses of ice that struck and grazed each other with a formidable sound. The look of the river in this condition made it impossible to believe that cavalry could be passed over it in small boats, and when we received orders to embark I thought that our passage would be marked by more than one catastrophe.

Each of the boats provided for us held four horses placed across, and four men standing between the horses' necks, for their hocks touched one side of the boat while their heads extended beyond the other. There were also three boatmen; two in the bow holding long poles with iron points, and one in the stern to steer; the two men in the bow pushed off the masses of ice with their poles, jumping on the large ones and keeping hold of the gunwale of the boat, making it pass round till a free space of the stream was reached; but the ice came down without interval, and a continual struggle had to be maintained against them, and also against the furious current that was taking the boat down below the only possible landing place—that is to say, one of the two wooden slopes that led to the bridge.

The horses were frightened at the noise of the ice, and especially at its appearance, when they were drawn up a little way from the boats. At last, after much labour and a long time, a thousand horses were safe on the left bank of the Elbe, without the occurrence of a single accident, and the boatmen of Hamburg, in this instance, justified their reputation for skill.

The object of Marshal Davoust was to dislodge the enemy from the villages that he occupied near Harburg, to carry off the forage and to burn the aforesaid villages, and this was done after giving the inhabitants time to remove their furniture, and especially their sick, who were very numerous. It was a sad sight, and I was not present at it, having been detached on the road to Bremen, for a corps of the enemy of unknown strength was advancing resolutely along it. A few cannon shots and our skirmishers served to keep them at a distance, and this did not amount to a serious engagement.

That day I lost my servant. Either he was captured by a party of

HAMBURG

während der Belagerung von 1813 bis 1814.

Sternschanze

Vor dem Ba...

Heiligengeistfeld

A L T O N A

Krankenhof

Reeperbahn

HAMBURGER BERG

Hornwerk

Blaue Hafen

ELBE

Norder Sand

Kuhwärder

Kleiner Grasbrock

HAMBURG

GROSSE ALSTER

Hohesfeld

BINNEN ALSTER

ST GEORG

HAMMERBROCK

Gänsebrook

Holz Hafen

Billbrook

Alter Holzhafen

Wilhelmburg

HARBURG

Cossacks, as he told me afterwards, (for I met him again) or he was frightened by the ill-omened rumours afloat in Hamburg, of the treatment in store for Germans in the French service when we should be overcome. He disappeared under the excuse of going to look for potatoes in a wood on our right, and never returned, nor, of course, the mare he was riding, and a very good one she was. I was grieved by the loss; this man had been five years in my service, he was very clever and very strong, he had followed me in Spain, in Italy, and in Austria, and though I had been obliged to blame him severely on one or two occasions, I felt I should not be able to replace him.

When I returned to Paris in 1815 he was a hussar in a Prussian regiment, and our meeting which happened in the Palais Royal caused quite a crowd there, for he rushed up to me and before I had time to see who he was, he seized my hands and kissed them with such transports that a crowd instantly formed round us, astonished at such an unusual spectacle. A Prussian hussar kissing the hands of a French officer in the open Palais Royal was indeed a fine story for the loungers.

We went back into Harburg, and made expeditions from time to time without much loss, for the enemy always retired at our approach. We had to send several foraging parties along the dike on the left bank of the Elbe upstream. This was a somewhat difficult duty, for the Elbe had burst the dike above the point we had to go to, and inundated the whole plain to a considerable depth, and this had caused some lamentable accidents. The muddy water of the river was running with great impetuosity on a level with the dike, and the Russians had planted a battery of four guns upon an island at a very short distance, and fired upon anything that made its appearance upon the dike.

I was again put in command of the regiment for these expeditions, and they took place at night. The men were ordered to keep silence, but it was very difficult to secure absolute obedience to this command sufficiently to keep our approach entirely concealed from the enemy; and so, we always had to receive some discharges from him. These results were not serious, for besides the protection of the darkness, we took care to make the men march in single file, with orders to keep a distance of at least a horse's length between them, and this gave a good chance for the shots to pass in the spaces left for them. Only one horse was killed, and a man had his leg broken by a musket shot.

But though there was not much danger to be found in these expeditions, I myself ran a risk, whence my escape seems quite miraculous. I have mentioned that the dike was very narrow, in a very dark night a little cannon that was being carried on men's shoulders was unexpectedly presented under the nose of my horse; he was surprised at this apparition, reared, and tried to fling himself on one side. The instinct of danger at the sight of the Elbe below him, and probably my efforts to prevent him falling into the river, caused him to make a prodigious effort to make a half turn, and get his fore feet upon the ground, but for a moment we were hanging over the void, above twenty feet of water running sharp enough to turn a mill. Wrapped in my cloak with all my military trappings there would have been no chance of escape, if we had fallen in.

I may here notice a fact insignificant in itself that, with others of the same kind, conduced to show what is often the real value of some military reputations. On the same expedition, there came behind my regiment the Provisional 2nd Regiment of Cuirassiers, led by a major whose bravery was cried up and who would willingly relate with great animation exploits of his own that were tolerably fabulous. The first time we marched together he came to me at the head of my regiment, and told me that if I would undertake to conduct the two regiments to their destination he would stop to see all our people pass, and ascertain that they were marching in proper order, and that he would join us afterwards.

There seemed no reason why I should not consent to this proposal, and it was made to me just at the moment when we were coming upon the narrow dike, and began to be exposed to the fire of the Russian battery. So, I led the two regiments to the spot, on a very small space surrounded with water, where I had all the trouble in the world to draw up rather more than eight hundred men and horses on a dark night and send them to forage in order.

As to the famous major he did not come; but as we returned, a peasant, belonging to a farm a little in the rear of the spot where our conversation had taken place, requested to speak to me, and told me that two soldiers had stopped at the farm as we went by the first time, and they had been taken so ill that they must be carried either in a carriage or on stretchers. These were the major and his orderly, who had gone into the farm, asked for something to drink and were dead drunk. I told the senior captain of the 2nd Regiment of the information I had received, and we left them there.

We made several expeditions to go and burn villages where the enemy was quartered, and obtained supplies. The marshal himself conducted these forays, and used to make harangues to the inhabitants telling them how much he regretted being obliged to come to this extremity. However, before setting fire to the houses, time was always given to carry off all their contents; but everything had to be taken into the fields, without shelter, and these poor people watched the burning of the roofs that had sheltered them all their lives from the weather.

We kept on having encounters, none of them serious, but almost daily. When the Elbe was free from ice that drifted long enough after the break up, for the frost did not yield till later in the higher parts of Bohemia and Moravia, the English also came to torment us. They ascended the river with gunboats, and when within range of Harburg, they turned round and fired from the large gun in the stern, keeping up this fire as they returned to their starting point; but this retreat was accompanied by the shot that the fort sent after them and that several times hit them.

Two sank in our sight, for we used to look on at this interesting sight. The boats that sank did not disappear; they made their way to the bank as soon as they felt that they were mortally wounded, and there they were heeled over till their masts and yards were secured upon the dikes still held by the Russians. Then men set to work to save their contents, an operation that it was necessary to carry on at night on account of the fire of the forts.

Strange rumours reached us, though we had no news from France. We had imperfect information that a great battle had taken place in the preceding month of October, and thenceforward we were in a state of uncertainty and perplexity, not knowing the result of this battle. So, our curiosity was very much excited by the faint reports that were in circulation; there was talk of the abdication of the Emperor, and the formation of a provisional government. At last the ignorance in which we were plunged ceased on the reading of the Order of the day by Marshal Davoust, the text of which I can remember.

The Emperor Napoleon has abdicated for himself and his son. The House of Bourbon again ascends the throne of its ancestors. Tomorrow the tri-coloured flag, wherever it is hoisted, will be replaced by the white banner with the ancient arms of France, and be saluted with a hundred and twenty-one guns. From this day forward the fortress of Hamburg will be defended in the name of His Majesty Louis XVIII.

This order was carried into effect in silence and with very different feelings. It would seem natural for the most part of the army to submit to it as a necessity, but it put an end to the anxiety that had been the fate of the garrison of Hamburg for seven months, and it presaged the re-opening of communications with France, and consequently the re-opening of family intercourse and affection that had been prohibited so long. It must have been felt to be properly imagined. I have mentioned that the order was executed in silence; indeed, the different ways of looking at the great event changing the position and destinies of France, and having its influence upon those of each person, did not permit of any manifestation.

As for me, the appearance of the white standard hoisted on a beautiful day, and tossed by a gentle breeze that waved its *fleurs-de-lys* re-awakened my ancient royalist feelings and the love for the House of Bourbon that had been inculcated into me from infancy, and that had caused my family so many sacrifices. Though a great admirer of the talents of the Emperor, I had never felt the devotion for him that he inspired in many; I should have felt myself proud at attracting his attention by some spirited action, without the smallest wish for him to have been its object in person. After his fall I felt more sympathy and attachment for him, without its going, be it well understood, so far as to make me desire his return to power.

The news of the peace followed immediately upon the order that I have mentioned, and there was at the same time a suspension of hostilities between the Russians and ourselves. There was an event that happened that gave opportunity for Marshal Davoust's enemies to accuse him to the new government, for a matter that in strict impartial justice should have rather brought him praise than blame. This is what it was.

When once the armistice was concluded the Russians put forth a pretension to establish themselves on the glacis of the fortifications until they should be handed over to them; but the marshal replied that he intended to keep his line of defence, and that if they did not act in accordance with his determination they should be fired upon.

It was a matter of simple conceit in the general commanding them, and to gratify it he thought that if he advanced with white standards the marshal would not dare to carry his threat into execution. In consequence, one fine morning, a line of white standards, followed by the troops in battle-array, advanced to take up the desired position. A volley of bullets fired at long range informed the Russians that they must not approach any nearer, and they took the hint; but General Benigsen did not fail to write to Paris that Marshal Davoust had fired on the flag of France, and he was much blamed for it. And yet this happened several days after this flag had been hoisted on the ramparts of Hamburg and saluted with a hundred and twenty-one guns.

The marshal was also blamed for having laid hands on the funds deposited in the Bank of Hamburg; the fact is true, but this pretended robbery only took place in order to furnish the means of paying the army and providing for the expenses necessary in our position, separated from France, and not having any possibility of communication with her. Besides this operation was performed in the most legal manner, by a commission composed of the superior servants of the said bank, notable merchants of the city, and generals and commissaries belonging to the army.

An inventory and valuation was made of all the property seized, the employment of them was carefully verified; but notwithstanding the material proofs of the most complete loyalty, the government did nothing to contradict the calumnies that had been heaped on him with a sort of zealous hatred. By this unjust and stupid behaviour, the Restoration alienated a man of consideration and of great influence over the army who would have served them faithfully, independently of his opinions and affections, because he was an honest man.

A few days afterwards we beheld the arrival of General Gérard, appointed to relieve Marshal Davoust of his command, and to bring the army back to France. This was a gratuitous insult to the person to whom the preservation of twenty thousand men in good order and a numerous artillery was due, in the midst of general disaster.

Five columns were formed to enter France by three different routes. My regiment was a part of the first to leave Hamburg; the departure of each to take place at intervals of two days. This column, besides my regiment, was made up of two regiments of infantry and three batteries; we brought back a hundred guns and two loaded waggons to each gun, the whole very well horsed.

I was appointed to march a day in front, with an adjutant-major and an adjutant sub-officer of each corps, with some orderlies. My duty was to arrange the daily cantonments, and continue to do this quite till our arrival in France, when the break-up would take place, as every corps was then to be sent to its appointed garrison. I found no difficulty as far as Bremen; but there, for the first time, we found ourselves in the midst of the allied forces, for the corps that had blockaded Hamburg had been collected on the right bank of the Elbe to leave the passage to the Weser free to us.

On our arrival at Bremen we found the garrison under arms; it was very numerous, and lined all the streets we had to pass along. This garrison was composed of Hanoverian forces in English pay, and it was an English colonel that commanded the place. I had to arrange with him for the lodging of my column. I was given the part of Bremen situated on the left bank of the Weser, and sufficient villages to make up our billets. We both put sentries on the bridge, to prevent communication between the troops of the two nations.

When we entered Bremen, we were in the proportion of twenty-five to thirty, and they had given us all military honours; the band of a regiment marched in front of us, and the troops carried arms as we came opposite to them; but behind the troops was a mass of furious people, ruined by the Continental system, and they did not spare us demonstrations of their hatred.

Among them figured, at least a third of the fifteen thousand inhabitants of Hamburg, who had been expelled for want of food and been received by the city of Bremen. From this, some notion may be formed of the reception that these people were inclined to give us if they had been free to obey their instinct.

However, all went well enough, though there was very near being an exception in my case. Having been obliged to cross the bridge alone, for a matter of duty that had not been quite settled with the English colonel, it was necessary to force a passage through the compact crowd of hostile persons, and I became the object of malevolence that would have turned out ill for me, but for the intervention of some Hanoverian *chasseurs* and some honest and, certainly, brave inhabitants.

The very natural emotion I felt at the bad position in which I found myself, was very soon altered by the anger I felt at the conduct of a very well-dressed man, standing on a door-step, with full command of the performance, and looking as if he applauded it, contemplating me with an insolent and ironical expression. If I had been able to get at him, I should have been glad to give him a buffet and have taken the chance of the consequences.

At Bremen I had a sharp altercation with General Guiton, commanding our column, as he sent for me after a dispute with the master of the house where he was lodged, and blamed me for not having selected his lodging with sufficient care. As this was entirely the business of his *aide-de-camp*, whom he kept with him instead of sending him to march ahead with me, as he should have done, I gave him roundly to understand, without going beyond the rules of discipline, that not only would I no longer take any pains to secure a convenient lodging for him, but that for the future I would not concern myself with it at all.

I had already been under this general's orders when I rejoined the 6th Cuirassiers after General d'Avenay's death, as that and the 4th composed his brigade. As colonel of the 1st Cuirassiers he had been a member of the court-martial that sentenced the Duke d'Enghien; and so, his thoughts were sad enough on the return of the House of Bourbon to power. He was a very vulgar man, without education, and his advancement to the rank of colonel had taken place in the early days of the Revolution. At the time I speak of he was old and very inactive. After our return to France I completely lost sight of him.

Leaving Bremen, we marched by Osnabrück, Holern, and Darstein, upon Wesel, where we passed the Rhine. During all this journey our reception by the inhabitants everywhere was very good. They pushed their courtesy so far as to desire that billets should not be issued for lodging or food. The villages where we were to lodge sent deputations to the spot where the column was broken up; and each deputation took possession of the troops appointed to go to their quarter, guided them, and on their arrival each head of a house took with him as many as he could put up, and feasted his guests as best he could; and so, during this long march not a single complaint was made against the soldiers of this column, and on their side, they had not a single insult to repress.

It seems to me to be an act of justice to speak highly of the German population of this country, for they had suffered cruelly by their annexation to France, both through the conscription, and through the passing of troops that had been a crushing burden to them. In this instance they displayed magnanimity, for though we individually had not been conquered, France had lost all her power, and with the support of the allied forces surrounding us on all sides, the inhabitants might have behaved very badly to us without our being able to ask them the reason why.

We crossed the Meuse at Venloo, and were equally well received by the Belgians, they were still uncertain what was their destined fate, and generally expressed to us their regret at not continuing to belong to France, all haste having been made to inform them on this point. When we arrived at Wesel, each of the bodies composing our column was sent in a different direction, ours was Lille, passing through Louvain and Ghent.

At our first stage from Venloo, I was informed that a Belgian who had served in one of our dragoon regiments had deserted from it, carrying off three of his captain's horses, whose orderly he was, and that he was living in this place, and had got out of the way on our approach. Next day, after we had started a quarter of an hour, the guide I had received to conduct me to the place of meeting, told me that a man to be seen talking to a woman at the door of a tavern was the stealer of the three horses. I instantly gave orders for his arrest; but just as one of the two corporals that I had sent on this duty was going to seize him, he darted on one side, jumped a ditch, and ran into a field of wheat.

The corporal followed him there, and as he could not induce him to surrender, he knocked him down with a blow of his sword on the head. We took hold of him, dressed his wound, which was not serious, tied him and handed him over to the advanced guard, my intention being to have him taken to the regiment he had left, to be tried there. As we passed through Belgium in the middle of the allied troops, the presence of this man in irons and with his head tied up, did not fail to cause me some trouble. Colonel de Saint-Sauveur having got leave to go to Paris, I was in command of the regiment.

At Ghent we found the gates shut, and we were made to wait four hours before they were opened; this arose from the omission to make military preparations for our passing through this great city. While we were waiting, some of my men had a quarrel with those of a guard outside the walls, and drove them away. I was considerably uneasy as to what the results of this accident might be, not being informed of it till too late to interfere.

At last we were allowed to come in. The whole garrison was under arms, and lined the streets for the whole distance we had to pass through this enormous city. In the open spaces guns were ranged; it might be supposed that Ghent and its numerous garrison thought the passage of four squadrons was a considerable risk.

When we got to Denain, near the frontier, four leagues from Lille, we received the order for breaking up, sending the four squadrons that composed the regiment that I was bringing back to their respective corps. Mine, in consequence of its number being the first, was required to make a part of the provisional guard of the new sovereign, Louis XVIII, and so I went to Paris.

Before we left Denain I had the mortification of losing my prisoner, for he found means to make his escape during the night. I severely punished the corporal commanding the guard where he was placed for safe custody. This corporal probably was no stranger to his escape, and ought to have had more than a regimental punishment.

CHAPTER 12

Arrival at Paris

I found Paris crowded with petitioners besieging all the offices. Marshal Davoust not being in favour, all his acts were strictly inquired into, and especially the promotions he had made in his army. Mine to the rank of major was questioned, while promotions of all sorts were showered upon persons who presented very delusive claims, but Marshal Suchet interfered in my favour; I was confirmed in my rank, and put on the strength of my regiment, which, as I have said, did duty for guards. I was not to remain long in it.

I met General Bruslart in Paris, formerly *aide-de-camp* to the Duke d'Enghien; he had always followed the fortune, or rather misfortune, of the house of Bourbon, and given them numerous proofs of devotion. Having been Chief of the Staff to the Royal Army of Normandy at the time of the Civil Wars, he had been successor to Count de Frotté in the command of that army, when he with seven chiefs under his orders was shot at Verneuil through an infamous act of treachery.

A short time after this event, the Royal Army having sent in its submission to the Government, M. de Bruslart signed it, excepting himself personally in a very haughty letter, which he wrote to the First Consul Bonaparte; he reproached him for what had taken place at Verneuil, though perhaps in strict justice the responsibility should fall on General Chambarlhac, as he directed and precipitated the events in question, in hopes that he would get credit for having acted on the principle there shown; that there are punishments that an adroit sovereign never orders, but by which he profits, and sets them down to the credit of the actors.

If this calculation was made by Chambarlhac it had no success, for thenceforward he disappeared from the scene, was never employed in the armies of operations in the glorious campaigns that followed, and finished his career in obscurity, in command of a division in the country. So, he was most likely blamed for the useless crime he had laid on his conscience, and it was probably owing to his good intention that he was not entirely disgraced.

My father had taken an important part in the war in Normandy, and I myself, though quite a child, had been entrusted with such commissions as I could perform, for my youth put me out of the range of the supervision of the government agents. So, I was privately known to General Bruslart, and he being appointed Governor of Corsica, and newly come to the army, was desirous of having a person who had been a long time in the army, to be intermediate between him and the troops he would have under his orders; he proposed to me to go with him as his Chief of the Staff, an office vested in the rank of Colonel, and he intended to ask for this rank for me.

Even if I had not esteemed General Bruslart so highly, the proposition was too advantageous to be refused; but besides the value of my promotion, I felt a lively satisfaction at being under the orders of a man whose loyal and chivalrous character had inspired me with a veritable enthusiasm, at the time I had known him, braving with the gaiety of a hero the dangers surrounding him every minute—for a price had been set upon his head.

And I was by no means sorry to leave my regiment, for the new colonel did very improper things in the administration of it, taking advantage for that purpose of the want of supervision inherent in a change of government under such extraordinary circumstances. So, I accepted the offer, and the War Minister did not raise objections when the request was made for the rank of colonel for me, but he wished to see me before giving his final determination.

I had an appointment with him, and was very well received. It was the General Dupont to whose headquarters I had been conducted by the Count de Moltke on leaving the fort of Pillau, when I had been prisoner to the Prussians. He invited me to breakfast, placed me by him, and talked a great deal to me; then he took me into his private office and told me that I should have the rank of colonel given me in two months at farthest, but that he preferred to send my appointment when I had gone to Corsica, on account of the claims he had to contend against, that would make my early promotion a support to the requests for similar favours, while when I was at a distance the matter would not be noticed.

I thought it my duty to give way to these kind words, spoken with so much confidence; but I was wrong not to insist, for in the minister's temper he would have yielded, especially if I had reminded him of our former interview on the banks of the Passarges. Now in six weeks' time he was no longer minister; and Marshal Soult, his successor, showed himself very much disinclined to grant promotion; so, my rank of colonel was deferred to a future occasion yet to be narrated.

I was appointed chief of a staff made up as follows, M. de Lamberville, colonel; d'Esparbès and de Perrin, lieutenant-colonels; de Boishulan and Galloni, majors: Grosson de Truc and my brother Félix de Gonneville, captains. My brother had not been in the service under the Empire, but he had just been made captain in recognition of the services rendered to the Royal cause by my father.

Besides the persons I have mentioned, General de Bruslart had two *aides-de-camp*, de Beausac and Louis de Lanet. Such a numerous staff had never before been seen in Corsica. Unhappily the general had also five or six persons attached to him, who, having done him some personal service, had adhered to his fortunes, and he paid their expenses. Among them there were several whose conduct and language disgraced him considerably in the country.

As soon as I was appointed chief of the staff I set to work to study Corsica. My experience as *aide-de-camp* had already initiated me into the duties I should have to perform, the *Manual of a Chief of the Staff*, by General Thiébault completed my education and after a month's stay at Toulon, detained by contrary winds, I became nearly certain that I should be able to do the business.

I had been fortunate enough to find a map of Corsica on a large scale at Paris, perhaps there is not another of the same dimensions made yet; and yet more, by the energy of Boishulan, who knew one of the new heads of departments in the War Office, I got a manuscript report on Corsica. I fancy it was the only one in the archives of the War Office, for many copies of the same work are not usually to be found there. So, I obtained a perfect knowledge of the localities, and this to begin with, raised my position in the eyes of the inhabitants, for they are more vain of their country than could possibly be supposed, and think a great deal of any information that a person has about it.

My position would have been anomalous towards the greater part of the officers of my staff; for three of them were my superiors in rank, and two held the same, if there had not been the advantage on my side of having seen service, and the habit of commanding soldiers, while they, newly admitted into the army by the Restoration, had never had, or had entirely lost all military tradition. The general's *aides-de-camp* were in the same case, and that immediately gave me an influence that no one disputed, and I found equal obedience in the officers of higher rank to that I did in the others.

A young Corsican on half-pay had been attached to my predecessor as secretary; I kept him in the same position. He was perfectly acquainted with the office work in all matters concerning the reports of condition to be sent to the Ministry, and he had been recommended to me as an intelligent and honest man, and I found this to be the case.

We had landed at Ajaccio on the 13th of November, 1814, after having had to encounter a fearful storm. We were received by General Cesar Berthier, whom General Bruslart came to relieve. He gave us a grand dinner, and was very amiable, but all the time much annoyed; for the Emperor had placed him in a splendid position, pecuniarily, in Corsica to get rid of him, and in consideration of his brother, the Prince of Neufchatel. Besides his appointments as General of Division, he had four thousand pounds as table-money, and lived at Ajaccio with a population of six thousand souls, not one of whom had an income of two hundred and forty pounds a year.

Till then Ajaccio had been the capital of the country, but we were ordered to transfer it to Bastia. In the existing state of affairs, besides its importance as a town, it was right for much more weighty reasons that Bastia should for the future be the residence of the military chief of Corsica, as he had special charge to keep watch over the island of Elba. This island, as is well known, had become the abode and kingdom of the Emperor Napoleon, and a brig of war had been left to him, named the *Inconstant*, with a full crew and officers chosen by him.

The naval station, under the orders of General Bruslart, was composed of the frigates *Fleur-de-Lys* and *Melpomene*, the corvette *Egeria*, the brig *Zephyr* a schooner, the tender No. 12, and two despatch boats. It was an actual fleet, but we had not got it always at hand; for the port of Bastia would only just allow the brig and smaller vessels to anchor in it, and the eastern side of Corsica presents no shelter to large vessels, but Porto Vecchio, a desert place with no supplies. So, the frigates and the corvette were obliged to remain at sea, or anchor in the Gulf of Saint Florent to the west of Cape Corsica, and messages had to be sent overland to communicate with them; and when they were at sea, orders were conveyed by light boats that were often a long time finding them, having perhaps gone in chase of other vessels by mistake.

As soon as we were installed at Bastia, I set to work to unravel the matters my predecessor had left in great arrear when he quitted his post; for in the interim the business had been carried on very negligently, in consequence of the carelessness of General Berthier, who had got information at long range that he would be relieved, though Lieutenant Serra, the secretary I have mentioned, had worked with all possible good will.

I was nearly forgetting to say that a more solemn entry into Bastia had been prepared for us than at Ajaccio; we were received with the sound of cannon, and all the bells. All along the road from Ajaccio to Bastia, the inhabitants came in crowds as we passed by, saluting the general with acclamations, and adding the cry *Viva la Justicia!*

This love of justice displayed by the Corsican people was a recollection of the Genoese dominion, when this justice had always been pitilessly denied them; and this imported into Corsican manners a habit of doing justice to themselves, either to revenge an injury, or in vengeance when any harm was done to their interest; and in this, always considering the matter as personal from their point of view, justice never seemed good to them except when sentence was given in, their favour; and so the impartiality of native judges is generally more or less under the dominion of their fear of the parties between whom they have to adjudicate.

A short time before our arrival at Ajaccio, a judge of the civil court had been killed in open day, on the public parade, by a man who had lost his case and accused him of being the reason of it. After this exploit, the assassin retired quietly, and not one of the numerous witnesses thought of arresting him. Examination into this affair was proceeding; but it is most likely that if this man has not died a natural death, or has not been assassinated in his turn, he is in actual enjoyment of the benefits of the laws of limitation, like so many others in the same case.

On our way to Ajaccio, a M. Pietri came before General de Bruslart and begged of him a safe conduct for his two sons, who were refugees in Sardinia. Before 1789 M. Pietri had been Colonel of the Royal Corsican Regiment, and this implied that he was a man of consideration, both personally and by family position. He was about seventy and lived near Sarthene. As for the two men for whom he requested a safe-conduct, they had nothing more on their conscience than having on the preceding Easter-day, in their parish church at the moment of the elevation of the host, stabbed the son of a smith.

The unfortunate young man ran towards the altar on receiving the first blow, but the brothers Pietri followed him there and finished him at the feet of the priest. After the completion of this crime, in the midst of a population of fifteen hundred souls assembled in the church, the two brothers went out without hindrance, and proceeded to Sardinia, the haven of refuge of Corsican murderers, if they do not like to live in the woods, as is Corsica for Sardinian murderers.

This is the history of the occurrence. The smith was a rich man, and had sent his son to France to receive a very good education. He was a handsome youth, and Mademoiselle Pietri, considering him superior to any men she had met before, encouraged the feelings she had caused to arise in him, and this inspired hopes in him of marrying her, which he probably allowed to be visible. Public opinion did not cast the least suspicion on Mademoiselle Pietri of having conducted herself in such a way as to give her brothers any cause for suspicion that they had the family honour to revenge. I mention these two facts to give a notion of the character of the people we had to deal with; I can remember several others of the same kind.

At the time we came to Corsica, the island was still under special regulations beyond the common law. The governor-general was invested with all the highest powers of police; trial by jury had not been instituted, and deputies were not sent to the Legislative body. The military authorities were indisputably the highest, and were approached with many attentions, not to say flatteries, in the hope of obtaining protection or favour. So, we had to hold ourselves very much aloof from these insinuating personages, as clever men as possible in discovering the weak side by which they might manage to gain the good graces of such persons as they might have some interest in gaining over.

Unhappily, the general did not keep sufficiently on his guard to resist the assaults continually made upon him, as he ought to have done. Having lived for many years out of France, he was not acquainted with new laws, and the changes of customs that had taken place in the course of time. At Aix he had met a briefless barrister of very bad repute, even suspected of having murdered his father-in-law, and only set at liberty for want of proof. The general brought this person to Corsica with him on some sort of recommendation, hoping to make some use of him in the questions of law that he might have to decide.

This man had the title of secretary, but he could not prepare a clear, or even legible, report. He was a stupid blunderer, of no education, and wanted to hoist himself into the post of protector. As his antecedents were soon known at Bastia, questions were put to me as to how the general could have come to take him up. As was natural, I repulsed the inquirers; but I represented to the general how much blame might be thrown on him through such a man, by the disgrace attaching to him by his indiscretion, possibly by his treason; and so at last he decided on dismissing him. It was with great difficulty that I procured this necessary decision.

General Pozzo di Borgo, *aide-de-camp* to the Emperor of Russia, and a Corsican, as everybody knows, having obtained promotion to the rank of major for his cousin Galloni, had begged General de Bruslart to take him to Corsica, as his family was there. No worse selection could have been made. I very soon perceived that this Galloni was generally despised and hated by his countrymen. Base and cringing to his superiors, he was harsh and arrogant to all who depended on him in any way. He was not trustworthy to me in the smallest point; and it was quite impossible to give him any duty, for he could not write, besides that I mistrusted him.

I think Lieutenant-Colonel Perrin had been a sub-lieutenant in his youth. He had passed the whole time of the emigration in England, and only returned to France with the Bourbons, bringing an English wife and two charming little daughters of three and four years old. I never knew how he came to get the rank he had obtained. His was what is called a happy life, quite taken up with his wife and children; not wanting in cleverness, contriving, and ready enough to be liberal in anything not concerning himself; uneducated, with no habits of occupation of any sort, and knowing absolutely nothing of military matters.

The other lieutenant-colonel, M. d'Esparbès, had never seen service; his brother, the king's almoner, had procured his appointment as sub-lieutenant in the Royal Grenadiers, and this gave him the rank of lieutenant-colonel. It was soon seen that he was quite incapable of performing his duties in that position, and so it was thought convenient to get rid of him by sending him with us. He was a scamp in the full meaning of the word, and it was impossible to get anything out of him. He was fifty years old, and kept in his service a tall Albanian girl of twenty, who waited on him as chambermaid and a pair of a kind of sharpers, of about thirty; and they all lived mysteriously together in not a very moral manner, if report is to be believed.

I had known Colonel de Lamberville a long time; he had got leave, and never joined, in consequence of the events I shall relate further on.

Boishulan, the second major, was an energetic man, and bold, but his special element was in dangerous commissions—there was not much else to expect of him. In other respects, he was full of loyalty and discretion, and had served in the Royal army in Normandy during the Civil War, where I had known him as well as M. de Lamberville. He had not the slightest notion of regular military organisation, and could not have given any account of the duties of any rank, in any situation.

Captain Grosson de Truc wore uniform for the first time in his life, and he was nearly sixty. He was a very pleasant man, but greatly embarrassed by his epaulets, his hat, and specially his sword hitting his legs. His uniform was half civil and half military, like that worn by Louis XVIII., and it had great pockets across that were always gaping open. The children used to laugh as he went by.

My brother was also wearing uniform for the first time, but he was twenty-six, of an elegant appearance and suitable figure, and he seemed as much at ease in his new dress as if he had never worn any other. He had uncommonly good abilities, a capital memory, and could draw reports with great facility; he was the only officer that was of any real use all the time we were in Corsica.

I have mentioned that it was very pressing to get to work; besides the arrears of my predecessor's correspondence, I had to conduct the general's with the War Office in all matters concerning the garrison, the movements and future operations of the troops, for the defence of the island, and the maintenance of order within it. Besides, I had all the communications with the *gendarmerie* on my hands for the following reason: Colonel Charlot, the commander of the Corsican Legion, when a major in the same force, had arrested the Duke d'Enghien at Ettenheim.

General Bruslart sent for him on our arrival, and told him with the utmost consideration that, having himself been one of that prince's *aides-de-camp,* he could not have any direct communication with the man who had led him to his death, though unwillingly, and that in consequence all. communications connected with the service must be made to the chief of the staff. This increased my work to an extent that cannot be imagined by anyone unused to Corsica. For this one department it had been considered requisite to have a whole legion of *gendarmerie*, while in the midst of France a legion was enough for four or five departments. And though the numbers in proportion were so much greater, there was more work for the men in Corsica, as crimes and misdemeanours were so frequently repeated there.

General Bruny commanding at Ajaccio wrote to me by every courier, and so I had to answer him. He was a very brave man, and before the Revolution had been a sergeant in the company commanded by General Bruslart, and it was to him that he owed his employment in Corsica, at a time when the number of general officers was quite out of proportion to the employments for them, and several had to be placed on the retired list.

So General Bruslart had asked for him and had no reason to regret it. General Bruny military matters, and he soon understood the Corsican character, and the duties he had to perform towards the inhabitants. Though I sometimes had to complain of his activity in writing letters, entailing a good deal more trouble upon me, I was also several times indebted to his correspondence for useful and wise advice that I profited by.

Another major-general commanded the district of Bastia, I think his name was Bellanger, he was a man of elegant manners but we had not time to know him thoroughly, for he was soon recalled to France.

To Captain Grosson de Truc were entrusted the higher duties of police. He had to send in a daily report on this matter to me, and every morning at nine o'clock I used to see him come into my office with bundles of papers sticking out of his great pockets. It would be quite impossible to relate the quantity of childish folly that was the result of his investigations during five months. But the poor good man acted conscientiously, and did himself a great deal of harm; but his work was always worse than nothing, and not wishing to vex him, I submitted to the terrible bruising he used to come and inflict upon me every day at a certain hour.

I have been desirous of making known the elements that went to make up the most numerous staff ever seen in Corsica, elements so heterogeneous that it was impossible to guide them to a common purpose; and I saw at once that all the work would fall upon me, with the help of my brother and my secretary, Serra. Ten hours of constant work daily during the first months, enabled us to bring up the arrears to the present time, meanwhile, we had not a moment's rest; but after that, although there was always plenty to do, we could manage to make acquaintance with the inhabitants of the best standing, some of them having elegant wives. There was a good deal of music, and my brother was very well received, as he had one of the finest voices I ever heard.

But in the midst of all this, the Corsican character would break out at any moment, and I will give some specimens. The Sub-Prefect of Corsica had given us a grand dinner, and I was seated at table next to a man with a long beard, a very peculiar thing at that time when no one wore them. This Corsican's name was Gaffori, and he belonged to one of the best families of the quarter.

When we rose from table, I asked the *sub-prefect* what could be the reason that had made him adopt a beard so entirely out of fashion. The *sub-prefect* replied to me,

> It is only that he has taken an oath, as is quite customary in our ways, not to shave his beard till he has killed his enemy, a man who would have dined with us if I had not been unwilling to bring them together.

A short time afterwards Gaffori appeared fresh shaved, looking proud and pleased, and the body of his enemy was found at the gate of the town pierced with a ball that had struck him behind. Justice took cognisance of the matter with no result, as always happens, and Gaffori was not even arrested.

Here is another example of a different kind. Bearing arms was strictly forbidden without a permit obtained from the military authorities in virtue of the exceptional laws governing Corsica. So, this was put under our authority, and was announced in all the divisions by the administrative power. Then the Major of Bastia came to me, and told me that it would be impossible for him to refuse the certificate necessary for obtaining a permit to carry arms to any person, because if he did he would be exposed to terrible vengeance.

In order to avoid this risk, I told him to write the date at the bottom of any certificate he wished me to consider as void, and this was done to my great trouble, for the countenance of bearers of certificates dated in this manner may be imagined when they found that they were rejected. This may give a notion of the situation of the authorities towards their administrators.

A few days after my arrival at Bastia I was waited upon by Pompei, the major that had been intimate with me on the journey from Valentia to France. I was very glad to see him again, and he showed pleasure at having found me out. He was well known and much respected in the country, and his reports about me concerning my services with the army of Aragon, contributed to raise me in the opinion of the garrison as well as of the inhabitants.

Pompei was separated from his wife, and she lived in a town called

Porta, eight leagues from Bastia, and we had a company in garrison there relieved every three months. The captain commanding it was a charming young man, and he was assassinated just as he was leaving Madame Pompei's house at nine in the evening, while a maid was lighting him down the doorsteps. He received two balls in the chest and was killed on the spot.

A cousin of the lady's was arrested on suspicion of having committed this crime, and as is always the case there were no proofs, so he was dismissed. Some enemies of Pompei, for everyone has enemies in Corsica, tried to find him guilty of this action, but public opinion undertook the refutation of this calumny, and he seemed as if he never troubled himself about it.

Time passed, and with it a number of events of greater or less importance, that kept up the necessity for office work, that, as far as I was concerned, never averaged less than ten hours a day. The War Minister had ordered the raising of a Corsican battalion of *chasseurs*, intended to assist the *gendarmerie* in the island; General Bruslart had been entrusted with the organisation, and delegated his powers to that effect to me, as well as the regulation of the duties this regiment would have to perform.

This news produced an immense sensation in Corsica, as there were in the island at home more than four hundred officers on half pay, desirous of being employed in their own country, and aiming at this poor battalion though it was only sufficient to satisfy the desire of about thirty of them at most. And so, to obtain the object of their wishes, parents, friends, and acquaintances were set to work with long accounts of very doubtful exploits and notable actions that made every one of them a hero, such as ancient and modern times have never beheld. Many of them also proved their profound devotion to the Bourbon dynasty.

M. Deshorties, the major commanding at Jaca when I left Spain, came to command the battalion; we renewed our acquaintance, and events proved to me that he was a man of honour, imbued with a feeling of duty. But grave events were soon coming to deprive him of the eventual command of the battalion, and me of its formation.

We were at the end of February, and the echo of the uneasiness and hopes that were displayed in France extended to us. Besides our attention was excited by events passing under our own eyes. The general, in his private correspondence with the Chancellor Dambray, had just received a letter from him, that gave no precise details, but seemed to prophecy great and sad events in the immediate future. All this caused us to watch the island of Elba with greater care than ever, and we soon had information that a battery of six guns had been shifted from its station at Porto Longone to Porto Ferrajo, and this was a proof of some hostile intention.

General Bruslart sent information of this incident to Paris and Toulon, and desired me to convey orders to the commanders of the vessels on the station to exercise the greatest vigilance over everything that should leave the island of Elba, and especially Porto Ferrajo. Orders were also given to seize anything suspicious, and especially the *Inconstant* brig if it were met with. All the vessels were at sea except the *Fleur-de-Lys*, she had just put into port at Saint Florent, and the captain had invited the general and staff to dinner onboard; it was settled they should attend so as not to seem to be concerned about what might appear menacing.

Two days before, a detachment, under the orders of Galloni, had been sent to Cervione, ten hours from Bastia; he had orders to arrest a certain adventurer who had landed in Corsica some days before. We had seen him at Bastia, but though suspicious that he was a Bonapartist agent, we had not arrested him, because he was the bearer of perfectly regular papers. He was expected at Cervione, and on his arrival put on a general's uniform though he had never been in the service, distributed a large quantity of tri-coloured cockades and proclamations, calling upon the people to revolt, and announcing the immediate return of a state of things that they regretted, and that must produce a season of prosperity to Corsica such as she had never before experienced.

This man had been received at Cervione by the widow of General Cervoni, a kind of *virago*, exercising considerable influence in the country from the name she bore, from a fortune of considerable amount in proportion to others, and because her character, habits, and manners were Corsican in the full meaning of the word. Her husband had been killed in the campaign of 1806 against Austria, leaving a most honourable reputation, and the Emperor, having liked him very much, had added an annuity of two hundred and forty pounds from his private purse to the widow's pension.

Now the Emperor's private purse was no longer in a condition to provide for such annuities, and the king's had many other debts to pay, and not being obliged to take up the Emperor's promises, Madame Cervoni found herself deprived of a considerable portion of her income; this loss, added perhaps to the attachment and gratitude she had vowed to the benefactor of her husband and herself, made her the determined enemy of the Bourbon Government.

It was to my great regret that Galloni had been selected by the general to direct the operation, for he was compromised in the eyes of the Bonapartist party, and pretended to have an influence capable of contending with that of Madame Cervoni in the country that has Cervione for its capital, and besides knew the country well.

He arrived at my house just as we were starting for Saint Florent; he had marched all night, and told me that he had retired without having accomplished his object, because some shots had been fired at him from the house of Madame Cervoni. In acting in this manner Galloni had failed in his military duty and caused the king's soldiers to suffer an affront. I was very angry, abused him considerably, and ran to the general, who shared my indignation.

It was settled that I should not go to Saint Florent, and I received full power to organise a second expedition, and give such instructions as I should think requisite.

Two roads led from Bastia to Cervione, one along the sea, as the village is not half a league from it, and the other following a range of hills, the first spurs of the mountains that almost entirely line the island. I arranged the march of the two little columns that I despatched that evening so that they might reach their destination together at daybreak, though marching by different routes.

They were received as Galloni had been, but their orders were special; Madame Cervoni's house was carried after no further resistance than a few shots, fired at the approach of the troops, and it was completely pillaged. We were informed that the people of Cervione, one of the largest villages in Corsica, had promised their assistance to Madame Cervoni, but they were intimidated by the simultaneous arrival of the two detachments, and did not dare to make any hostile demonstration. As to the lady, she found means to escape either with or without the adventurer, for we were not informed whether he was at her house at the time of the action. A store of colours and tri-coloured cockades were found in the house and burnt.

The day after this expedition took place, the general returned to Bastia, enchanted with his reception on board the *Fleur-de-Lys*. The sailors manned the yards, and replied to his call for the king's health by enthusiastic cheers, and the town of Saint Florent appeared to do the same. It was a false prophecy. Two days later we heard of Napoleon's departure from the island of Elba, and at the same time an order was sent from Toulon for all the vessels on the station to return there, except the tender and two despatch boats. Nevertheless General Bruslart gave orders to the *Fleur-de-Lys*, still at Saint Florent, to get under weigh, and capture or sink the brig *Inconstant*, if she met her at sea with the troops of Napoleon's guard on board.

This frigate reached the Gulf of Saint John some hours after the landing of Napoleon in France, and anchored near the island of Sainte Marguerite to await events. M. de Garat, her captain, was an emigrant, and had served in the English Navy, and yet was much beloved by his officers and crew, as they found he was a real sailor.

The *Melpomene* and *Zephyr* had met the orders from Toulon at sea, and had gone there with the schooner. The *Zephyr* met the *Inconstant* brig, hailed her, as is customary with two vessels meeting within the range of voice, and let her pass without suspecting what she carried.

If Napoleon's return to France had been prevented, it is clear what would have been the result; no new coalition, no Waterloo, nor the subsequent invasion with its ruinous consequences, and above all, party spirit would not have been awakened or augmented, and perhaps we should not have had the Revolution of 1830 nor that of 1848.

However, the Revolution was in progress at the spot we occupied. Emissaries came from the island of Elba and proclaimed the departure of Napoleon; asserted that he had been recalled to France by the whole nation, with the assent of the Foreign Powers. At the same time a proclamation was issued in Corsica, depriving General Bruslart of his command, and giving orders that he should be arrested and sent to Paris, making an appeal to the troops and the people. The general replied with a counter proclamation, reminding the regiments of the oath they had taken when they received the standard they had sworn to protect a few days ago.

Napoleon's enterprise was there represented as an adventure that could only have a temporary success; and it was shown that if the king's authority were maintained in Corsica during the storm, incontestable rights to his gratitude, and to that of the nation, would be obtained. This proclamation had a good effect, and perhaps would have attained the result we hoped for, had not a certain General Simon—sent us, as he said, for an inspector—made it his principal object to rally the troops to Napoleon's cause. He came to Bastia a little later; his position as inspector enabled him to collect the officers, reviewing the troops in detail in their barracks, and he soon got a following whose efforts altogether changed the spirit of the 34th Regiment, forming the garrison of Bastia.

The country was also in a state of agitation, and the company on detachment at Porta returned to Bastia, under the pretext of fears of an attack and its retreat cut off. This first breach of discipline, at such a time, provoked me greatly, and I proposed a severe punishment for the officer who was to blame; but it was not inflicted, for General Simon took advantage of his title of inspector to prevent it, at least as long as his pretended inspection should last, with the probable intention of inducing him to join his adherents—as did not fail to take place.

There was a tolerable number of Royalists in Corsica, and they might have been depended on to resist the party that was rising, as it was composed of their enemies; but no cohesion existed among the Royalists, as they did not expect any struggle and were surprised by the recent events, having no means of organising resistance; but this could only take place by dependence upon the troops, and no confidence could be placed in them.

General Bruslart called a council of war, composed of the colonel of the 34th Regiment, the colonels in command of the Engineers and Artillery, the Inspector of Reviews, and the secretary to this council. The questions put to it were confined to these: the defence of the island, and obtaining supplies of food for the citadel, as it contained a considerable quantity of munitions of war. We were forced to see what was coming, and had not long to wait.

Next day, we were informed that a large number of peasants, led by half-pay officers, and with Colonel Casabianca at their head, whom I knew and we all knew, were marching upon Bastia, and were only two leagues from it. The thing seemed to me so extraordinary that I begged the general to allow me to go and see for myself. I went with four *gendarmes* and Major Deshorties, at his own request to go with me. We saw the fires of a bivouac from some distance, at the spot we had been told, and as we came nearer, the advanced posts covering it got under arms.

As soon as we were in range, the guard on the road we were coming by, about twenty men in number, took aim at us without any questions. I made signs to them not to fire, and went on alone; then, passing the guard, I got into the middle of the bivouac, and was soon surrounded by those I knew and by all the curious. First, I asked Colonel Casabianca what was the object of this assembly; and if he thought that it was a good way of proceeding to present himself, in arms, at the gates of the city where the military authority was stationed with more than sufficient means to repress any insurrectionary movement.

He replied that his only intention, and that of the brave men with him, was to deprive General Bruslart of his authority, whether he liked it or not, as they were sure he intended to hand over the island to the English; that that was their whole motive, purely French and free from any party spirit. I had good reasons to give in refutation of this infamous calumny, and the discussion was continued on this head; but I knew very well that their innermost intention was to act after the style of Napoleon's proclamation.

Casablanca's brother, and several Corsicans whom I did not know, took part in the discussion and showed great regard for me. Having exhausted every means of proving to them that they had nothing to do but to go home, I left them, expressing my regret at the necessary results of their persistence.

Then the colonel said to me, "Shall you attack us this evening?"

"Very likely," I answered.

"Then," said he, "tell General Bruslart that my first shots shall be for him."

One incident had occurred during our debate; to the imaginary complaint at the project of delivering Corsica to the English, was added the attack and pillage of Madame Cervoni's house, and this was brought up as a crime against General Bruslart. One copy of the orders given to the *commandants* of the two columns had been lost, and turned up in the hands of one of the insurgents who gave it to the colonel in my presence.

But as this order bore only my signature, I expressly assumed the responsibility, declaring that had the general not been absent from Bastia, he could not have avoided giving one of the same tenor, to avenge the affront offered to the first detachment sent to Cervione, and to cut short the intrigues of Madame Cervoni and her ridiculous acolyte. There was a moment of great excitement during this discussion, and Dehorties who had followed me, took his part with decision. At last all became quiet, and I thought I saw that they considered we had reason on our side though they maintained the contrary. I have a very distinct recollection of the spectacle that was presented by this collection. The brigands of a melodrama would be but a feeble copy.

The insurgents were armed with long guns, pistols, and daggers, and the variety of their dress made the whole a picture of a savage kind, that did not seem to promise an absolute respect for the law of nations. They were in a considerable ferment during our presence, forming groups around us, pressing us sometimes too closely, and their chiefs could hardly keep them off.

I had a violent altercation with a Corsican major, commandant of the fort of Saint Florent, who had deserted his post to join the rebels. He was a stupid man, and I had previously had a sharp conversation with him on a matter of duty. In the midst of his friends he thought himself in an advantageous situation, but he found he was wrong, for I showed rather more than surprise at the breach of the laws of discipline and honour that had brought him to the spot where I found him. Nevertheless, I should have been glad if the adventure had not taken place, for it gave the signal for a disturbance, that might have had serious consequences, in such company.

After our departure, a family that was closely connected with another that was there already, came in bringing its following. A quarrel arose, the two families fired on each other, and five men were killed.

I found General Bruslart in front of Bastia and the 54th Regiment on parade. I reported the result of my expedition to the general, and the number and position of the rebels. I asked him for two companies of *voltigeurs*, to attack them from the heights on the right, while he should leave a battalion at Bastia, and march upon them with the rest of the regiment by the road I had traversed. I answered for the success of the operation, and the plan was approved but just as the order was being given for its execution, Colonel Figier, commanding the 54th, took me on one side and told me that to his great regret he must say that not only his regiment would refuse to march against the rebels, but that if there were a collision he would side with them. If lightning had struck the ground at my feet, it would certainly have caused me less emotion than did this declaration. Anger and indignation made me dumb for the moment.

At last I was able to master myself sufficiently to ask the colonel, with all the coolness I could muster, if he had weighed the consequences of such a treason. The thought of being obliged to transmit the blow I had just received to the general, made me employ all the arguments I could to endeavour to destroy the work of General Simon, and the bitter fruits we had to reap. It is certain that some very fine promises had been made to the colonel in the Emperor's name, and he answered me that there were some circumstances stronger than human will and calculation, and that his regiment was obliged to yield to necessity.

I ought to have advised the general to take no notice of the colonel's statement, to have formed the regiment in square, and to have addressed the officers and men with some of those fiery words, that at the moment of incurring danger, or proceeding to action rarely fail of their effect. And the situation was such that other cords besides those of duty and honour might have been. made to vibrate. We were in a state of uncertainty about the result of Napoleon's attempt, and might therefore presume that it would not be successful.

Supposing that the army should rally round him, its reorganisation, after all the disasters, was not yet in a state of sufficient advancement to put it in condition to make head against Europe again in arms; the representatives now in congress at Vienna could not fail instantly to take the proper measures to prevent the return of a dominion they had long groaned under and had just broken down. Perhaps the regiment might have been persuaded that glory and profit would be its share, if it assisted to maintain the royal power in such a province as Corsica during the storm; and if we had succeeded in bringing them over, three hours would have been enough to put down the insurrection, for the regiment at Ajaccio was at that very moment giving proofs of its fidelity, and that at Calvi would certainly have followed the other two's example.

Had it been thus, probably the *dauphin*, after the capitulation of Drôme, would have come to Corsica instead of taking refuge in Spain, and so continued to reside in a French land, surrounded by French troops—a living protest against the treason which brought so many ills on France that now in 1861, the year these lines are written, the traces of them are far from being effaced.

Perhaps the notion of seeing General Bruslart fall a victim to an alliance between the troops and the half savage band I had just left, exaggerated in my eyes the horror of the scene that might take place; and I also fancy that the thought that my brother was going to run risks to which he was not accustomed, exercised a bad influence upon me. At last I was obliged to inform the general of the declaration that had been made to me. He showed his fierce indignation to the colonel and all around him; but when all was said, we returned into Bastia, to the great delight of the partisans of revolt, and the consternation of the opposite party.

It was a lost game perhaps for want of decision, as often happens in similar circumstances. I have a kind of remorse at not having acted as I have since thought I might have done. General Bruslart on many occasions had given proof of such intrepidity and remarkable coolness, that no suspicion of cowardice can fall on his memory. He was strange to the army and had even fought against them, so an instinctive feeling made him believe that he had not the sympathy of the troops under his command.

I was the only connecting link between him and the troops, as I was the only person in his numerous staff who had served with them. He felt it, and so did I; and that is the reason I must think myself to blame for not having persuaded him to adopt an energetic line of conduct, that would have done him the greatest honour if successful, and might have had the result I have mentioned above.

We returned to Bastia, and some officers of the staff and myself met at the general's, to try to find out what could be done in the desperate position that we found ourselves; while there, information was brought us that a meeting had been called by General Simon, that the civil authorities were present at it, the administrative branches, the judicial authorities, and the chiefs of the various branches of the military service, that they were deliberating and would send a deputation to inform General Bruslart of the result.

On quitting the island of Elba, Napoleon had sent forth the proclamation that all the world knows, and as I have mentioned before, this proclamation contained orders to arrest General Bruslart, and to send him to Paris under a strong escort. This was matter for grave reflection! Vincennes and the Duke d'Enghien recurred to my memory.

At last the deputation was announced. It was composed of the colonels in command of the artillery and engineers, who had always been on good terms with us, of the adjutant-general and the review inspector; of the sub-prefect, as the seat of the prefecture was at Ajaccio; of the Mayor of Bastia, and the president of the Civil Tribunal. They presented themselves with respectful bearing, and the colonel of artillery read the declaration in a perturbed voice, often interrupted with emotion, informing General Bruslart that the authorities being convinced that his intention was to make over the island to the English, they ceased to recognise him as their head, and gave him till, that evening to embark on board the corvette *Egeria*, which had been signalled in the offing since the morning, but that after that time they could no longer answer for the security of his person. That as to the officers of his staff, they remained free to continue their functions till further orders and would not be disturbed.

The general coolly took the declaration, wrote at the bottom a proper and firm protest, declaring that he only resigned his appointment on compulsion by superior force, and taking no account of the dangers that threatened him. He then returned it, requesting that they would send him a properly certified copy. I declared that all the officers composing the general staff refused the favour that they had the presumption to offer, and that they followed the general's fortunes.

Time passed, the corvette neared the land; her great white flag continued to fly at her peak, and this did not fail to make the busybodies uneasy who had acted on the supposition of Napoleon's success, and they were far from being sure of it yet. We hastily made our preparations for departure, and I went to the citadel to get a sum of five hundred pounds that was placed at the general's disposal on my receipt. But when the moment for embarkation had come, they told me they would keep me as a hostage till five Corsicans on board the *Egeria*, to be taken to Toulon, were given up. My brother wanted to stay with me; I obliged him to embark, making him understand that if there was any danger to run, we must not both be exposed to it on our parents' account; but Louis de Lanet, the general's first *aide-de-camp*, would not consent to leave me.

Only two officers of the general staff were missing at the roll-call, one, Lieutenant-Colonel Perrin, was on a mission to Toulon, his wife and two little daughters had remained at Bastia, and were embarked by us and taken to the *Egeria*: the other, Lieutenant-Colonel d'Esparbès, had kept quiet during the storm, but we shall hear of him again.

Lanet and I went down to the port to accompany the general, and we saw him embark, with my brother, Major Boishulan, Captain Grosson de Truc, Aide-de-Camp de Beausac, Madame Perrin and her two children; the boat was to bring back the five Corsicans. Having looked after them as long as the darkness would allow, I returned home, and a disagreeable surprise awaited me. The door of my rooms had been forced by the application of so much violence, that a strong iron bar fixed at one end in the wall, and supporting the leaf of the folding door that was not generally opened, had been torn off, and with it a portion of the wall it was fixed to; the floor was covered with rubbish.

Otherwise not an article of furniture was broken, and my pistols that I had left on the table, after loading them, had not been touched. And yet the housebreakers could not have had malice against my person, for under observation as we were, it was impossible that it should not be known that I was away from home when the crime was committed. My servant was also absent, having been employed with the general's in carrying baggage down to the boat.

Lanet had come with me, and went away after helping me to put some papers in order and destroy others. In Corsica, as at Genoa, the best rooms are at the top of the houses; my lodgings were on the third story. Lanet had only just got into the street when I heard him give a stifled shout, and fighting amid great noise. I seized my pistols, rushed down the stairs of my three storeys in the dark, and fell into the midst of a group composed, as I afterwards learnt, of half-pay officers, who I knew were all violent in their opposition to the Bourbon Government.

I knocked down the first one my hand touched, and cried out to his comrades, who came to help him, that I would shoot him if anyone came near me. I was quite determined that I would, I held him under one of my knees and by his neckcloth, drawing it tight enough to prevent his making the slightest movement to get away. This scene of violence could not last, and I should certainly have ended by falling a victim if an infantry guard had not come up from a short distance at the noise. I put the officer I had treated so badly into their hands, and they arrested three or four more, and heard from them that they had seized Lanet and taken him to General Simon.

I ran there under the influence of the action that had just taken place, and entered his *salon* with one pistol in my hand, and the other in my coat, and my sword trailing. This ridiculous equipment, which I never recollected, produced a great sensation that was displayed by an air of fright on the features of Madame Simon and her daughter, and the paternal tone that the general assumed to try to calm me.

I warmly complained of Lanet's abduction, the violation of my domicile, and the aggression of the half-pay officers, as it certainly would have caused more than one death if the guard had not come up. He assured me that all this had taken place without his complicity, and that an inquiry should be made. He added that Lanet, whom I had been looking for in vain, had really been brought to him and sent home with an escort.

Then General Simon opened another question, he told me that I was in such an exceptional situation with regard to all the component parts of the General Staff in Corsica, that it only depended on myself to remain and continue my duties, that he knew my services, and that I ought not to break up my career. After he had tried persuasion, he even made use of flattery. I naturally replied as was my duty, and I left him as soon as possible to go to Lanet, and make sure he had not been subjected to any further violence.

Lanet told me that on leaving my house he had been seized so suddenly that it was quite impossible for him to make the least resistance, and that at the first moment a hand had been laid on his mouth to prevent his calling me, and this gave his shouts the accents of distress that had moved me so much. This crisis was past; had we others to undergo? The affirmative seemed the most probable answer to this question. We spent the night together at my house, without going to bed.

Next day early, General Simon's *aide-de-camp* came to tell me that the five Corsicans on board the *Egeria* had been given up and I was free to depart. Very anxious to take advantage of our liberty, we were on our way to the port to take boat, when we were informed that the *Egeria* was no longer in sight, nor was any other vessel within the horizon. We ourselves made sure that we were left behind, and tried in vain to understand the reason, then we went sadly back to my house.

We had only just returned, when Lieutenant-Colonel d'Esparbès presented himself. He appeared greatly embarrassed, and at first, I attributed this to the reproaches his conscience might have made him on his retreat during the events of the previous day, and I expressed my astonishment to him at it. At first, he stammered, and then he told me, that on my refusal to retain my employment, General Simon being invested with the authority of Governor by the Commission, had confided to him the functions of chief of the general staff, and that he was come to ask me to hand over to him all that concerned his duties.

I looked at the wretch; his legs trembled, and he seemed like a criminal expecting sentence. I had despised him a long time, he was a disgustingly immoral man, but I did not expect such treason. As I said, the Abbé d'Esparbès, his brother, the king's almoner, had got him the rank of Lieutenant-Colonel without his having ever served, so he owed everything to the Restoration, for it had found him in a complete state of destitution in consequence of his misconduct. I reminded him of all this, and added that, as I did not recognise the authority that had invested him with these new duties, I would never hand over to him anything concerning them, that after I was gone all would be found, for I did not intend to carry anything off.

On a further display of Lanet's indignation at this base desertion, he replied, in a tone showing the greatest meanness, that he was forced to act in this way, for he had no money, and so was in no condition to pay the cost of the necessary journey to Paris.

We stopped a moment looking at him with pity and disgust; then all at once Lanet, seized with a generous impulse, put his purse into his hand with more than forty pounds in gold in it, telling him angrily,

"There, you blackguard! take that, and do not disgrace yourself."

Lanet was only a captain, and not twenty-five; d'Esparbès was more than fifty and was a lieutenant-colonel. This abrupt speech addressed to a man of such an age, and so much higher rank, was so character-istic of the situation that I seem still to hear Louis de Lanet's voice. D'Esparbès, far from being offended, weighed the purse in his hand with a pleasure that did not escape my notice, and was going to put it in his pocket; but I snatched it from him and gave it to Lanet, telling him,

"Do not you see that he will keep your money and will not go?"

Not a word was said in answer to this last affront, and the man it was addressed to, in obedience to my orders, went out hanging his head.

He afterwards sent me the two rogues he had to wait on him, and they presented themselves to me in a most impudent way, asking me, in their master's name, for the papers relating to the formation of the Corsican battalion. I showed them the door and heard no more of them.

About mid-day, information was sent us that a small sail was in sight, and was tacking about in front of Bastia, her manoeuvres evi-dently showing that she did not intend to come in. She was soon recognised as the tender, No. 12, one of the vessels on the station, and she was waiting for us. We had made a bargain with the owner of a harbour-boat, to put us on board the *Egeria* if she returned, we sent for him to tell him to hold himself in readiness to take us out to the tender.

On the pretext that the course of events had been so much more violent since we had made our bargain with him, and that he might be compromised, and run a risk himself by our being in danger, he insisted that the price he had asked was not a sufficient recompense, and as his ultimatum told us a fabulous sum that we were obliged to accept.

We learnt that a hostile assemblage had collected at the port on the news of our departure, and we were advised to choose another place of embarkation. Two or three hundred paces from my lodging was a beach, crowded with loungers in the evening, but nearly deserted during the day, and we could go there without crossing any part of the town. The boat came to this beach to take us off, and we went there escorted by Pompei and my secretary Serra, who both chose to accompany us, though I begged them not.

This mark of devotion was the more touching that Pompei was suffering from serious illness and had that morning broken a blood-vessel in his chest, and was obliged to keep his handkerchief to his mouth all the time, to catch the blood that came from it. As for Serra, a half-pay officer, he was exposing himself to the vengeance of his comrades, by this protest against their conduct and feelings towards me, displayed by threats and exaggerations of the occurrence of the previous evening. Serra had been married eighteen months and had a little child.

We were considerably disappointed on reaching the landing-place to find a large and dense crowd obstructing the approach to the boat, and that we must pass through them to get to it. The information we had received about the assemblage at the port made us considerably suspicious of this one, and I again begged Pompei and Serra to go away; but they refused, and that in a tone which showed me that they thought their honour concerned not to leave us at such a time, and this seemed to me a fresh proof that they thought there was danger.

A circumstance that seemed childish, but that might have had seri-ous consequences, added to my anxiety; I was carrying my pistols in my hand, and there was some apprehension that this might be taken for a preparation either for attack or defence, and might excite an at-tack, but I did not like to put weapons that I might want out of my power. With these various thoughts I walked towards the group, sup-ported by Lanet, Pompei, and Serra, and followed by my servant as pale as death and trembling like a leaf.

The crowd opened as we drew near, it was the critical moment; we passed through them and they remained silent. On reaching the edge of the sea I embraced Pompei and Serra with great affection. The boat could not come close enough to get into it without stepping into the water. Three sailors were there and they offered us their backs. I jumped upon one, Lanet on another, and my servant on the third, and in a few moments, we were on board and had pushed off.

The tender was under sail about a league and a half off; she was commanded by a nasty rogue called Clément, turned out of the navy during the Empire for a series of dirty tricks, but at a later time he had married a woman at Avranches, whose father had done service to the Royal cause; and this woman, a very pretty person, had come to

Paris and found out General Bruslart, and he procured the restoration of her husband to his rank of lieutenant in the navy, and got him a command on the Corsican station, but this had the worst effect upon the navy.

The importance of the Corsican station had put me in communication with a great number of officers of that service, and they spoke of Clément to me with the greatest contempt, and would not have any communication with him. Vulgar and ill-educated, he had the tone and decided manners of a bad melodramatic actor. I never met a more disgusting being. I had been obliged to give him a considerable scolding at Toulon, and as it came round to me that he said that, but for the difference of our rank, he would ask me the reason why, I told him that if such was his desire I was ready to give him satisfaction and sign a letter stating that I was the aggressor.

Then he pretended to be melted, praised my magnanimity, and swore that he was for me in life and death. Thenceforward he was disgustingly obsequious to me. In this affair I behaved like a school-boy, and if I tell the tale it is certainly not to boast of it, nor to induce anyone to copy my proceedings in similar circumstances.

I have forgotten to say that Major Deshorties had united himself to our fate, and that he had joined us on the beach and embarked with us.

The *commandant* of the tender, on seeing us coming, like a mountebank as he was, had the drum beat to clear for action, and sent the thirty men of his crew to quarters. When we got on board I asked him the meaning of these formidable preparations, and he answered me that seeing a boat approach full of men, he had been afraid of a surprise and of being boarded by the rebels of the island, whose success he knew. This boat, the very inoffensive object of the suspicions of Captain Clément, carried the owner, four rowers, Deshorties, Lanet, my servant, and myself—in all, nine persons.

On setting foot on the deck of the tender, I found myself in my brother's arms. Captain Clément had been sent to reconnoitre, and meeting the *Egeria*, was told to go in search of us. To make sure of the commission being properly executed, and to gain more speedy intelligence of our fate, my brother had left the *Egeria* and come to meet me. We embraced with much pleasure.

Next day we entered the Gulf of Saint John, and we should have been capsized in it but for the quickness with which Captain Clément let go the main sheet, and enabled the tender to right from her beam ends. At the moment there was a disorder that gave me a notion of the excitement of a shipwreck. All faces expressed an intense fear. It was in this very Gulf of Saint John that Napoleon had landed a few days previously, still uncertain as to what might be the result of his disastrous attempt. We made two tacks to get out of the gulf, where a French frigate was lying at anchor, still flying the white standard. At last we reached Toulon and joined the *Egeria*; General Bruslart was waiting on board for us before landing, as we then did without further loss of time.

As soon as we landed we went to Marshal Masséna, holding the command of the Southern Provinces of France from the king. He received us very well, and seemed determined to make head against the storm; and told us, among other things, that the white cockade was nailed to his hat, and would never be replaced by any other. As we took our leave, he asked me to bring him the state of the troops we had left in Corsica; and when I brought it the next day, he kept me nearly an hour, putting questions to me about the various points held by the regiments, and the events that had led to our expulsion from the island. All the time I spent with him, I was examining him closely, as was natural with such a great personage; there was something of the eagle in his features, as has been said; his nose was very prominent, and his eyes piercing.

By his orders we proceeded to Marseilles, where he himself was soon to go. During the day there came in some grenadiers of the party Napoleon had brought from the Island of Elba; and they had abandoned the cause and deserted, being quite demoralised by their more than chilly reception by the population. It was naturally supposed that the desertion would continue; and it is very likely that, if a mournful example of defection had not been set by a regiment of infantry and a company of Engineers sent to Sisteron to meet the expedition and fight it, Napoleon would soon have been abandoned by the chief part of his own men, and have had no chance of safety but in flight—and where could he have gone?

But the course of events was otherwise. The Count d'Artois came to Lyons, and retired precipitately; the *dauphin* capitulated at the bridge of the Drôme, betrayed by the troops under his orders, except the 9th Foot, whose fidelity could not be shaken; and at last Napoleon reached Paris. The rest is well known.

We had gone to Marseilles with the intention of joining the corps that had the *dauphin* at its head. The inhabitants and the National

Guard at Marseilles showed an absolute devotion to the Bourbon cause; and talked of a resistance that should make their city a second Saragossa, if it became necessary. This military ardour, that had caused us to be warmly welcomed, fell before a slight check that was experienced by three thousand National Guards, weakly attacked by two companies of *voltigeurs* and two guns. Then Marshal Masséna gave orders for the recognition of the Emperor, and the hoisting of the tricolour flag and cockade; although a few days before he had sworn that the white cockade was nailed for ever to his hat.

After the *dauphin* had capitulated to General Grouchy, the Emperor's messenger, General Bruslart was naturally obliged to remove himself out of the way of the threats held out against him in proclamations. He embarked for Spain with Beausac, his second *aide-de-camp*, and Louis Lanet returned to Berry to his old castle of Garde-Giron. He was a devoted and clever man, of a chivalrous spirit, and at the time I am writing this he remains one of my best friends. Deshorties, my brother, and myself at once set out for Paris.

Here I mean to indulge myself in a little digression, that will be found to contain a study of the human heart. We had brought back Lieutenant-Colonel Perrin's wife, his two children, and even down to a very ugly and very nasty little dog. To get all these onboard ship all on a sudden, leaving nothing behind, and in our situation! Heaven only knows the trouble and difficulty this family caused us; especially as Madame Perrin was possessed of the most impassable inertia in the world. At Marseilles, Perrin resolved to embark with his whole family for some place that I forget, and took his passage in a small vessel. Just at the start his wife and children disappeared, and we assisted him in unsuccessful efforts to find them.

Time pressed and night approached. At last, just in the dim twilight, we saw in the harbour, and some distance from the quay, a boat that attracted our attention by its uncertain movements. We thought we could see a woman and two children in it. We jumped into another boat lying there and told the waterman to row as hard as he could to catch the other boat. Perrin was half mad, but when we reached the boat, we had the great pleasure of finding the objects of our search. Madame Perrin had been down at the port, where her husband had told her to meet him, and had been frightened by a quarrel between some sailors; she had taken refuge in a boat begging the waterman to put off, and was rowing about in uncertainty what was to be done. We took her off to the vessel where their passage was taken; she was getting out towards the entrance of the harbour, crowded by the quantity of foreign vessels that were in haste to escape the consequences that a revolution might entail.

We had hardly gone a hundred fathoms towards land, when Perrin called me back in a despairing voice. We came alongside his vessel as soon as we could, and he told me that if we did not help him, he and all his party would be starved. The captain had told him that he had not a single mouthful of food to give his passengers, for even the crew had not enough to eat for the five days their passage would take at the very least. We went on shore. I ran to the Hôtel Beauvau where we were staying, had a great basket filled with bread, pies, cold meat, and wine; it was carried down to the boat that was waiting for us, and we put off to find our people.

But the little vessel we were in search of had gone out of harbour and was in the roads, making tacks with several more to gain an offing, for the wind was contrary and freshening much. The night was very dark, and the sea rough; we had to take the greatest care to avoid being run down by vessels that were running every way, and hailing each other loudly as a warning of their mutual danger, and the risk was much greater for our poor boat, as they would have run over it without finding it out. These hails prevented ours being recognised, as we shouted out the name of the vessel we wanted, and the search took us so long that at one time I was in despair of success.

At last, by a chance that may be called providential, in consideration of the darkness, and the disorder in the roads, we reached the object we sought, and were received with an explosion of thankfulness that almost made me shed tears. We still had considerable difficulties to overcome in getting back to harbour. I had to pay the boatman handsomely, and the provisions in the basket would cost about four pounds. Some months afterwards I met Perrin at Paris; he seemed confused and displeased to meet me, seemed hardly to recognise me, and never said a word about the scene in the roads, nor about repaying me for what I had spent for him. I turned my back upon him and never spoke to him again.

General Grouchy had fixed his headquarters at Aix, after the *dauphin's* capitulation, and taking the appearance of submission at Marseilles into his consideration, was in no hurry to take military possession of that city, probably dreading that the troops and the populace might come into collision, as the state of exasperation of the latter had been increased by the check that the National Guard had experienced.

We did not very well see how we could manage to return to Normandy; the diligence was not running, in consequence of the operations of war that had taken place on the line we should have to follow, and then: we disliked the notion of crossing the country held by General Grouchy's forces. Meanwhile I received a deputation from the Marseilles merchants that pleased me very much. They came to propose to me and the other staff officers still there to remain at Marseilles, and supposing that we were unable to make use of our private resources from our families, or any other sources, to request that we would be willing to accept any sum I might mention under the name of loan.

I received this offer in a proper spirit, and expressed our intention of setting out as soon as we could find means of transport; when one of the merchants composing the deputation told me of a *vetturino*, a very honest man and a thorough royalist, who was just starting for Paris, and would certainly be glad to have such travellers as we were, with him. This was a very slow means of travelling, and did not answer at all to our impatience; but in our present circumstances it had the advantage of enabling us to travel without attracting attention.

So we made a bargain with the *vetturino*, and two days afterwards we started on our journey in a capital *berline* with two strong horses to draw it, with our trunks upon the imperial, and four long barrels of oil from Aix in a boot behind; our driver was a dealer in this, and with his passengers it gave him a good income. The carriage had room for six, and we were four in it, Deshorties, my brother, and myself, and a child of fourteen, whom General Bruslart had taken with him to Corsica at his parents' request, to teach him a secretary's duties.

At Aix we took up a very pleasant lady of sixty. We were joined by a carriage containing six ladies from the island of Elba, belonging to officers or persons of the Emperor's household. We became objects of suspicion to them, and among other tricks they tried to play us, only just escaped arrest at Lyons on their denunciation. Just as we entered the city their carriage passed us, and on our arrival, we were surrounded by *gendarmes*. The quartermaster commanding began by taking up an insolent tone, so I got angry, generally an unsuccessful proceeding, but on the present occasion it was quite successful, to the great amazement of my brother and Deshorties, who laughed when it was all over, but had been very anxious during my anger.

At one of our resting places, one of the ladies from Elba came with tears in her eyes to beg us to take her into our carriage, for her companions kept on humiliating her, because her husband was in an inferior position to theirs. We took pity on this pretty woman, only about twenty years old, and very willingly granted her request.

This method of travelling by short journeys is not without its pleasures, but for the impatience sometimes caused by it. The horses go at a walk when the road is net quite level, the passengers can walk as much as they like, with a shelter ready if rain comes on, and there is a good chance of seeing the country well. Deshorties knew the names of nearly all the owners of properties of importance that we saw from the road, and told us their family histories.

Our driver had his appointed hostelries where he was expected at certain hours. We found our meals and rooms ready, and as he had been on the road more than twenty years it was important to him that his passengers should be contented, and we had no ground of complaint on this head during the fortnight that our journey from Marseilles to Paris lasted.

Chapter 13

State of Normandy During the Hundred Days

As we expected, we found Paris in a state of trouble and anxiety, the inevitable consequence of a revolution like this brought to pass in a few days. The United Congress of Vienna had spoken; war was to be renewed, and the French Army was far from being reorganised. The old Imperial Guard, whom the Restoration had been foolish enough to disgust, were recalled to Paris, and had an appearance of melancholy and resignation, like the look of tried soldiers going to meet a danger without any chance of success. They knew that their small numbers would again have to strive with all the forces of Europe.

They might be seen collecting in groups, conversing animatedly but with a sorrowful expression that struck me and made me melancholy. I could not desire that the cause they were going to support should triumph, and yet having run the same risks as they did for ten years, I groaned in prospect at the infallible defeat that would bring back the foreign armies upon France. The contest of these two different feelings distracted my mind for three months.

My brother and I proceeded to Normandy, when we had spent a few days at Paris making observations and getting news. I was there subjected to a kind of persecution that was not pushed to extremity, on account of the uncertainty of the new authorities as to the issue of the events in preparation. However, one night in my absence, my father's house at Maizet, near Caen, was surrounded by a considerable armed force, accompanied by *gendarmes*.

At the break of day, they forced an entrance, and asked where I was. On receiving answer that I was not at home, they had all the rooms opened and searched the cupboards, and even the desks, examining the papers. Not having found anything suspicious they went away, and the Civil Commissioner with them said that it was known that I was at Condé-sur-Moireau to make plans and raise an insurrection, and that M. de Bruslart would come and put himself at its head. They did me more honour than I deserved.

A few days afterwards a *gendarme* brought me a letter from the prefect, that very politely requested me to call at his office the first time I went to Caen. It might have been a snare, but if I did not go I should have seemed to be afraid, and so I went. The *prefect* received me with ceremonious politeness; and told me, with a certain amount of embarrassment, that he advised me for my own sake and for that of my family to do nothing of a nature to excite the suspicions of the government, that he had received very strict instructions in this matter, and was very desirous not to be obliged to put them into execution.

I thanked him, and made a strong complaint of the brutality of the behaviour of the agents who had conducted the domiciliary visit at my father's house a few days before. He excused himself, telling me that he had got wind of how things were done, and had not waited for my complaint to show his anger.

As far as I remember, this *prefect's* name was Ramel, and he was brother to the general of that name, who was some weeks afterwards murdered in his bed in a cowardly way at Toulon or Montauban. The reaction after the first restoration was not free from blots of this kind. Marshal Brune died in this manner at Avignon, and others as well, who fell victims to private hatred and revenge, under the veil of political opinion. It was a great misfortune for the Royal cause that its enemies made it responsible for atrocities that could never have been foreseen or prevented.

Time brought just, what was expected, a declaration of war from all the foreign powers, and their armies advanced towards our frontiers. Just at the time of the Battle of Waterloo the Duke d'Aumont landed on the coast of Normandy, near Bayeux, with several officers who had gone to Ghent to join the Royal family in their well-known refuge there. This expedition of the Duke d'Aumont had no solid base of operations. It had not been announced, and so did not at first find any support from possible sympathisers.

As soon as we were informed of this, my brother and I, and some of my relations, taking some peasants with us, proceeded to Livry, near Villers-Bocage, a spot pointed out to the Duke d'Aumont as likely for some time to be favourable for a petty sort of a war with the feeble means he had been able to collect. His materials were inferior to anything that can be imagined, and must have dispersed at the smallest attack. There was a want of arms; pocket pistols and bad rusty swords were almost the only means of attack and defence of those who figured in this assembly; so, when our little troop appeared armed with double-barrelled guns, it was considered as a good reinforcement.

The Duke d'Aumont, poor man, had no military reputation. He had shut himself up in the castle of Livry, and did not even take the pains to organise, well or ill, the few hundreds of men that came from different sides, who made their bivouac in the yards, and did not know what directions they were to receive, or where they could go in case of the silence of the authority that they had voluntarily joined and submitted to.

But though this authority abstained from making his will known, to make up for it there was a perfect outburst of personal pretensions, such as I suppose had never been seen till then. It was curious to see everyone assuming beforehand a large proportion of the promotions and favours of all kinds, and counting on a fresh Restoration, that the events of war made almost certain.

People who had never done anything, and most of whom seemed unfit to do anything, tried to persuade themselves that joining the Duke d'Aumont under such *perilous* circumstances was an act of devotion and heroism that would justify the highest pretensions. Finally, to do them justice, those who dreamed of the epaulets of a general, or of a *prefecture*, accepted a donation of fifty pounds, or some equivalent employment, without any shame. The greatest part of them got nothing, and that was justice.

One meeting I had there deserves to be reported. Eugene d'Hautefeuille of whom I have already spoken, had been made colonel by the most speedy promotion recorded in the archives of the War Office, he had gone with General Grouchy as second chief of the staff in the expedition against the *dauphin*. I knew he was against us, when we were just making our arrangements to meet this expedition. My astonishment may therefore be imagined when I found him, three months afterwards, landing on the coast of Normandy to support the other side. We came to an explanation on this point, that showed me that he had acted with an address on which I could not congratulate him. He was a very clever man, but his character had never pleased me though we had been very intimate.

The king's speedy return to Paris called me there; I wished to get my position and my brother's established. I had resigned, and the rank he had obtained, had not been recognised; so we had to get ourselves replaced on the War Minister's list. It seemed a simple thing, and I even thought that the promise made to me before I went to Corsica, my conduct there, and lastly, the sacrifice I had made of my rank gained by eleven campaigns and a thousand dangers, would procure me the promotion, that, I was told on all sides, was my indisputable right.

It was even said that one step would most likely be thought insufficient for my reward, and that I should have two given me in the remodelling of the army that was to take place. Without allowing myself altogether to rely upon this hope, I must own that I should not have been much surprised had the thing taken place; but it was not so.

My brother's re-appointment that I asked for at the same time as my own was granted without difficulty; he was at once nominated to an office of his rank in the staff of the 4th Division, with its headquarters at Nancy, and he went to his new post. As for me, after spending two months in applications, warmly supported by the recommendations of General Bruslart and several other generals, under whose orders I had served, I, with great difficulty, managed to get appointed with my actual rank to the 6th Regiment of Cuirassiers, bearing the name of Condé, and being raised at Arras.

I had such a reception at the War Ministry, and at the offices of the staff when I presented myself to support my brother's application—I had held such a position in Corsica when entrusted with a great deal of power through the confidence of General Bruslart, that I therefore considered this new appointment as a disgrace, and with the more reason that I saw promotions, decorations, and favours of all sorts lavished on all kinds of intriguers, on happy petitioners—some of whom presented no vouchers nor claims, and others could only put forward a devotion that perhaps was real, but they would have had much trouble to find proofs.

The avenues to authority were obstructed, there were lines of attendance formed at the doors of the ministers' offices, especially at the War Ministry; and on reaching even the ante-chamber of the head of a department, or even of an office, it was found to be so crowded that it was impossible to get a turn for an audience the first day. It was necessary to come ten times to get one, and with the probability, too often realised, of being listened to inattentively and wearily, and only receiving evasive replies. Besides the crimes of venality and corruption must be put down, unhappily, in such circumstances, they fill too many sad pages. It was disgusting.

The Duke d'Aumont, I prefer to believe without his own knowledge, served as a stepping stone to many people who made use of the last method; it was notorious that a major who had received his promotion at the Restoration and had been his *aide-de-camp*, made use of the duke's name in a most ignominious way. Money was not enough for him, and he even attacked ladies who came with petitions. One of them cried out at his violence and help came; a complaint was sent up, and the major dismissed. I do not know what became of him; he was more than fifty and horribly ugly. This business caused an evil report.

At Arras I joined the Regiment of Condé under the command of Colonel de Baillancourt, a brave and worthy soldier -whom I had known first in 1805, and in the Prussian campaign in 1806 and 1807—he was then a captain in the 8th Cuirassiers. He received me capitally, and handed over the officers' drill and instruction to me, a duty that I performed during all the time that I served in that regiment, that is to say from 1816 to 1825.

We remained three years at Arras, and I became very intimate with General Fleury commanding the 2nd Regiment of Engineers; he had married Mademoiselle de Sèze, and my intimacy with this family is still existing at the time I write these lines in June 1862. Madame de Fleury, an admirable woman in every respect, died a few years ago.

A short time before we left Arras I fought a duel with an ex-captain of Chasseurs of the Imperial Guard, named Vallée, and wounded him with a sword cut. This man was disposed to be hostile to all those who did not share his opinions, had been exiled for having attempted to cause a mutiny in an infantry regiment in garrison at Arras, and he had just returned in virtue of a declaration of amnesty; but he was subjected to an active supervision, for banishment was far from calming his political feelings, and had only exaggerated them.

Two years afterwards, at Marseilles, he again attempted to seduce a regiment, but was caught in the act, arrested, tried, condemned to death, and executed. It is on account of this last circumstance that I recall an incident of little interest by itself. However, this affair made a great noise in the country, and I received a great many compliments, for Vallée was feared for his great strength and skill in fencing. He had spent the period of his exile at Brussels, and had obtained the reputation of an excellent master of arms. He was very much my superior in that art, and I only owed my success to his becoming impatient when he saw that I did not lose my coolness, and so avoided the snares he laid for me.

We left Arras in the month of April, 1819, and went first to Colmar, staying there till May, 1822, and then to Dijon. War with Spain having been resolved on, the Regiment of Condé was named as one of the *cuirassier* division attached to the army of invasion that was to march under the orders of the *dauphin*. We left Dijon at the beginning of February, 1823, to go to the neighbourhood of Pau, the place of assembly for the division.

It was frightful weather all the time of this march, lasting a month. Our route had been thoughtlessly drawn out, and made us go by tracks that had never been travelled in Winter within the memory of man. We had horses stuck in the mud; the rivers were in flood, and the smallest water-courses in such a state as to be difficult to cross. We passed over one on a plank hardly two feet wide and at least fifteen high.

We crossed the Garonne at Langon in sailing boats, stretching up over flooded meadows far above the landing-place, as we should never have made it by going directly into the course of the river. When the sail jibed on the other tack the horses were scared by its noise and its rubbing their backs, and threw themselves backwards or forwards, making the boats rock in a very alarming manner, and the boatmen cried out that if we could not manage to keep the horses quiet they would not answer for the consequences. We were fortunate enough not to have to lament over a single accident, it was quite a miracle, Crossing the Elbe at Hamburg had been much less difficult or dangerous.

To give a just idea of this march of a month, it must be added the men hardly ever had time or means to dry their clothes, getting them wet through with rain or snow every day; in several places between the Dordogne and the Garonne fuel was so scarce that even the superior officers could not have a fire in their quarters, for the very small quantity of wood that could be procured was kept for cooking. Our sufferings here, in the centre of France at this time, caused by the carelessness of the officer in charge of the movements of troops, are inexplicable.

The bad weather pursued us in our cantonments at Pau, and we did not see two fine days together in this climate though it is so famous for its mildness and sun.

The *dauphin* had established his headquarters at Pau, and he addressed a very good proclamation to the people of Spain, announcing that he did not enter their territory as an enemy, but only to restore order, put down the disturbance of a factious minority, and deliver their sovereign from the oppression that he groaned under.

We entered Spain by the Bayonne road. One *corps d'armée* under the orders of Marshal Molitor entered by the eastern road, and marched upon Saragossa and the Kingdom of Valentia. The main body of the army took the road to Madrid with the *dauphin*. A very slight encounter took place near Logroño; we took no part in it and reached Madrid without meeting the smallest resistance.

Our entrance into the capital by the gates of Alcala and Toledo was very brilliant. The streets, as we marched along, were covered with hangings as for Easter-day; all the windows were lined with women in their best clothes, waving their handkerchiefs, crying out *Viva la Francia*, and throwing flowers to us. The populace pressed upon our steps, and also kept shouting; but among the shouts in our honour, many could be distinguished crying out for one person or another's death, for in Spain it takes shedding of blood to make a fine gala day; and so, we saw some groups of sinister figures with bare and bloody arms, that had probably taken advantage of the stir occasioned by our presence to gratify their personal hatred.

We crossed the city one way, while another column crossed it in the opposite direction, and we went to take up our cantonment at Leganes, a large village two leagues from Madrid, where there is a fine barrack, usually occupied by the Walloon Guard; but we did not enter it on account of its dilapidated condition. We and the 5th Cuirassiers were billeted on the inhabitants, and I was appointed *commandant* of the place, that is to say put in charge of the police, in all matters concerning exterior discipline, and intercourse with the inhabitants. Not a single complaint was made on either side during the few months we spent there.

I remarked that many of the inhabitants of Leganes were fair, which is very unusual in Spain, and their complexion especially in the women is of exceptional beauty. I would add that the Walloon Guards were recruited in Belgium, and great care was taken to select the handsomest men.

About the month of July, we received orders to go to Alcala d'Henares, to relieve a battalion of the Grenadiers of the Guard, ordered to form a part of the expedition to Cadiz. We had a march of eleven hours to reach our destination, in a heat so great that if the naked hand touched the *cuirass* it was drawn back as hastily and suffer-

CUIRASSIER OFFICER OUTSIDE A VILLAGE HOUSE

ing as much as if it had touched a red hot iron. Alcala is a pretty town, and then contained about twelve thousand inhabitants. Its university is of wide-spread fame, and Cardinal Ximenes was especially fond of it, and lies in a magnificent tomb in the middle of the University Chapel.

I was again *commandant* of the place at Alcala. During our stay at Leganes, Colonel de Baillancourt had been appointed to the command of the 2nd Regiment of Cuirassiers of the Guard, in garrison at Madrid. This favour was clearly due to him, if for no other reason, because it had been for several years considered by all that he ought to be promoted to major-general, and though I was sorry to see him go away, I received this tardy and half justice with pleasure. During the seven years I had served under his orders, our intercourse had always been full of mutual confidence.

He was succeeded by a Monsieur Patarin, Lieutenant-Colonel in this very 2nd Cuirassiers of the Guard that Colonel de Baillancourt had just entered. The command of the 6th Cuirassiers had been left in my hands, and I gave it over to M. Patarin; he was a good sort of man, but a boaster and liar in the most trivial matters. He had emigrated when a sub-officer-adjutant, and at the Restoration, after a long interval of service, had been appointed Lieutenant-Colonel of the 4th Cuirassiers, and then soon got transferred to the Guard. He was very wearisome to me at first, sending for me continually for matters of very little consequence; but at last he got to understand things as well as was in his power, and at last our intercourse was always pleasant during the years I served with him.

While we were at Alcala an incident took place that deserves mention. A *cuirassier* of the regiment had been brought up, while we were at Leganes, before a court-martial for violence towards a corporal and sergeant. He was a man of very bad character. I had been attracted by the sound of the struggle at a tolerably early hour of the night, and had given the culprit some blows with the flat of my sword to make him let go, for he had hold of the corporal and was trying to throw him down, He was immediately taken to the prison at Madrid.

Just after our arrival at Alcala, information was obtained that three hundred mounted officers of the Spanish corps that Marshal Molitor was in pursuit of, had come to Guadalaxara, a town twelve leagues to the north of Alcala, on the road to Saragossa that we had not occupied. We received orders to detail a detachment of a hundred and fifty horses, and hold ourselves in readiness to march on this assemblage of officers on the first information that they occupied a position where there would be any chance of a fight.

I was appointed to command this expedition, and was impatiently expecting the signal to start; though there was such disproportion of numbers, I was quite sure of success if we met, for the body I was to find was composed of officers of all arms, even of infantry, and in con sequence it could not act with the union and combination that actuates troops accustomed to obey a single commander.

In this state of expectation, I was ordered to Madrid to appear as a witness at the court-martial on the affair of the grenadier. I requested to be excused from giving evidence, on the ground of the possibility and even probability of an order for my detachment to start. This reason seemed good, and I was exempted. But Colonel Montcalm, the president of the court-martial that tried the *cuirassier*, managed matters so badly that the man was acquitted to the general astonishment. Then Lieutenant-General Roussel d'Hurbal, commanding the *cuirassier* division, wrote to General Deschamps, the commander of our brigade, that the acquittal of the prisoner rendered me liable to a judgment that would entail my dismissal, two years' imprisonment, and incapacity to be recalled to the ranks of the army.

General Deschamps had come to take up his quarters with us at Alcala; he sent for me on the receipt of this letter, and with an air of the greatest consternation handed it to me to read. I ought to have perceived in it nothing but a proof of aberration of intellect on the part of its author, to have taken no account of it, and quietly let things take their course; but I made the mistake of being too hasty at the cool indifference with which they threw to the dogs the honour and career of an officer in the higher ranks, whose conscience told him that he had always been guided by feelings of duty.

Besides, in the case in question, I was perfectly within the law, and so I should have been even if I had killed the man who was struggling with his corporal and striking him; and the colonel who was present at the occurrence, (for it took place on our return from Madrid where we had been spending the day together, and we were attracted by the noise of it), loudly expressed his approbation of the correction I had given, and even wished it had been more.

Indignant and irritated to the last extremity, I wrote in anger to General Roussel d'Hurbal, telling him that I was certain I had acted legally, and that far from claiming his indulgence, I earnestly requested him to have me brought before a court-martial, and to call it with the least possible delay. I was quite sure he would not dare to do it, and if he did I should be acquitted with great credit. The matter rested there, but I was deeply wounded, and thenceforward my thoughts took a gloomy turn, to which I was already inclined by matters foreign to the military recollections that are the only things to be contained in this narrative. (In 1816 M. de Gonneville had lost his wife; in 1819 his son; in 1821 his father; in 1822 his daughter; and lastly his mother died during the Spanish campaign in 1823.) I lost both appetite and sleep, and to finish me I had two days afterwards to repress a rising occasioned by the passage of some political prisoners.

The people had gone to the prison to cut the prisoners' throats as they came out. I ran thither with three or four officers, without having time to fetch our arms, for it was in the morning and the information came to us at the hotel where we breakfasted. We had to make our way through the crowd, always a hideous sight when agitated by evil passions. Shouts of death were heard around, impatient hands were brandishing knives; all foretold a scene of blood, and murder would have been done without an intervention.

We reached the prison-door just as the gaoler, under the influence of fear or perhaps his own instinct, was going to hand over the prisoners to the multitude, under pretence of giving them in charge to five or six wretched horsemen of the Army of Faith, whose swords were hung on with rope, and who trembled as much as the men they were to guard. The steps in front of the prison-door had not been invaded, and we arrived in time to send the prisoners back just as the first appeared on the door sill with the look of a man led to execution. I was impatiently expecting the arrival of the picket of fifteen *cuirassiers*, always kept ready to mount; they soon came up at a gallop and cleared the approaches to the prison, so that I could get the prisoners brought out, and I sent the detachment that came to help on escort duty as far as two leagues from Alcala.

In my condition this scene had a great effect on me, and there was an increase in the malady I had been suffering under for several days; I had a fever, and our surgeon-major could not detect its character. We left Alcala to go to Carabanchel, one league from Madrid. It was only one day's march, but I suffered very much from the heat during it. I had been able to touch nothing but cold water for a week; and the fatigue was much greater for me than for persons in their usual health. I went to bed on my arrival, and next day jaundice was declared, and such a severe jaundice that the doctor had never seen one like it.

While I was suffering from this trial, my regiment received orders to join an expedition sent to the left bank of the Tagus, where it was thought they might find a party of the enemy, said to have been seen in that quarter. This marching order made me rather more yellow. During all the course of my campaigns no cause had ever prevented my joining the service portion of the corps I belonged to, and, consequently, I had been present at all the affairs in which it had taken part; there were even some that I could enumerate besides that I was personally concerned in.

So, the idea that the Regiment of Condé might go into action and I not be with them, caused me so much vexation that I had great difficulty to prevent myself from weeping when all the officers came to express their regret at going without me. I remained alone at Carabanchel, and treated my jaundice so well, by eating four or five pounds of grapes a day, that on my regiment's return in five or six weeks' time, if not quite well, I was on foot and feeling my strength return.

I made a very pleasant acquaintance during my illness. I was in the house of the Marchioness of Hanos, for she was at Madrid, and I was lodged in the first story of her country house. Some days after I had taken up my quarters there, an unusual noise took place on the ground floor, and I thought that the *marchioness* had come to Carabanchel from Madrid; the porter informed me that she had not come, but had allowed a general, a friend of hers, to occupy the disposable part of the house with his family.

Now this personage was General Black (Blake). In the War of Independence, he had been President of the *junta* that governed Spain during King Ferdinand's captivity; *generalissimo* of all the forces raised against us; and especially had commanded the army we had been opposed to in the conquest of the Kingdom of Valentia. In these later times he was President of the insurgent *junta* sitting at Cadiz, whither they had taken the king; and after the capitulation that put the king and the town into our hands, he had abandoned any participation in business, and went to Madrid before the return of the king and the *dauphin*.

His wife was with him, the husband of the eldest daughter, and her two young children. They arrived destitute of everything, for all their baggage had been taken by a band of brigands in the Sierra Morena. I paid them a visit, though I was still quite yellow, and was so well received that I saw them every day, at all hours, for the three weeks I spent near them.

The general was a plain man, modest, and of great learning; he talked little, but spoke with a benevolent air that did not look like a wish to avoid a longer conversation. As we had always beaten him, I did not like to be the first to talk to him of the conquest of Valentia; when he asked me in what corps I had served in that war, I was obliged to tell him that it was in the very one that had been against him and had caused all his disasters, for he and the rest of his army had fallen into our hands in consequence of the fall of Valentia.

He did not draw back from a subject that must have had such painful memories for him, and even enjoyed putting questions to me about the details of matters that had passed there, and giving me information of the highest interest on these matters or others connected with them. He told me that at the Battle of Saguntum he had at first thought himself secure of victory, and that probably he should have secured it but for the defeat of his cavalry. He had never understood how they were routed in the way I have described in my account of this battle—neither have I myself. He had a very great respect for the 13th Regiment of Cuirassiers, and said they had caused him severe loss.

We often, also, spoke of the existing condition of Spain in consequence of our intervention; and the succession of events since then showed me that his judgment was correct, and was a perfect justification for the resolution he had taken, and adhered to, of disappearing altogether from the stage of politics. I fancy that his name never appeared in a newspaper after 1823, though it had been so famous; I never even saw a mention have taken place. We parted with reciprocal promises not to forget one another; I do not know whether he kept it on his side, but as for myself, I have often thought of him and his family.

My regiment returned to Carabanchel without having had occasion to draw swords, or having seen the shadow of an enemy. I was delighted that it was so, and took advantage of the rest that was given them, to repair and set in order all the mischief done by a three weeks' march. After we left Dijon, I performed the duties of lieutenant-colonel, as the officer bearing that rank was away on duty, and only joined us on our return to France. We received orders to march rapidly to Manzanares, in the southern part of La Mancha, at the foot of the Sierra Morena, but this order was withdrawn, and we stopped some days at Aranjuez, and had time to explore it at our ease.

The Casa Labrador was falling into ruins for want of necessary repairs, and the millions that were buried by Charles IV. in this fancy, seemed to us to be very nearly lost. Masses of gold and the most exquisite pictures are lavished on the interior, and the rain had already found its way into the roofs, and was threatening mischief to the splendid ceilings, and all the ornaments that make this abode one of the most magnificent that have ever existed. The actual palace is very common, and the inside was so dirty that a private person, even though not at all particular, would have looked twice before he received his friends in the state apartments. But great historical events have taken place there, and they give great interest to this residence.

I took much more interest in visiting the field of the Battle of Acaña, where Marshal Soult, with twenty thousand men, defeated eighty thousand Spaniards and took twenty-two thousand prisoners. I knew the marshal's manoeuvres, and a sight of the ground made me understand this immense and magnificent success which may thus be sketched, to the south, two leagues from Aranjuez, the valley of the Tagus is bounded by a steep of moderate height, with the town of Acaña at its top on the route into Andalusia. The Spanish Army, marching on Madrid and thinking they were sure of conquest, encamped on the height; Marshal Soult had hastened from Madrid on the news of this aggressive march, he boldly crossed the Tagus, and ranged his troops in order of battle in the plain, so that the enemy from his commanding position could count the small proportionate numbers of his adversaries, and think he would crush them next day. But during the night Marshal Soult having rested his troops some hours, climbed the steep that protected the camp by very abrupt slopes a little on the Spanish right, and attacked the right with the vigour that French soldiers always display when they feel they are well led.

A change of front to the rear had to be made to meet the attack, as the ground admitted of nothing else; Ballasteros, the general in command of the Spaniards, probably tried it, but his troops were poorly drilled and led by bad officers, and came to meet French valour with hesitation and disorder. The result to them was a frightful rout, entailing the loss of all their artillery, of twenty-two thousand prisoners, and a great number of killed and wounded.

And so, the army that a few hours ago had a certainty of victory in prospect, and of a triumphant entry into Madrid, found it was so much beaten and dispersed that its remnants could not be rallied, and it was never heard of again. The inhabitants of Madrid had thought Marshal Soult's little army sent forth for a prey to their liberators, and at the dull sound of the guns they made preparations for a splendid triumph for the conquerors. They were quite incredulous at the first news of the defeat, but at last they had to yield to the force of evidence, and return of Marshal Soult's army with its twenty-two thousand prisoners as an incontestable fact.

Our stay at Aranjuez was not long, and we marched to the Sierra Morena, crossing the province of La Mancha from north to south, a well cultivated and rich country with not a tree to be seen in it. The villages are almost towns their population is so numerous; they are at great distances apart, and in the intervals, there is not a house to be found, and that is one reason why the police in Spain have never been able to protect those very few houses that stand alone against brigandages; and so all these large villages are solidly built and show a sort of defence; the entrances are few in number and could easily be barricaded; the houses are continuous and have no openings towards the country; the windows are almost all furnished with strong iron bars, and the doors thick enough to resist a violent attack for a long time. Within, the appearance denotes comfortable circumstances, and there is a neatness to be found there, that is nowhere else to be seen in Spain except in the Kingdom of Valentia.

We stopped at Manzanares where the 4th Regiment of Cuirassiers joined us, and we received the submission of the Lithuanian Mounted Chasseurs. Colonel Aymar, their commander, had acquired some celebrity by beating a body of partisans in our pay who had been desirous of penetrating into Madrid contrary to orders, the day before we made our entrance into it. Colonel Aymar, under the very plausible pretext that this was a violation of the convention of occupation, fell upon them between the Prado and the Alcala Gate, and served them the worse, because he had a personal hatred against the adventurer who was their chief; and, besides, these partisans being Spaniards, the encounter naturally took the stamp usual in civil wars.

We gave a dinner to Colonel Aymar and his staff; I sat next him at table, and though he was naturally dull and silent, I managed at last to engage him in conversation; we talked of the war of independence, and he also had served in it. He told me that his mother and sister had perished by the hands of the French, under circumstances I do not remember. His regiment seemed to me in better order than most Spanish regiments I had seen.

From Manzanares I went with a squadron to lead a column of prisoners made in Andalusia, as far as Madrid-Lejos, half way to Aranjuez. and handed them over to a squadron of the 5th Cuirassiers that came to meet them and escort them to Madrid. There were a hundred officers, four hundred soldiers and sub-officers, and some forty women and children. This employment gave me considerable trouble, in consequence of the carelessness of the officers about their men, they would have been starved to death had I not looked after them myself.

Among these prisoners I found a colonel of Engineers from Valentia, he had been in the army that had surrendered at the taking of that city. Conversing with him on the occurrences of that time, I told him about the young lieutenant-colonel I had left, to my great regret, lying on the field at Saguntum, and with real pleasure learnt that he was not dead. After we had left the field of battle, some persons who had seen him fall, returned at night and carried him off. This colonel also gave me satisfactory news of the Muños family, with whom I had lodged in Valentia and who had made friends with me.

I had only just returned to Manzanares when my regiment received orders to return to Madrid. We had again to traverse the interminable plain of La Mancha that shows not a single undulation of the ground, but a very curious phenomenon is to be found a few leagues from Manzanares. The Guadiana rising in the mountains of Alcaraz, after a course of considerable length, disappears all at once, without leaving the smallest trace that it has in former times flowed over the ground, then it re-appears at some distance, at a spot by the side of the road we had to travel; there it issues from three small lakes in the midst of an immense lagoon of reeds that would be impenetrable, but fishermen cut little alleys in them to get their boats along, and reach the little lakes; no one has ever been able to sound their depth, and they give out such a quantity of water that the Guadiana is a considerable river when it issues from them; these lakes are called Ojos de la Guadiana—the eyes of the Guadiana.

We resumed our encampment at Carabanchel near Madrid, but I did not find General Black still there. We received orders to return to France, and go into garrison at Joigny, and we got there at the end of November, 1823. As soon as the frontier was passed, the march was nothing but a long and wearisome ovation for us. The authorities of the towns we stopped in came to meet us with such specimens of National Guards and bands as they could collect. We had to undergo long addresses in praise of our exploits, our valour, and our victories.

It may be imagined that knowing what our performances had been during this campaign, and our great wish to pull off our boots after a day's march, we found these daily receptions sufficiently tiresome. Again, it was not all over with that; there was a banquet awaiting us; and then it was the turn of the poets of the place to laud us, and combine the words glory and victory with the name of Condé that the regiment bore. At last we arrived at Joigny, it put a fitting crown on the edifice, and it was done.

Garrison life began again in all its uniformity. When we had repaired the damage caused by our marches, the recruits and horses sent to us had to be drilled. Eighteen months passed thus, and during that time our lieutenant-colonel had been made colonel and replaced by an old major, a good sort of man, but quite wanting in manners and education.

For ten years, at all inspections, I had been nominated for this rank, and I had comforted myself that no other person would fill this post in my regiment, when it became vacant. So, I was sadly disappointed at this fresh discomfiture; but I was used to disappointment, and in this instance, as in others, I kept a brave heart against fortune.

Probably to keep me patient, I had in the course of these ten years been appointed officer of the Legion of Honour, and had received the crosses of Saint Louis, and Saint Ferdinand of Spain.

At last, eighteen months after our return to Joigny, I received my appointment as major in the 1st Regiment of Cuirassiers of the Royal Guard, and this gave me lieutenant-colonel's rank, while leaving me the duties I had performed for eleven years. I received proofs of attachment and regret from the officers of the Regiment of Condé, that affected me much, and I left Joigny at the beginning of the year 1825.

The regiment I joined was commanded by Colonel de Lepinay, a narrow-minded and vain man. He received me very well, and immediately gave me charge of all relating to the drill, including the theoretical instruction of officers. I did not know one of them, there were men of very good, not to say very high, families among them; others had been taken from the class of sub-officers. Nevertheless, there was a united spirit ruling among them, and the regiment looked thoroughly well.

It was in garrison at Meaux when I joined, and out of each eight months spent two at Paris, to be on duty near the king, and this duty for the heavy cavalry consisted of giving the king's escort in Paris only, and taking a share with the other troops of the guards at the Tuileries. The major on duty commanded the escort, and kept at the left door of the carriage; this post was not without its dangers, for the carriage was always driven at full speed, whatever might be the condition of the road and width of the street, and it compelled the major and the officer on guard who was at the other door, to perform evolutions that sometimes caused serious accidents.

None happened to me during the three years I passed in the Guard, and I did more escort duty than any of the other majors, as they were all sometimes ill; during one of our tours of duty there were only two of us, and as the king went out every day, we had only one off duty. We spent twenty-four hours at the guard in the Rue de Rivoli, facing the Pavilion de Marsan, and besides the cavalry, a hundred horses strong, we had three companies of infantry on picket, and the outer guards of that arm under our command.

The king's general escort was composed of fourteen bodyguards commanded by a sergeant, of fourteen *cuirassiers*, or horse grenadiers, also commanded by a sergeant. The officer of the Guards and the major only appeared there for etiquette; one of the king's esquires, usually a general officer, went in front of the carriage; the heavy cavalry only escorted the king as far as the barriers, and there it was relieved by the light cavalry in waiting at the spot; for the king's return, the detachment of the former and the major on duty had to wait at the barrier and took the king back to the Tuileries; he went out every day as I have mentioned; in the hunting season especially, Charles X. would have thought his day lost if it had been spent without a hunt.

In bad weather there was this nuisance in the escort duty, that it was done in full dress in all weathers at a gallop, and that one received the mud from the horses and the wheels as well as any rain falling. On returning to the guardroom, one had to change with all speed to go to the breakfast or dinner of the officers on duty, for these meals took place exactly at the moment when we got back to the barrier; one of the king's stewards presided, a court office, and the royal servants waited.

Nothing especial happened to me during the three years I served in the Guard, except commanding the regiment at an inspection, and this got me a good many compliments, and I fancy also the ill-will of Colonel Lepinay. The officers did not like him, and freely expressed their opinion that the regiment had never before shown off to so much advantage, or worked so easily. As I have said before the colonel was a narrow-minded sort of man, and this probably wounded him, for on his return till I left the regiment he treated me very coldly, whereas he had not before this.

And yet I may say that I never made or listened to any improper speeches about him; and even when I heard anyone making allusion to his nonsense, while engaged in the theoretical instruction of the officers, I always repressed it.

There were three majors, de Mons, de Ploeür, and myself. One day when I was with de Mons, de Ploeür came in with a serious and displeased look. He said good morning to us, and afterwards instead of sitting down as de Mons asked him, he kept walking up and down the room at a quick pace. At last we asked him what was the matter, and then he stopped and said in a solemn voice,

> We cannot go any more to the Café des Célestins. I have just come from it; all the officers were there and talked of the colonel in a way that was unbearable, and I—I did the same.

A rather peculiar joke was played on M. de Villequier, President of the Court of Rouen, by the Bodyguards. He had come to Paris to reprove his son who had got in debt; all his son's comrades came in a body to visit M. Villequier, and begged him to do them the honour of dining with them. The President was delighted at these proofs of respect, and was most happy to accept the invitation. The Bodyguards drank his health first, and then several more, combining the sword and the gown in their toasts. M. de Villequier drank with them, found them charming and full of respect for him. He even sang a song to be like them, and at last allowed a sword and sabretache to be buckled round his waist. Next morning the poor President remembered the events of the previous evening, paid his son's debts without saying a word, and very soon went back to Rouen.

Several months afterwards he was presented to the *dauphiness*, and she said to him, "I am astonished, Monsieur le President, that you are not in full dress to come to court."

M. de Villequier, in consternation, passed his eye rapidly over his clothes, but could not see any omission.

"You have forgotten your sabretache," added the *dauphiness*; and then she bowed to the President, and he has probably never consoled himself for this adventure.

Every Sunday, as the king came from chapel he used to say a few words to the courtiers he passed. The old Marquis de Raigecourt was one of the most constant attendants; and as he was afflicted with a chronic cough, Charles X. generally said to him, "Well, my lord marquis, how is your cough?" But one day he asked him how the *marchioness* was, and M. de Raigecourt, being deaf, never suspected that the king had changed his usual inquiry, and answered, "Sire, much as usual by day, but the night wears me out."

In the month of May, 1828, I was appointed Lieutenant-colonel in the 12th Regiment of Chasseurs. During the three years I had spent in the Guard, I had time to become known to the king and the *dauphin*, as they were very particular in having information about all the officers of the Guard, especially the superiors. I had often attended them out hunting, and had been treated with the kindness they generally displayed to all that approached them. The *dauphiness* alone always showed me the most marked coldness, and she never said one word to me during these three years.

This was very unusual with her, and I felt the bitterness of it the more severely because I had really worshipped her from my youth. This orphan of the Temple, an object of interest to the whole world, held the place of a divinity in my fancy. The smallest details of her mournful history were engraven in my memory, and I never saw her without calling to mind her image during the most terrible seasons of her life. I should have been glad to be able to give her some proof of great devotion; and when I left the Guards, though at my own request, I thought with regret that perhaps I should thus lose the opportunity.

Events only too clearly proved that my good will was never to find any means of expression. I joined the 12th Chasseurs at Verdun. The Lieutenant-Colonel de Nettancourt having been appointed to the Guards, gave over the command to me. The colonel, Count de Maillé, had been placed on the retired list at his own request, and had gone away a fortnight ago. My friend Colonel Blin, the head of the Cavalry Office, had shown me the inspector's notes about all the officers of the regiment. I had taken copies of them and studied them, so as to have a previous knowledge of the men I was to meet.

Colonel Jourdan, appointed to relieve M. de Maillé, had obtained leave, and was not to join for three months at Lunéville, and I had orders to send four squadrons there for a camp of manoeuvres. I had been informed at the War Ministry that the regiment had been for a long time very much neglected by Colonel de Maillé; his conduct was very irregular and his mind had been entirely distracted from his military duties by an unfortunate passion for music. As for Lieutenant-Colonel de Nettancourt he was quite taken up with a great law suit he had in hand against the house of Rohan and thought of nothing else. All the furniture was loaded with bundles of papers in the room where he received me, and I could not get him to talk about anything

CUIRASSIERS IN CAMP

but the law suit; he told me all the stages of it, from its beginning in the reign of Louis XIV.

I set to work at once to get the regiment forward, so that it should not appear to too great disadvantage at the camp at Lunéville, where there were already three other light cavalry regiments. When the body of officers came to call upon me on my arrival, I addressed them in such a way as I thought most likely to stir up their individual zeal; but I had been warned that their habits were fixed, especially the captains', and they generally took very little notice of the orders they received. I myself very soon received a proof of it in a matter of dress. I put the six captains-*commandant* under arrest, and never but once again had I occasion to resort to extreme measures.

When the time came, the four squadrons told off for the camp, started on their march, and I had the pleasure of hearing that when they arrived they were considered in a satisfactory condition. I remained at Verdun with the two remaining squadrons, and the colonel returned with those from Lunéville about the month of October. The usual garrison duties occupied the Winter; about the following month of June, the four squadrons went back to Lunéville, and I stayed at Verdun as I had done the year before.

The celebrated journey of Charles X. into Lorraine and Alsace took place a few days afterwards; and the frenzied enthusiasm of the people at every stage, gave hopes of stability soon to be cruelly disappointed. The king, accompanied by the *dauphin*, heard mass at Verdun, and dined and slept there. I had gone two miles to meet him with all the cavalry under my command, according to the standing orders, and I escorted him the same distance on his departure. The king and the *dauphin* were very civil to me, and treated me as an old acquaintance.

The next week the *dauphiness* also arrived at Verdun, she came from Metz and had desired that there should be no public reception; but the *sub-prefect* with an excess of zeal that did not come from the heart, ranged the National Guard upon the glacis, and made them surround the princess's open travelling carriage, the drums marched in front. Now these National Guards were wearing the same uniform as those who in and the children of France on the journey from Versailles to Paris, and this wretched notion of the *sub-prefect* must have reminded her of that disastrous time, and so she was very much annoyed, and let it be seen rather too much. What, then, was my astonishment, and I may say emotion, when she showed a great deal of kindness towards me, and spoke to hardly anyone else when we paid her a visit!

The like favours were renewed during the breakfast. General Vathier, the *commandant* of the Department of the Meuse, and residing at Verdun, had gone to Bar to await the king's return, the *dauphiness* caused me to be seated next to her at table; and an especial mark of favour that she showed me in the presence of all, just as the troops in garrison were marching past before her, was a very great honour, and I preserve a respectful and affectionate remembrance of that honour. The troops were the 50th Regiment of Foot, and two squadrons left by me under the command of Major Schaüenburg; all the authorities were ranged in order fifteen paces to the rear of the *dauphiness* for the march past, and just as the troops were beginning to move, she turned, looked for me among the group, and called me by name. I hastened up, thinking she had some orders to give, and when I came near, she said, with an expression of kindness and almost of affection that I shall never forget in my life,

"Monsieur de Gonneville, remain near me."

Perhaps from my very youth, my heart had exceeded all others in the devoted worship paid to the sorrows of this princess, and her royal character; and now she thought of me under circumstances where such distinction had perhaps never been conferred. I was exceedingly gratified at it. She spoke to me several times during the march past, asking what I thought of the 50th Regiment, as she considered that they were not very good. I answered that she must make some excuse for people that were too much taken up with her to think of keeping line or distance.

But as some officers' wives had rushed into the column to their husbands' sides, and were marching and keeping step with them to get a better sight of her, she said to me,

"Now you must allow that is a little too much."

The *dauphiness* got into her carriage after the review, and as she went away, bowed to me in a way that seemed the more gracious to me, as she never had accustomed me to any favours from her while I was in the Guards. What could be the reason of the change? I shall never know. I never saw her again, and was much grieved at her death; I had kept up a vague hope that the time of her trials might end, and Divine justice confer a crown on her in this world, in expectation of her certain inheritance in Heaven.

In the month of August, 1829, I received orders to take the command of the depot for remounts at Saint Maixent. Colonel Blin, the chief of the cavalry office, had advised me to accept this appointment, for, as he wrote to me, it ought to ensure my promotion to the rank of colonel in two years at most.

So I started for Saint Maixent, and as I went through Paris I had an interview with the Count de Caux, War Minister at the time, and I received some very flattering speeches from him, and some information for the re-organisation and future work of the depots, as he said they were going from bad to worse.

A few days afterwards, Major Méan de Saint-Prix gave me over the command, I spent nearly a year in traversing the whole of the district attached to the depot, and managed to make some good purchases, and also did my best to conform to the instructions I had received.

Chapter 14

The Revolution of 1830

In the month of May, 1830, I got leave to go to Paris to fetch my wife and daughter. (In 1825 M. de Gonneville had married as his second wife, Mademoiselle de Bacourt, sister of M. de Bacourt, ambassador in the reign of Louis Philippe, and legatee of Prince de Talleyrand's *Memoirs*.)

There was at this time a dull murmuring of political storm; the expedition to Algeria in preparation might make a diversion, and prevent the revolutionary projects being put in operation; but the king had made the immense mistake of putting the Duke de Polignac at the head of the government, and their mistakes, the absence of any precautions against danger, the alienation of several of the regiments of the Guards, and the undeserved distrust of those of the Line, all were causes that induced the revolution of July, depriving the elder branch of the Bourbons of the throne, when all around them, except Marshal Marmont, Generals Vincent and Saint Chaman, were one worse than another in incapacity, cowardice, or treason.

I have no intention to relate the well-known history of the catastrophe; but I wish to repeat that all real soldiers have never ceased to say that at the time Charles X. made an abdication of his rights for himself and his heirs, and consented to leave the soil of France, a man of spirit, if there had only been one to be found, would have been able to bring the king back in triumph to his capital with nothing but a couple of guns and a squadron of cavalry.

I left Paris just as the portion of the population attached to legitimate loyalty as the symbol of order in the State and in families, was agitated by vague and dismal rumours. I had only just got to Normandy to spend the rest of my leave, when the famous Ordinances suspending the constitution were published. I was staying with one of my oldest and best friends, M. de Dampierre, and he asked me to stay with him till daylight should appear; but the notion of being absent from my post at a moment when a difficulty might arise, prevented me from accepting this proposal, and the day after we heard of the publication of the Ordinances I set out for Saint Maixent, taking my wife and child with me.

As far as Tours I perceived a certain agitation in the places we passed through; and there it became much more apparent. It was night when we arrived there; the whole population was crowding the Rue Royale as we entered. My carriage was instantly stopped and surrounded by this crowd in their anxiety for news, as they had already heard of the fighting in Paris, and everyone was anxiously awaiting the event with different feelings.

I found considerable difficulty in making the inquirers understand that I knew nothing. At last we were able to get into the Pheasant Hotel, and next day I had a visit from Count Borgarelli d'Ison, a good friend of mine, commanding the 16th Regiment of Infantry at Tours. He did not seem to me as uneasy as the circumstances seemed to demand; he was an Italian, and though naturalised in France, he could not have the patriotic feelings ingrafted by the traditions of many generations. Hence naturally arose a little indifference for the destinies of the country, and the dynasties as they rose and fell.

We left Tours about nine in the morning to go to Poitiers. No certain information had been received there; it was only known that there was fighting in Paris. At Châtellerault, while we were stopping at a wheelwright's, and I had some small repairs done to my carriage, I saw a man come at full speed by the road we had just passed in the greatest disorder; his clothes were torn, his nankeen pantaloons were drawn up to his knees, allowing his bare legs to appear with the blood almost starting from them through the friction of the stirrup leather and saddle flaps. His face was swollen and purple, and seemed to look like a case of apoplexy.

As soon as he was assisted from his horse, for he could not dismount without help, he came tottering to me and begged me to let him have a place in my carriage to continue his journey; he told me that he could not possibly continue on horseback any longer, as he was not used to it, and that he was in the greatest haste to get to his family at Bordeaux and reassure them, as if they heard what was going on at Paris they might suppose he was among the number of the thousands of neutral persons who fell under the shots of the two parties.

He showed me a printed bulletin; it was signed by the principal revolutionists, and without any positive expressions, it made me think that the defence of order had not obtained, the success that in my inmost thoughts I wished should be established most indubitably; it was clear that when the bulletin was published there were two opposing directories in being at Paris, and victory had not declared for either side I pointed out to the unfortunate individual that as I had my wife in my carriage, my daughter lying in her cradle, and two servants on the box, it was physically impossible to give him a place, but that he might get a cabriolet at the first house that would take him to Poitiers at least.

He followed my advice, and before we started I had the pleasure of seeing horses put to the cabriolet I had told him of. I fancy the poor wretch had never been on horseback before, and he had just accomplished without stopping seventy-five leagues at full speed of posting in all sorts of saddles, and this in nankeen trousers without straps, and wearing shoes.

We reached Poitiers on the evening of the same day, and there also I was anxiously questioned by all who came near me. I saw the *prefect* and General de Marchangy commanding the division. I informed them of the bulletin of four lines shown me by the Bordeaux merchant, for the man was a merchant, and they thought the same of it as I did.

Next day between Lusignan and Niort, I met Madame de Beaumont and five of her children; her husband, the *prefect* of the Two Sèvres, was sending her to her own family near Vendôme, as a precaution against the risks he might be exposed to. While we were changing our horses, she communicated her fears for her husband to me, and as I still hoped that the crisis would terminate in conformity with my wishes, I gave her a little encouragement. She begged me to write to the *prefect* in this style, as soon as I got to Saint Maixent, and I promised that I would. I knew Monsieur and Madame de Beaumont very well, they had received me very pleasantly at Niort as soon as I arrived in the country.

Everything was very quiet at Maixent. During the ten months I had passed in this little town, the inhabitants had seemed to me to be persons of such pacific nature that I never had an idea that they could take part in a revolutionary movement. I had never seen anything there but placid and good-humoured faces. So, the day after my arrival, just as Captain Schaff, one of the depot for remounts was come to give me some particulars relating to the duty, I was greatly surprised to see my secretary come in hastily and much agitated; he came to tell me that a crowd of rioters were rushing to the Town Hall to hoist the tricoloured flag.

I instantly ran thither followed by Captain Schaff; the mayor and the municipal council all seemed stunned. Their answer to my reproaches for having allowed this sign of rebellion to be hoisted, was to show me the crowd collected before the Town Hall door, that I had passed through to get to them, and had to push my way, that is to say that they had only yielded to force.

There was a person among them bearing himself so proudly as to attract my notice. He began to speak in justification of the events; but as soon as I could make out the subject of his speech, I opened the door leading to the steps outside, and made a speech to the assembly to try and bring them back to better feelings. I was received by menacing cries and shouts, they tried to get the gendarmes to fire on me. At these threats, several of the persons I had left in the interior of the Town Hall came to beg me to come inside, and even tried to force me; but I got away from their hands, and running, or rather jumping down the stairs that divided me from the throng, I quietly stepped into the midst of them.

My heart was beating fast, and I was choking with anger, for nothing has ever seemed so hideous to me as a popular rising; the worst passions are displayed in a most repulsive manner on faces that have usually a look merely foolish, and if it was my duty to put down a similar movement, with sufficient means, I should be pitiless.

However, as soon as I descended into this ignoble arena, their vociferations ceased; they listened to me, and even when a man attempted to approach me with insult on his lips, the others kept him back. When I had made the best speech I could, but without persuading them to haul down the colour, I went away declaring that the white standard and white cockade should remain the colours of the depot for remounts, and that any attempt at the contrary should be repulsed by force. By force! And I had not a single cartridge, nor even a flint; the some thirty carbines that were the arms of the men of the depot had only wooden flints, and twenty Lancers of the Guard waiting for the horses to be given them, had not even their swords.

I went to the barracks from the place where I had such bad success; assembled my men, told them their duty, and said I had no doubt they would fulfil it. They gave me their promise and kept their word, except two Lancers of the Guard who deserted. I immediately sent an account of the events to General Marchangy and asked for his orders, for my present position could not be maintained for long.

Niort was at boiling heat, and was threatening to march to Saint Maixent to bring the *commandant* of the depot to reason. The *prefect* had printed and posted up my letter written to him on my arrival, and this had slightly checked the revolutionary movement, and caused some uneasiness to its promoters. The rioters would not forgive me this uneasiness. In their front rank appeared a certain Leclerc La Salle, editor of an opposition newspaper that continually had a crow to pick with the opposition.

I waited in vain for the general's reply; on the news of the revolution he had deserted his post without thinking of anything he left behind him, but afraid of the people of Poitiers, though they did nothing.

The new government became established during the subsequent week, it relieved the authorities who had not accepted it, and sent commissioners into the departments to hold inquests and receive adhesions or resignations. My mind then became exceedingly perplexed; I was filled with profound disgust at the new order of things, at the people who had fomented it, and the herd that crowded to support it; but I hesitated at quitting a career that I had embraced with enthusiasm; and at losing twenty-five years' service and the fruit of all my campaigns; I also felt a repugnance at making a voluntary surrender of the fortress to the hungry mass that are raised by a revolution.

All these reasons urged me to delay. I also said to myself that if there was any chance of the elder branch of the Bourbons regaining their place, they ought to approve of their most devoted servants having remained in the ranks of the army, though they had unfortunately not relied sufficiently upon it.

So, I went to Niort to the general that had been sent there, and whom I knew to have been prejudiced against me. Nevertheless, he received me very well, and seemed satisfied when I told him of my intention to remain in the service, without the least concealing my opinions or what I had done.

After that the tri-colour flag had to be hoisted at Saint Maixent. I had followed this flag in every war that I had seen, but for sixteen years it had not been the flag of France, and I felt a great sinking of heart at giving orders for it to be resumed.

I had often received threatening messages during the few preceding days; sometimes my house was to be attacked at night, sometimes insults and violence to my person were promised when I went out. But nothing of the sort took place. I made preparations for defence in the event of an attack upon my house, because it was the shelter of my wife and child; but I continued to go out at all hours as usual, not a bit the less.

My brother was on the Staff of the King's Guards, and I had been very anxious on his account, but was relieved by a letter from him. He had been hurt by his horse falling in the Place du Carrousel at the time of the fighting, and had been in great danger, but he was then in health and safety at his own house.

I had several days to wait in suspense and anxiety, then I received a letter from the Ministry, giving me orders to go and take the command of the depot of remounts at Alençon. I expected to have been put on the inactive list, and that would have suited me well enough, as employment must necessarily put me in contact with the new authorities, whose opinions and behaviour were very hateful to me.

However, I obeyed, and my journey from Saint Maixent to Alençon was sorrowful in a moral point of view. I was painfully struck at every change of horses with the continual repetition of popular tumult, disturbing and bringing to the surface the most abject-dregs of society, and we were exposed to the malicious curiosity characteristic of this class during the few minutes required for changing horses.

Alençon too, had its reactionary movement; the *prefect*, M. de Kersain, had been obliged to flee, and the mayor, M. de Chambray, had been menaced with death. The general sent to Alençon by the new government was a very brave man, who had before been in command of a brigade at the camp at Saint Omer, that was summoned to the king's assistance when it was too late. I heard from him that the troops from this camp had marched to Paris animated with a most excellent spirit, and the insinuations of the people of the towns they passed through were quite powerless against it.

Indeed, it had been necessary to moderate their spirit, when they desired to break down obstacles raised in several places to delay their march, and wished to fire upon the post-offices decorated with the tri-colour flag. The cavalry started from Lunéville under the orders of General Bourbon Busset, and marched upon Paris with the same feelings; but it had been sent for too late, and was stopped on the road by the accomplishment of the events of Rambouillet.

The day after my arrival at Alençon I received my promotion to the rank of colonel, and orders to go and take the command of the 4th Regiment of Hussars at Pontivy. My astonishment may be imagined at receiving this appointment, because I was expecting at least to be put on the retired list. I had for several days been suffering an increasing pain in the foot, and I could not proceed to my appointed post. The surgeon I called in ascertained the formation of an abscess under the sole of the foot, and the necessity for several weeks' rest. I asked for leave and obtained it, going to Calvados, to the Château de Bray, the house of my friend Dampierre, whom I had left a month before; this had been time enough for France to alter its face, and millions of lives to be completely changed.

The ministers' offices were soon besieged by a crowd who had lost their bread by the revolution; but this crowd was but a trifle compared to that scrambling for places; the Minister for Home Affairs in a few days received three thousand requests for *prefectures*, and forty thousand for *sub-prefectures*. It was the same everywhere, regiments turned out their officers, and Marshal Gérard, the new War Minister, instead of treating these acts of insubordination with rigour, filled up the places of these officers by their inferiors, the instigators of the revolt. The army was falling to pieces, for such examples, even if exceptional, must necessarily at last corrupt the whole, always on the watch for change, especially when opening the door to ambition.

Meanwhile during the progress of my cure, the minister informed me that he had made a change in my destination, and that as soon as I was able I was to go to Dôle and take the command of the 13th Regiment of Chasseurs. A short time after receiving this order I started on my journey, and went to the War Ministry as I went through Paris. The new head of the cavalry office was the son of the actress Branchu, and he gave me a sort of admonition based upon the affair at Saint Maixent; I considered this very improper, and showed my displeasure pretty sharply.

Going home I wrote to the minister, and told him that if the words of the head of the office had been intended to call forth from me any explanations of my conduct as needing excuse, they had completely failed of their effect; for my conscience told me that I had done my duty, and that under the same circumstances I should do the same again I added that if this frank declaration made me appear in opposition to the ideas of the government I was ready to submit to the consequences, and I stated at the end that as I had heard that the 13th

Chasseurs had obliged several officers to retire, particularly the colonel, my first care on joining them would be to discover the authors of such a breach of discipline, and that as long as I was in command of the regiment, they would be put on one side and not receive any favour or promotion. I received no reply, and went to Dôle.

Lieutenant-Colonel de Brack received me there, a man who had been brought again into the service after an interval of sixteen years; and had been appointed in his nominal rank although he had only been a captain before. De Brack had a certain kind of notoriety, especially due to his amours with Mademoiselle Mars of the *Théâtre François*, After the fall of the Empire, he had attached himself to Napoleon's family, especially Queen Hortense, and had attended in the capacity of gentleman of honour upon the daughter of Prince Eugène de Beauharnais, married to the Emperor Don Pedro on her voyage to Brazil.

He was just married; his wife was a charming woman, daughter of General Farine; he had been one of the handsomest men to be seen, and at his present age, forty, was still very good-looking. He was clever and wrote in the papers, but was a man always about some intrigue and trying to throw dust in people's eyes. He received me very pleasantly, and introduced me at his own house in the evening to the three majors of the regiment, the fourth to return to France. I was pleased enough with the appearance of these three persons, as they seemed honest men; as for the lieutenant-colonel, I thought that, in the midst of his civilities, there was some awkwardness which did not look as if all was quite above-board.

It was arranged that I should receive the body of officers next day at noon; I had been informed during the course of the evening that the regiment had just been inspected by General Sémelé, and he had left Dôle two days before my arrival, and the lieutenant-colonel told me nothing particular about the inspection. Next day at noon I received a letter from General Sémelé, giving me orders to go to Besançon to await the determination of the War Minister, as he had forwarded his opinion that at the present time he thought it undesirable to entrust me with the command of a regiment.

On the receipt of his letter I hastened to the lieutenant-colonel, and strictly questioned him as to whether he knew anything of the contents of the letter he had forwarded to me. By his behaviour, I felt sure that he knew the tenor of it; but he took all sorts of oaths to me that he knew nothing about it, and that gave me an opportunity of making him understand what I should have thought of his silence on the evening before, if General Sémelé had taken him into his confidence.

And then I used some pretty plain language to him, as if I had full confidence in his assertion, whilst it really was on his observations and his information of my conduct at Saint-Maixent, that General Sémelé, a notorious enemy of the Restoration, had come to his determination concerning me.

So, I was obliged to go to Besançon to General Morand, commanding the division, who had been informed of my coming. I found him very well disposed towards me, and yet he had been completely neglected during the sixteen years of the reign of the elder branch of the Bourbons. He had passed all that time in complete retirement, he was a man of great merit, and his name was among the generals of the Empire who were elected by public opinion to become marshals of France, and he had commanded a *corps d'armée* in the last campaigns with great distinction.

I very soon saw that he did not approve of Sémelé's hasty way of proceeding; he often asked me to dinner and to visit him while I was at Besançon; we talked of fighting, and I was very glad to show him that I had studied the matter from good authorities, and understood it on a sufficiently comprehensive scale.

His wife was a Pole, beautiful as they generally are, and very fond of society with its brilliancy and pleasures; she could never forgive the Restoration for condemning her to retirement during the pleasantest years of her life, and so she was most violent in her political opinions. She and her daughter of fifteen were bedizened with tricoloured ribbons; her son was only five and wore the uniform of the Civic National Guard. I immediately found an enemy in her; but her influence over the general had diminished in proportion to the advance of years, and certain matters that report said he had a right to reproach her with, and indeed he cast a pretty sharp sneer at her on the subject in my presence at the dinner table.

I was waiting the minister's decision on the matters laid before him by General Sémelé when I received a large official packet. It contained an order for me to go to Haguenau to preside over a commission appointed to receive three thousand horses for the cavalry. And with this order were sent instructions as to my duties as president of this commission, and a copy of the bargain made with the Jew contractors. I alone was to decide on receiving or rejecting the horses offered.

The letter was addressed to me as Colonel of the 13th Regiment of Chasseurs, and as nothing was said in it about General Sémelé's decision, I thought it had not been thought worthy of consideration; besides, it seemed to me very unlikely that a commission of such great importance, implying great confidence, and at a time when war seemed imminent, should be entrusted to an officer who was to be set aside. So, I wrote to Lieutenant-Colonel de Brack to inform him of my temporary destination, and to desire him to send me a detailed report every week about all the regimental duties, insisting especially on such as were in preparation for a speedy start on a campaign.

I reached Haguenau before the other members of the commission, and found the 7th Regiment of Chasseurs, then under marching orders to leave the barracks free to receive the remount horses. The regiment left Haguenau three days after I arrived; it was under the command of M. de Mornay. The members of the commission soon arrived, they were three in number—a major, a lieutenant, and a veterinary surgeon.

I have mentioned that they were only empowered to give their opinion when consulted; and I must add that during the whole of the examination not one of them said a word to me about the horses I passed. Before they came I had received a visit from a Strasburg Jew, who was to show me the horses as agent for the sellers. He was a very polite man, well dressed and holding a high position among his people at Strasburg, his name was Afft.

On taking leave of me he put five-and-twenty shillings into my servant's hand as he opened the door for him, and so astonished him by his generosity that he came to tell me about it. I thought it was a kind of feather to try how the wind blew, and I sent him at once to carry back the thirty *francs*, and this probably cut short any attempt of the same kind.

At last we began to receive the horses, and so many were rejected that Aaron, the famous Paris horse-dealer, and one of the principal speculators in the transaction, hurried to Haguenau to see if he could not persuade me by his intervention to be more yielding.

I had made a rule that I would not allow any observations to be made by the contractors about horses I would not receive. On the first occasion when he was present, Aaron, in a somewhat too peremptory manner, tried to make me see that a bad horse was a good one; and I told him that, if he said another word, I would put a stop to the inspection; and that would have caused them a considerable loss, as all the horses from Germany stood at their expense.

He attended another inspection and kept silence, then he went back to Paris, leaving his son with whom I had no cause to be dissatisfied. I have related this small detail, because experience has shown me that it is quite impossible to act properly in receiving remounts, if any discussion is allowed to be opened by the interested parties. At Haguenau I received or rejected a horse with a single wave of the hand, and there was no sort of contest. Unfortunately, this principle is not followed by all heads of inspection of remounts.

The purchase of horses at Haguenau began in the month of January, 1831, and was not ended till the month of May, for the bad weather at times prevented the inspection, and the same cause delayed the arrival of the troops of horses. The Winter had been very rainy; inspections always took place out of doors, as the horses' action had to be considered after a trial on the hard road; they began at eleven o'clock and continued till four.

I never could see above sixty in the day. They came from Mecklenburg, Jutland, Hanover, and Oldenburg; and as some good horses from Würtemburg had been shown to me on approval, I obtained authority from the minister to receive some from that country also.

All the time this inspection of horses had been going on I had received the weekly reports of my regiment, and kept up an active correspondence with the lieutenant-colonel, so I was preparing to return to the 13th Chasseurs, when the War Minister wrote to me that the king was desirous of expressing his satisfaction to me at the manner in which I had discharged the duty entrusted to me, and he added that His Majesty desired to make use of my services at a later time, but that being *compelled* for the moment to deprive himself of them, he had decided that I should return to my home and be in the receipt of half-pay.

I raised no objections; only in replying to the minister to inform him of the place where I intended to reside, I told him that it seemed hard to me to appear to be sent into disgrace, just as I had performed a duty that entailed great moral responsibility, and had caused me to receive such a proof of satisfaction at its performance as had been given to me.

Then the minister sent me a second letter in still more laudatory language than before, and assured me of his good will for the immediate future. A few days afterwards I heard from General Wolf that the minister was desirous of seeing me as I passed through Paris, and that General Préval, Under-Secretary of State to the War Office, had desired him to inform me that he would go with me to the minister, and this took place.

We were both invited to breakfast; on rising from table the minister took me into his private office, and told me that he was much distressed at the measures taken with respect to me, under an influence that he much regretted, but he gave me his word that I should have the first regiment vacant. This was intermixed with expressions of great good-will, and I remember them the more thankfully for it was a matter of notoriety that Marshal Soult was not liberal in expressions of that kind.

According to my taste, the command of a regiment would certainly have suited me best, but in the existing disposition of the army, with the noise that my business at Saint Maixent had made, and my being placed on the inactive list, I might have encountered great difficulties in such a command. I felt so much irritation against persons who had taken advantage of the revolutionary movement to obtain promotion, that I was conscious of incapacity for the impartiality that is the first duty of a chief. I spoke my thoughts openly to the minister, and he admitted their justice. We parted, with the assurance on his side that he would not forget me, and on mine that I was much gratified by his reception of me.

Six weeks afterwards I received my appointment to the command of the depot of remounts at Alençon. I did the work for two years, and might perhaps have stopped there till I became general of brigade or retired; but the office of remounts was removed from the cavalry office, and the chief placed at the head of this important branch of the service understood nothing about it; he gave orders that would have thrown it all into confusion, I got annoyed, perhaps unreasonably, and I requested to be put on the inactive list until my retirement.

I also had to contend with the ill-will of the authorities at Alençon, excepting however General Cavalier, the Commandant of the Department, all my intercourse with him was very pleasant. The *prefect* had denounced me, and I had a most violent epistolary quarrel with the king's advocate; he forwarded my letter to the advocate-general, and was very much blamed by him.

A short time after my arrival at Alençon, I had also been denounced in the Chamber of Deputies by a deputy from the Two Sèvres named Le Clerc, Casimir Périer, then President of the Council of Ministers, and Marshal Soult made him sharp replies, and he was silenced, the

Quotidienne, a Legitimist newspaper, took advantage of this incident to make a eulogium on me, and all this, as may be supposed, contributed to excited the ill-will of the radicals of the day still more against me. The only place in Alençon where I found any sympathy was in the house of the Count de Chambray, where the aristocracy met to live entirely apart, from the authorities. (In France, in Louis Philippe's time, it was a kind of mark of disaffection not to visit at the houses of the government officials and attend their receptions.)

I received permission to give up the command of the depot at Alençon and retired to Caen, where my brother was already settled.

This is the end of my military recollections; the pleasure I have felt at occasionally finding traces of my ancestors' deeds have induced me to write as I have done. This feeling has been so acute as to make me think that perhaps my modest part in the midst of the memorable events of the wonderful period in which my life has been passed, may have some interest for my descendants. And besides M. de Bacourt, my brother-in-law, has persuaded me to relate my experiences; and probably this advice was dictated by the kindly feeling of a desire to make a diversion for me in the state of uselessness produced by my retirement.

Yet I wish to say that this repose has not been a burden to me, and a proof is that this narrative was commenced a dozen years ago, and has been broken by long intervals, explaining the want of connexion, and the omissions in it. As for the style it must fall very short. I offer no excuse, only laying its roughness down to my being an unlearned soldier, and my small powers of writing.

Another object of mine, in committing this narrative to paper, has been to describe a military career, and to add the picture of its inseparable miseries to its attractions, to the youthful imagination. I have passed over in silence the short periods of repose I enjoyed during the stormy time of my life, with the variety they imparted into my life, because if I had gone into them, and the occurrences in my family, though they were my first interest in life, I should have been writing my own history and falsified the title of these memoirs, and this is just what I wished to guard against. If any of my descendants follow the career of arms, and find here matter for useful reflection, I shall not have altogether wasted my time, nor my brother-in-law his advice.

Sketch of a Soldier: Colonel De Gonneville

More honour than honours.
Old Motto.

"There were more trees of our ancient forest overthrown than up-rooted by the storms of the Revolution," was a true and philosophical thought of M. Bonald, guided by the light of a deep and lively faith.

The longer the succession of revolutions in our unhappy country, the clearer has it become to attentive minds that the storm that laid low the trees of the forest could not pluck up their roots.

Doubtless our country has been deeply convulsed, and the surface is strewn with ruins. The leaves have been torn down by the storm, but the roots remain alive and their sap is not dried up. They are almost universal though nearly invisible, and remain in those fields of our ancient France which bear the footprints of our ancestors. The roots of the old tree are still there, and these roots want only morning dew, fine sunny days and tranquil evenings to make them sprout afresh, expand, and grow so as to give a protecting shade to the men who may dwell beneath their shelter.

God alone can give us these things, when He deems that our trial has been long and painful enough.

These somewhat melancholy reflections have been suggested by a perusal of the writings of a noble who was a gallant soldier and a good man.

He too belonged to the ancient forest. Like so many others he was flung to the ground, but raised himself again by a mighty effort, and experienced the troubled life of our modern generations.

Much has been made of a saying of later days, which is in fact nothing but a cast-off rag of the Revolution, namely, the appearance of new orders of society. Have those who thus threaten the French community ever cast a look on the ancient orders of society? Have they ever studied the birth and growth of the French nation beneath the shade of the cross of the priesthood, and of the sword of the nobility? Have they measured the vast work of the religious orders in preserving art and science as a holy trust, in opening public schools, in tending the sick, in preaching morality, and struggling against barbarism? Have they reckoned up the blood shed by the nobility from Tolbiac down to Fontenoy, in order to create the fair realm of France, and to preserve our country from the assaults of the enemy?

The miserable ignorance alone of modern days could so much misconstrue the past as to believe that such as Suger, Sully, Colbert, Turenne, and Condé could have at once arisen from the common herd and envious multitude.

Nothing here on earth arises spontaneously. The cedar has been a sapling, and the river that encircles the boundaries of empires has flowed in silence, almost hidden in the grass of the meadow. Man cannot emancipate himself from this divine law governing the world, and directing all progress with far-seeing wisdom.

The subject of our *Memoir*, as we have said, belonged to the ancient *strata* of society. The moment these strata were broken up he hesitated not, but gallantly took his post among the ranks of the defenders of his country. He followed the tradition of his race, and was a soldier.

This was the time when Châteaubriand said, "The honour of France took refuge beneath her flag." Men took refuge in the camp to escape from politics. Camps were a neutral ground where the sons of France all lived like brave comrades, whether they came from cottage or from castle. A moment before, by a freak of fortune, the generals had laid their heads upon the block. But they were familiar with death, and received it from the revolutionary tribunal as easily as on the field of battle.

Not one of them thought of sacrificing military duty to his private ambition, or deserted the camp for the public platform—military honour remained unstained notwithstanding the Revolution. Hoche, Kleber, Desaix, Marceau, had all fallen in arms in the midst of their soldiers. Not a single one, whatever were his origin or his faith, had failed in fidelity to the chivalrous notions of the old captains of the ancient monarchy. They had received that mysterious inheritance, and handed it down intact to their successors. It was reserved for our time to see the sword of the general officer pass into the unwashed hands of an insurgent populace. For a captain to solicit the votes of the im-placable adversaries of the army is just the same thing as surrendering his sword to the enemy.

It was not thus when M. de Gonneville took his place in the army. He had to endure sufferings, but to brook no disgrace.

At that time many scions of the old aristocracy were entering the service as private soldiers. The list of their names would be long and glorious. It can easily be found by taking the names of the volunteers of the last war; thus, the fathers may be known by their sons.

M. de Gonneville's military recollections are not written with any artistic or scientific view. He confines himself to a simple narrative of the events of his military life, and passes by everything that has no connection with the service.

These recollections are very instructive, they penetrate into the inmost part of military life, and treat alike of the smallest details and of important matters. This book is really a page of history, an important page, letting in light on facts unknown in scientific works. We shall endeavour to bring some forward, but we must somewhat explain our modest share in these labours.

We had the honour to be well acquainted with him whom we are speaking of. With his manuscripts to aid the heart's memory it will be easy to shed a light upon this noble figure. His mental and corpo-real features were both deeply marked. The iron of his nature was so moulded by the Divine hand that tender lights were thrown into relief by the cold, dignified shadows, and the spectator was struck with the harmonious blending of paternal kindness and of the stern resolution which was the measure of his force of character.

La Bruyère has said that there are two sorts of greatness, true and false. True greatness is free, gentle, familiar and popular; it is easily accessible, and accepts sympathy, losing nothing by being seen close at hand. Nay, the better it is known, the more it is admired. It bends kindly towards its inferiors, and returns without effort to its natural position; sometimes it relaxes, neglects itself, withdraws from its ad-vantages, always sure of being able to resume them and make full use of them; it laughs, plays, and jokes, but in a dignified manner; it is ap-proached with a union of freedom and restraint; its noble and gentle temper inspires respect and confidence.

Such was the greatness of M. de Gonneville, and he knew how to keep himself great without making others feel themselves small. His recollections extend only to his entrance into the army, and he is silent about his twenty earlier years. But they should not be forgotten, and it is our duty to recall them.

The house of Le Harivel de Gonneville was of Danish origin, and belongs to the oldest nobility of Normandy. The surname is Le Harivel and is written Harwel. A warrior of this ancient race accompanied William the Conqueror to England, and became chief of the ducal house of Northumberland, even now bearing the same arms as the Harivel de Gonnevilles.

The father of Colonel de Gonneville was the King's Lieutenant at Caen, and was entangled in one of the most bloody episodes of the Revolution. The young and brilliant Count de Belzunce was his friend. This name, illustrious for piety, devotion, and charity, could not save the count from the blind fury of the populace.

Pursued by a maddened crowd, Belzunce fled for refuge to the governor. At the risk of sharing his death, M. de Gonneville received him in his house, and it was very soon besieged, and taken by assault. Belzunce was torn from his asylum, though he made a desperate resistance, was dragged through the streets, and massacred on the Place Saint Pierre.

Aymar Oliver Le Harivel de Gonneville, who was born in 1763, was then six years old, and it was by the merest chance that his father and he himself were not involved in the fate of the Count de Belzunce. Eighty years after this scene of blood, Colonel de Gonneville would shudder with indignation as he described it. He could remember the smallest details of that dreadful night, when his mother carried off her youngest son through the crowd which was yelling for more blood.

While this trembling mother was making her escape with her two children, the populace were tearing the body of the Count de Belzunce to pieces. A woman tore out his heart, held it up to the crowd on the point of a knife, put it on a grate full of charcoal, and devoured it at last with the rage of a tigress.

The only means of escape of Madame de Gonneville and her children was through the air-hole of a cellar. They were sheltered by the darkness of the night, and their progress was undisturbed, save by the cries threatening the governor's life. Aymar de Gonneville hurried after his mother, holding on to her dress.

Sometime afterwards, in spite of the penalties that were constantly re-enacted, the former Governor of Caen emigrated and became a lieutenant-colonel in the Army of Condé. His property was sold, and his wife obliged to take refuge in the hut of a fisherman near Rouen on the banks of the Seine.

This high-born lady bred up in riches and honours, now lived in obscurity and poverty, and we must add in sanctity.

The subject of our narrative was now nine years old. He went to Rouen every day in a little boat to fetch necessaries for his mother and brother. As this fisherman's hut was unlikely to attract observation, the chiefs of the Royalist Army of Normandy sometimes came at night to consult under this almost invisible roof. General Bruslart often wanted messengers to communicate with General de Frotté, but it soon became impossible to obtain any, as several had been taken and put to death.

Madame de Gonneville had taught her children to keep a secret. They were no restraints on the conversation, and their looks showed that they understood it all.

Aymar de Gonneville was eleven years old when, one evening, just on retiring to rest, General Bruslart expressed his regret at being unable to forward some important despatches to the department of L'Orne. The boy offered to carry them. Bruslart cast a long loving look on him and refused.

Then the mother took her son by the hand, led him to the Royalist chief, and said these simple words in an agitated voice. "Take him. I give him to you for the King's service." They disguised him at once, and hid the despatches under his peasant's garb; opened the door, his mother pressed him to her heart with blessings, and with a confident step he went out into the darkness.

This first journey occupied a fortnight; the child made the whole of it on foot, and brought back General de Frotté's answer.

For a period of two years he was thus employed on some important missions, going from Rouen to Caen, and from Caen to Alençon, never coming back unless his dangerous work was done. He often spent the night in woods or fields, sleeping beneath the shelter of a tree or hedge. Young as he was, attention had been directed to him and suspicion excited. This made him careful, and he never allowed himself to fall asleep without having hidden his despatches under stones. He would much sooner have given up his life than surrendered them.

Thus, he grew up among perils. Poverty, pain, weariness, and danger were all his mind had to feed on. He saw the heads of his mother's friends fall, he saw her tremble and pray for him. He supported and encouraged her when she mourned her absent husband, of whom she heard nothing for many years. Before he was grown up, he was a soldier and head of his family.

At last the Reign of Terror terminated, and M. de Gonneville returned to France about 1801.

We shall find the subject of our portrait a private in a cavalry regiment in 1804, and follow him over the battlefields without fear of being misled. But as he passes over in silence anything that has not an intimate connection with his military life, we will mention a few circumstances of his private life.

When captain of *cuirassiers*, on leave in 1810, he married his cousin Mademoiselle de Langle, by whom he had two children. In a period of six years he only spent a few months in Normandy with his wife, and she died in 1816. He lost his son in 1819, his father in 1821, his daughter in 1822, and his mother in 1823.

In 1825 he obtained the hand of the sister of M. de Bacourt, who had acted as ambassador in the time of Louis Philippe, and was the friend and testamentary executor of Prince Talleyrand.

Of this marriage was born after several years, a daughter, who became Countess de Mirabeau.

Before opening M. de Gonneville's manuscript, and making ourselves acquainted with the fortunes of the young soldier, let us pause to take a look at the old man of ninety. He died at Nancy, so that the veteran could hear the march of the enemy from the very first days of the war, God alone knows what echoes rang through his soul.

But when peace was signed, a large quantity of manuscript one day reached us written in a firm hand. The old man spent his last hours on his profession, and had written some interesting notes on the war for us; one especially, concerning the army at Metz, bore the mark of incontestable superiority. The old warrior spoke of our unhappy France with pious resignation. He mourned her errors, and concluding with Shakespeare's words, "*France is God's soldier,*" he added, "God will not forsake His soldier."

★★★★★★

The best side of the colonel's character came into play at the domestic hearth; in his latter years he took up his quarters there between the wife who had been for nearly fifty years the inseparable companion of his life, his daughter, and grandchildren. We have told what Christian feelings pervaded him, we have spoken of his courage, and endeavoured to describe his kindness.

Yet the portrait is not complete. In physiognomy there are slight tints which the eye guesses at, though nearly invisible, and which no words can express. The expression of the countenance is the reflection of the light from a hidden fire.

This man never led a useless life; from infancy he had been the support of his mother, and the devoted agent of the party to which he belonged by right of birth. Thirty years of his long career were entirely devoted to his country, and he was still in his full strength when he retired into the province of Normandy, that he loved so well. His lofty intellect was then, as always, employed in doing good. The Colonel lived with his brother, a few leagues from Caen, on an hereditary property; and he soon became the providence of the whole country, where his name will never be forgotten.

How can all his tenderness be told in words?—visits to the sick whom he nursed himself, consolation to the afflicted, paternal advice to those astray, alms to the miserable, charity to all?

But he was not entirely absorbed in this Christian life. The most charming hospitality and frank cheerfulness reigned under his roof. He and his brother were the only teachers of the Comtesse de Mirabeau, his daughter; the soldier thinking himself ignorant and unlettered, again, in a lonely neighbourhood, commenced his studies in order to direct the education of an only daughter, from whom he was unwilling to be separated. Along with a classical education there was moral teaching, and that direction of energy which he considered necessary above all. Lessons in drill, lessons in riding, exercises of all kinds, everything had its time, and the colonel used to laugh and say that the morning was devoted to classes on horseback.

He remembered 1793, and perhaps foresaw 1875. At the end of the year 1872 he perceived the approach of death, and did not turn aside his head. By that time the soldier had yielded to the Christian.

The malady that carried him off made its appearance on the very day of the Germans' entry into Nancy. His conflicting emotions were the more severe because the old captain had some intimate friendships among the ranks of the foreigners. He did not feel the blind sentiment of mere hatred of the conqueror. He knew what war is, and remembered his victories and his captivity. He had not forgotten the cruel mission of the soldier, and coolly and wisely weighed the dreadful duty of the man who bears the sword for his country's honour.

However noble were his feelings, none the less did he feel a mortal grief at the sight of conquered France. The foreigners themselves understood this grief, and the Prince Royal of Prussia paid him the honour of a visit, and reminded him that in 1808 the French were the conquerors of Germany.

The old soldier, a descendant of the illustrious captains of Louis XIV, a perfect gentleman, a veteran of the first empire, an heir of all our previous glories, who had always borne his head high, would not bend it either to the victorious enemy or to the Revolution.

God had reserved this last trial for him, and it brought him to death. When he saw his end approaching, and the priest had given the heavenly blessing, the old man in his turn gave his blessing to his family and servants, like a knight of ancient times. He said:

Above! I shall make my prayer that God may permit my soul to hover around you.

Then after a long silence his voice was heard again. He spoke of war, invasion, country. His last thoughts were for France and for God.

Such had been the death, three centuries and a half before, of Bayard, the knight without fear and without reproach.

But one last joy had been reserved for the old man. On the very day that the news of our first defeat arrived at Nancy, the only man of his family, Count Roger de Martel, the young husband of the beloved granddaughter of the colonel, came to announce to him that he was going to enter the army.

The colonel's countenance lighted up, his heart leapt in his bosom, while former days were recalled.

He whose portrait we are drawing had reached the age of seventy-five years, when we had the honour of knowing him. His mighty old age resembled those majestic rivers that seem to enlarge just before they fall into the ocean, and whose water is as clear and limpid as when it springs from its source.

One fine Autumn evening we were conversing with him under the trees of the favourite walk of King Stanislas, Duke of Lorraine.

Our minds were roaming at haphazard, passing from history to philosophy, from philosophy to art, from art to the curiosities of human life. I asked him what Fortune, the heathen goddess invoked by Christians, really was. He looked at me as if to divine my undercurrent of thought.

I said, "I am surprised that you did not attain to the height of it. Is Fortune really blind then?"

An imperceptible smile passed over his lips, but he spoke not.

I resumed, "I must remind you, my venerable master, of a story of the fifteenth century; a knight, whose name I have forgotten, had distinguished himself at the Battle of Fornova, under Charles VIII. Louis XII. sent him into Italy, and his blood flowed on the bridge of the Garigliano. The knight was again wounded at Agnadel, and covered himself with glory at Brescia in sight of Bayard. He returned to Italy in the time of Francis I., and fought with Prospero Colonna. At Marignano the knight protected his king, fell into the hands of the enemy and was led into captivity.

"Afterwards he returned home, with his body seamed with scars, and brought nothing with him but a broken lance and a helmet dinted with blows. The knight raised not a single complaint, but beneath his shield these words were traced by his comrades in arms, 'More honour than honours.' Has not the ancient gentleman of Marignano bequeathed to you his example and his motto? But how can four words recompense a long life of a good man?"

At that moment one last ray of the sun lighted up the colonel's countenance, a glory seemed to illuminate his white head, and his eyes shone bright. Then he stretched himself to his full height, raised his right hand and pointed to the sky.

General Baron Ambert

LEONAUR

ALSO FROM LEONAUR
AVAILABLE IN SOFTCOVER OR HARDCOVER WITH DUST JACKET

OFFICERS & GENTLEMEN *by Peter Hawker & William Graham*—Two Accounts of British Officers During the Peninsula War: Officer of Light Dragoons by Peter Hawker & Campaign in Portugal and Spain by William Graham .

THE WALCHEREN EXPEDITION *by Anonymous*—The Experiences of a British Officer of the 81st Regt. During the Campaign in the Low Countries of 1809.

LADIES OF WATERLOO *by Charlotte A. Eaton, Magdalene de Lancey & Juana Smith*—The Experiences of Three Women During the Campaign of 1815: Waterloo Days by Charlotte A. Eaton, A Week at Waterloo by Magdalene de Lancey & Juana's Story by Juana Smith.

JOURNAL OF AN OFFICER IN THE KING'S GERMAN LEGION *by John Frederick Hering*—Recollections of Campaigning During the Napoleonic Wars.

JOURNAL OF AN ARMY SURGEON IN THE PENINSULAR WAR *by Charles Boutflower*—The Recollections of a British Army Medical Man on Campaign During the Napoleonic Wars.

ON CAMPAIGN WITH MOORE AND WELLINGTON *by Anthony Hamilton*—The Experiences of a Soldier of the 43rd Regiment During the Peninsular War.

THE ROAD TO AUSTERLITZ *by R. G. Burton*—Napoleon's Campaign of 1805.

SOLDIERS OF NAPOLEON *by A. J. Doisy De Villargennes & Arthur Chuquet*—The Experiences of the Men of the French First Empire: Under the Eagles by A. J. Doisy De Villargennes & Voices of 1812 by Arthur Chuquet .

INVASION OF FRANCE, 1814 *by F. W. O. Maycock*—The Final Battles of the Napoleonic First Empire.

LEIPZIG—A CONFLICT OF TITANS *by Frederic Shoberl*—A Personal Experience of the 'Battle of the Nations' During the Napoleonic Wars, October 14th-19th, 1813.

SLASHERS *by Charles Cadell*—The Campaigns of the 28th Regiment of Foot During the Napoleonic Wars by a Serving Officer.

BATTLE IMPERIAL *by Charles William Vane*—The Campaigns in Germany & France for the Defeat of Napoleon 1813-1814.

SWIFT & BOLD *by Gibbes Rigaud*—The 60th Rifles During the Peninsula War.